ECONOMIC THEORY AND SOCIAL JUSTICE

Economic Theory and Social Justice

Edited by

Giancarlo Gandolfo
Professor of International Economics
University of Rome 'La Sapienza'

and

Ferruccio Marzano
Professor of Development Economics
University of Rome 'La Sapienza'

First published in Great Britain 1999 by
MACMILLAN PRESS LTD
Houndmills, Basingstoke, Hampshire RG21 6XS and London
Companies and representatives throughout the world

A catalogue record for this book is available from the British Library.

ISBN 0–333–72340–6

First published in the United States of America 1999 by
ST. MARTIN'S PRESS, INC.,
Scholarly and Reference Division,
175 Fifth Avenue, New York, N.Y. 10010

ISBN 0–312–21779–X

Library of Congress Cataloging-in-Publication Data
Economic theory and social justice / edited by Giancarlo Gandolfo and Ferruccio Marzano.
p. cm.
Includes bibliographical references and index.
ISBN 0–312–21779–X
1. Economics. 2. Social justice. I. Gandolfo, Giancarlo. II. Marzano, Ferruccio.
HB171.E247 1998
330.1—dc21 98–19153
CIP

This book is printed on paper suitable for recycling and made from fully managed and sustained forest sources.

10 9 8 7 6 5 4 3 2 1
08 07 06 05 04 03 02 01 00 99

Printed and bound in Great Britain by
Antony Rowe Ltd, Chippenham, Wiltshire

Contents

Preface

Giancarlo Gandolfo and Ferruccio Marzano

Ten years after the unexpected and untimely death of Fausto Vicarelli a conference was organized in his memory at the Faculty of Economics of the University of Rome I 'La Sapienza'. We are sure that Fausto would have warmly appreciated the readiness of so many scholars to contribute a paper to the conference – economists from Italy and from other countries.

The conference was attended by a great number of colleagues and students as well as by members of Fausto's family and several of his friends. In particular, we wish to thank the President of the Societa' Italiana degli Economisti, Professor Alberto Quadrio Curzio, and its three past Presidents who accepted to chair the Conference's four Sessions.

The conference was generously financed by the University of Rome I 'La Sapienza', the Consiglio Nazionale delle Ricerche (CNR), the Bank of Italy, the Banca di Roma. We sincerely thank all these institutions as well as all the participants in the conference, whose papers and other contributions have been published in the present book of proceedings. The usual disclaimer as to the responsibility for the published material obviously applies.

In the book papers and other contributions have been organized in much the same order in which they were presented in the conference; most papers and comments, though, have been revised in the light of the discussion. Hence, besides a Personal 'Reminiscence' by Giancarlo Gandolfo, an Introduction by Ferruccio Marzano, and an Opening Address by the Governor of the Bank of Italy, Antonio Fazio, the eight papers by Professors James Tobin, Ignazio Musu, Paul Davidson, Giorgio Lunghini, Jan A. Kregel, Giangiacomo Nardozzi, Anthony B. Atkinson, and Stefano Zamagni, as well as comments on them, will follow under the same headings of the four Sessions of the conference. Finally a special group of 'Testimonials' is included, whereby attention has been given to specific and less known sides of Vicarelli's life and general attitudes, besides his strict scientific work, in particular Professor Minsky's 'letter to the conference' which Hyman wrote and sent just one week before his sad decease, and then three short contributions by Antonino Tripoli, Franco Bentivogli, and Nicola Genovese. Some Concluding Remarks by Ferruccio Marzano will close the volume.

List of the Contributors

Giancarlo Gandolfo: Professor of International Economics, Faculty of Economics, and Director, CIDEI (Centro Interdipartimentale di Economia Internazionale), University of Rome I 'La Sapienza'

Ferruccio Marzano: Professor of Development Economics, Faculty of Economics, University of Rome I 'La Sapienza'

Antonio Fazio: Governor of the Bank of Italy, Rome

James Tobin: Emeritus Professor of Economics, Yale University, Nobel Laureate in Economics, 1981

Sergio Parrinello: Professor of Mathematical Economics, Faculty of Economics, University of Rome I 'La Sapienza'

Paolo Syslos Labini: Emeritus Professor of Political Economy, Faculty of Statistics, University of Rome I, 'La Sapienza'

Ignazio Musu: Professor of Political Economy, Faculty of Economics, University of Venice

Antonio Pedone: Professor of Public Finance, Faculty of Economics, University of Rome I 'La Sapienza'

Paul Davidson: Professor of Economics, University of Tennessee

Giorgio Lunghini: Professor of Political Economy, Faculty of Economics, University of Pavia

Claudio Gnesutta: Professor of Economic Policy, Faculty of Economics, University of Rome I 'La Sapienza'

Jan A. Kregel: Professor of Economics, Faculty of Political and Social Sciences, University of Bologna

Augusto Graziani: Professor of Political Economy, Faculty of Economics, University of Rome I 'La Sapienza'

Guido M. Rey: Professor of Economic Policy, Faculty of Economics, University of Rome III

Giangiacomo Nardozzi: Professor of Economics, Faculty of Engineering, Polytechnic of Milan

Marcello de Cecco: Professor of Monetary Economics, Faculty of Economics, University of Rome I 'La Sapienza'

Anthony B. Atkinson: Professor of Economics, Oxford University

Luigi Frey: Professor of Labour Economics, Faculty of Economics, University of Rome I 'La Sapienza'

Stefano Zamagni: Professor of Political Economy, Faculty of Economics, University of Bologna

Nicola Acocella: Professor of Economic Policy, Faculty of Economics, University of Rome I 'La Sapienza'

Alessandro Roncaglia: Professor of Political Economy, Faculty of Statistics, University of Rome I 'La Sapienza'

Felice R. Pizzuti: Associate Professor of Economic Policy, Faculty of Economics, University of Rome I 'La Sapienza'

Hyman P. Minsky: Late Professor of Economics, Jerome Levi Economics Institute, New York

Antonino Tripoli: President, Fausto Vicarelli Association, Rome

Franco Bentivogli: Former General Secretary, Italian Metalworkers Federation, Rome

Nicola Genovese: Associate Professor of Political Economy, Faculty of Economics, University of Messina

Fausto Vicarelli: A Personal Reminiscence

Giancarlo Gandolfo

Fausto Vicarelli was born on 18 January 1936 in Osimo (Ancona, Italy) and died in a solitary car accident in Rome, on 23 November 1986. He is survived by his wife, Gabriella, and three children (Claudio, Francesca and Stefano).

Fausto obtained his *laurea* in economics at the Faculty of Economics of the University of Rome in 1959 with a dissertation on 'Dynamic theory according to Hicks and the Swedish school'. In 1961–62 he spent one year at Harvard University attending graduate courses, and in 1962 he was appointed assistant professor of economics (tenured from 1965) at the Faculty of Economics of Rome, obtained the *libera docenza* in economics in 1968, and taught at the University of Ancona from 1970 to 1976. He won the competition to become a full professor of economics in 1976, and taught at the University of Florence (1976–81). In 1981 he was called to the chair of economics in his *alma mater*.

He was a much appreciated and influential consultant to the Bank of Italy and to the trade unions (CISL: Confederazione Italiana Sindacati Lavoratori). He did this not for money (it may look queer, but I can testify that, when he did not work for free, the money he got from this work was barely sufficient to cover his expenses) or lust for power, but out of a genuine social interest and altruism. The same altruism that made him use his free time personally to help people with disabilities. It was impressive how he managed to be an excellent teacher, much loved by his students, while finding the time to carry out excellent research work, excellent consulting work, excellent charitable work (this last he considered as part of his most intimate life, so that even his closest colleagues and friends including myself did not know of it). I suspect that the car accident in which he died after losing control of his small car (no other vehicle or living being was involved) was partly due to his exhaustion after a long day of such hard work.

I met Fausto in the early 1960s when we were both appointed

assistente volontario ('voluntary' assistant professor) at the Institute of Political Economy of the Faculty of Economics and Commerce of the University of Rome. 'Voluntary' meant that one had a formal position of assistant professor with certain official duties but with no salary. This was how one begun an academic career in Italy at that time. Of course, excluding the case of rich persons undertaking the academic career as a hobby, one had to have a paid job elsewhere. Fausto worked as a consultant to CNEN (Comitato Nazionale Energia Nucleare, now ENEA), I was a staff economist at the research department of the Bank of Italy.

In 1965 we entered the competition to become *assistente ordinario* ('ordinary' assistant professor, where the 'ordinary' meant that a salary, and tenure, were attached to the job). Fausto came out first, I was second, but fortunately for me there were two positions available, hence I could continue the academic career and work in the same Institute of Political Economy as Fausto.

Both of us had a flair for mathematics. However, at that time in Italy there weren't many economists familiar with advanced mathematical methods: on the contrary, 'mathematical' economists were considered with suspect by the mainstream majority of 'literary' economists, and to write mathematical papers wasn't the best way to foster one's own academic career. Notwithstanding this, Fausto and I freely used mathematical (and econometric) methods, and considered ourselves with pride as members of the 'sect' of mathematical economists. I still vividly remember our excitement and enthusiasm when we had the opportunity to attend the first World Congress of the Econometric Society (held in Rome in August 1965), and could listen to and meet those who for us were legendary figures (Ragnar Frisch, Richard Goodwin, John Hicks, Tijalling Koopmans, Paul Samuelson, just to mention a few).

Fortunately our membership to the sect was not held against us thanks to the open-mindedness of the professors with whom we worked at the Institute (Volrico Travaglini and Vittorio Marrama, respectively). In 1968 we both obtained the *libera docenza* in economics (a degree, now abolished, which at that time was a necessary step in the road to the full professorship). In 1970 our paths diverged: he obtained a professorship in Ancona, I got it in Siena.

Hence I can say that I am better acquainted with Fausto's early works rather than with the works of his maturity. This also derives from the fact that, as a consequence of the scarce diffusion of the knowledge of mathematical methods mentioned above, we subjected each other's papers to a close scrutiny, not only as regards the ideas, but also carefully to check their mathematics. This acquaintance gives me the opportunity to highlight some less considered but important aspects of his juvenile output that may put his scientific evolution into better perspective.

In fact, most of the several assessments of Fausto Vicarelli's scientific work (see below, in the Further Reading section) have stressed his important contributions to Keynesian economics and to economic policy issues. This is certainly correct, but it is not irrelevant that Fausto also had a deep knowledge of neoclassical economics, on which he wrote excellent papers at a high level of technical sophistication.

In his paper 'An attempt at a dynamic analysis of Pareto-optima and returns to scale', for example, he deals with the problem of whether a general equilibrium neoclassical system converges to the set of Pareto-optima through a dynamic adjustment mechanism of the *tâtonnement* type in competitive markets. Building on earlier work of Arrow, Hurwicz and others, he shows that in the case of constant returns to scale the convergence is ensured only if the production functions are strictly concave, whereas undamped oscillations arise in the case of simple concavity. Finally, the system is unstable in the case of increasing returns to scale, as it does not converge to equilibrium for any arbitrary initial position. It is, however, conditionally stable, since it converges for initial positions belonging to a certain set.

Another topic to which he gave an important contribution is the problem of the microfoundations of macroeconomics. In the 1960s this problem (nowadays so fashionable) attracted little or no attention in general economic theory, whereas it was already clearly set out in international economics under the name of 'the problem of integration between the pure theory of international trade and international monetary economics'. The former has an essential microeconomic nature, while the latter is essentially macroeconomic and is often identified with open-economy macroeconomics. Hence to talk of the problem of their integration is tantamount to dealing with a microfoundations problem. At that time I was already specializing in international economics, and in my scientific discussions with Fausto this came out as a topic worth investigating, as very few and unsatisfactory treatments (notably by Kemp, Travaglini and Cutilli) existed. This is what he did, and after a long gestation period he published his essay 'Verso un'integrazione fra teoria pura e teoria monetaria del commercio internazionale' (Towards an integration between the pure and monetary theory of international trade).

He first sets up a generalized neoclassical model of barter exchange whose short-run equilibrium may logically coexist with a non-zero *desired* trade balance. The (non-zero) equilibrium value of the trade balance is determined simultaneously with the international level of the interest rate on commercial credits.

He then builds a model with money, characterized by an interest-elastic demand for money and excess demands for goods sensitive to changes in real wealth. Here, as in the barter model, international equilibrium is compatible with a surplus or deficit in the trade balance, but now the non-zero trade balance is matched by capital flows between the two countries, whence changes in the stocks of money.

The fact is then stressed that short-run equilibrium of both models must be distinguished from long-run equilibrium, for the latter is achieved at a zero desired trade balance. The integration problem is then solved by showing that endogenous forces, which ensure the dynamic convergence to long-run equilibrium, are the same in the two models.

My personal recollections show that Fausto Vicarelli arrived at the scientific position of his maturity – that made him a leading figure in the field of Keynesian (without any *post, neo,* or other prefix, but in the etymological meaning of the adjective) economics – starting, like Keynes, from a deep theoretical knowledge of neoclassical economics, that he subsequently found incapable of contributing to the solution of the economic problems of our world, as detailed in his 1985 paper 'Natural Laws and Economic Policy: Some Considerations on the Theoretical Foundations of the New Classical Macroeconomics.'

FURTHER READING

Bentivogli, C. and Trento, S. (1990) Fausto Vicarelli: l'eredità keynesiana, *Il Progetto* **X**, 81–6.

Caffè, F. (1986) Ricordo di Fausto Vicarelli, *Politica Economica* **II**, 285–90 (with a bibliography).

Ciampi, C.A., Spaventa, L., Carniti, P. and Rey, G.M. (1987) Il libro di

Fausto Vicarelli 'La questione economica nella società italiana', *Politica Economica* **III**, 561–78.
Ciocca, P. *et al.*, (1988) Il contributo scientifico di Fausto Vicarelli: una prima valutazione (with a bibliography by M.T. Pandolfi), *Rivista di Storia Economica* **5**, 3–25.
Trento, S. (1991) Ricordando Fausto Vicarelli, *Lettera FIM* **II**, 11–13.

FAUSTO VICARELLI'S SCIENTIFIC WORKS

This list does not include articles in the general press (newspapers and magazines), book reviews, and so on. For a list of these, see the bibliography by M.T. Pandolfi published as an appendix to P. Ciocca *et al.*

Sull'impostazione duale di un modello di programmazione lineare applicato al settore elettrico, *Economia Internazionale,* 1964, **17**, 448–85.
(with A. Fazio) Un modello di domanda per beni d'investimento: formulazione teorica e applicazione al settore estrattivo e manifatturiero dell'economia italiana, *Rivista di Politica Economica*, 1966, **56**, 1515–51.
Interrelazione tra fenomeni reali e fenomeni monetari nel meccanismo ciclico, *Metroeconomica,* 1966, **18**, 239–61.
Ottimo paretiano e rendimenti di scala in un tentativo di analisi dinamica, *Economia Internazionale,* 1967, **20**, 1–35.
La funzione di produzione ad elasticità di sostituzione costante e la stima del tasso di progresso tecnico, *Rivista di Politica Economica,* 1967, **37**, 973–1060.
Moneta, ricchezza e bilancia dei pagamenti, Roma, Edizioni dell'Ateneo, 1970.
L'esportazione di banconote nell'esperienza italiana dell'ultimo decennio: una analisi quantitativa, *Studi economici,* 1970, **3–4**, 322–47.
Verso un'integrazione tra teoria pura e teoria monetaria del commercio internazionale, *Economia Internazionale,* 1972, **23**, 431–49 and 623–53.
II processo d'integrazione reale-finanziaria dell'economia italiana nella Cee, in Banca d'Italia, *Contributi alla ricerca economica*, 1973, **3**, 285–320.
Flussi finanziari internazionali. Uno schema teorico e un modello per l'economia italiana, in Ente per gli studi monetari, bancari e finanziari Luigi Einaudi, *Quaderni di ricerche*, 1974, **13**, 3–111.
Introduzione, in F. Vicarelli (ed.), *La controversia keynesiana,* Bologna, Il Mulino, 1974, 9–46.
Disoccupazione e prezzi relativi: un tentativo di reinterpretazione di Keynes, *ibid*., 207–32.
Tasso d'interesse e livello del reddito in un sistema chiuso agli scambi con l'estero, in F. Cotula and P. de' Stefani (eds), *Elementi per la politica monetaria,* Roma, Bulzoni, 1975, 59–61; also in F. Cotula and P. de' Stefani (eds), *La politica monetaria in Italia. Istituti e strumenti,* Bologna, Il Mulino, 1979, 287–316.
L'aggiustamento della bilancia dei pagamenti, in F. Cotula and P. de' Stefani (eds), *Elementi per le politica monetaria*, *op. cit*., 153–69.

Equilibrio interno ed esterno in regime di cambi fissi e flessibili, *ibid*., 430–49.

(with C. Caranza and C. Chiesa) A Model for the Banking System's Foreign Operations, in F. Masera, A. Fazio and T. Padoa-Schioppa (eds), *Econometric Research in European Central Banks,* Banca d'Italia, *Contributi alla ricerca economica*, Special Number, 1975, 283–95.

Struttura degli scambi internazionali e inflazione mondiale, in *Sviluppo economico, scambi internazionali e crisi monetaria,* Atti della XV Riunione Scientifica della Società Italiana degli Economisti, Milan, Giuffrè, 1975, 9–33; also in *Bancaria,* 1975, **31**, 1204–14.

Moneta, ricchezza e bilancia dei pagamenti: un modello per un'economia aperta, in *Contributi in memoria di M. Bandini,* Rome, Università degli Studi, Facoltà di Economia e Commercio, 1976, 189–209.

(with C. Gnesutta) Efficienza marginale del capitale, teoria monetaria di Yale ed ortodossia keynesiana, *Rivista di Politica Economica,* 1976, **66**, 733–52.

Keynes. L'instabilità del capitalismo, Milan, ETAS Libri, 1977; Engl. tr. *Keynes: The Instability of Capitalism,* Philadelphia, University of Pennsylvania Press, 1984, and London, Macmillan, 1984.

Moneta e valore nella 'Teoria Generale': verso una nuova interpretazione di Keynes, in R. Faucci (ed.), *John Maynard Keynes nel pensiero e nella politica economica,* Milan, Feltrinelli, 1977, 96–117.

Introduzione, in F. Vicarelli (ed.), *Capitale industriale e capitale finanziario: il caso italiano,* Bologna, Il Mulino, 1979, 15–57.

II modello keynesiano in un'economia aperta, in F. Cotula and P. de' Stefani (eds), *La politica monetaria in Italia. Istituti e strumenti,* Bologna, Il Mulino, 1979, 317–40.

(with M. Marconi) L'accumulazione di capitale nella visione della Cisl, in G. Baglioni (ed.), *Analisi della Cisl. Fatti e giudizi di un'esperienza sindacale,* Roma, EL, 1980, vol. 2, 445–94.

Preferenza per la liquidità e moltiplicatore nella 'Teoria Generale': una risposta a A. Campus e G. de Vivo, *Ricerche Economiche,* 1980, **34**, 237–42.

Intervento, in *Credit Systems in the Seventies*, Ente per gli studi monetari, bancari e finanziari Luigi Einaudi, *Quaderni di ricerche,* 1980, **17**, 399–404; also in G. Calabresi (ed.), *I sistemi creditizi degli anni settanta,* Roma, Bancaria (ed.), 1982, 477–81.

Note in tema di accumulazione di capitale in Italia (1947–63), in G. Lunghini (ed.), *Scelte politiche e teorie economiche in Italia 1945–1978*, Turin, Einaudi, 1981, 13–69.

Accumulazione, risparmio, sviluppo, in *Zero cinquanta. Pro e contro il fondo di solidarietà,* Roma, EL, 1981, 79–98.

Le economie industriali fra stagnazione e inflazione: quali vie di uscita dalla crisi, *Studi e Informazioni,* 1981, **4**, 56–66.

La crisi dell'accumulazione, in V. Merlo (ed.), *Controllare l'accumulazione,* Roma, EL, 1981, 20–4.

Disintermediazione bancaria e struttura del sistema finanziano, *Economia Italiana* 1982, **2**, 231–45; Engl. ver. *Review of Economic Conditions in Italy*, **0**, 235–49.

Struttura finanziaria e sviluppo economico tra teoria e prassi, *Informazioni Acri,* 1982, **6**, 22–5; also in *Gli intermediari finanziari e lo sviluppo economico,* Siena, Facoltà di Scienze Economiche e Bancarie, 1980, 61–73.

Dall'equilibrio alla probabilità: una rilettura del metodo della Teoria Generale, in F. Vicarelli (ed.), *Attualità di Keynes,* Rome-Bari, Laterza, 1983, 291–318; Engl. tr. From Equilibrium to Probability: A Reinterpretation of the Method of the General Theory, in F. Vicarelli (ed.), *Keynes's Relevance Today,* London, Macmillan, 1985.

Credito, in *Dizionario di economia politica,* G. Lunghini and M. D'Antonio (eds), Turin, Boringhieri, 1983, **III** , 11–111.

Modelli econometrici e realtà economica: osservazioni sui recenti sviluppi della macroeconomia, in *Ricerche sui modelli per la politica economica,* Banca d'Italia, *Contributi alle ricerca economica,* Special Number 1983, vol. 2, 727–35.

Incomes Policy and International Money: Comment on Davidson, in J.A. Kregel (ed.), *Distribution, Effective Demand and International Economic Relations,* London, Macmillan, 1983, 182–5.

Banchieri alla sbarra. Recensione a G. Nardozzi, Tre sistemi creditizi. Banche ed economia in Francia, Germania e Italia, in *Mondo Economico*, 21 December 1983.

Stagflation in the Seventies: A Relative Prices Theoretical Approach, *Metroeconomica,* 1984, **36**, 127–41; It. ver. Stagflazione e prezzi relativi: un tentativo di interpretazione della crisi degli anni settanta, in G. Gandolfo and F. Marzano (eds), *Keynesian Theory Planning Models and Quantitative Economics: Essays in Memory of Vittorio Marrama,* Milan, Giuffrè, 1987, vol. I, 365–83.

L'economia mondiale in mutamento e la capacità di adattamento dell' economia italiana, *Studi e informazioni,* 1984, **7**, 111–26.

Recensione a G. Rodano, *Il credito all'economia. R. Mattioli alla Banca Commerciale Italiana, Moneta e Credito,* 1984, **37**, 238–42.

Leggi di natura e politica economica: considerazioni sui fondamenti teorici della nuova macroeconomia classica, *Politica Economica,* 1985, **1**, 7–36; also in G. Rodano (ed.), *Ascesa e declino della nuova macroeconomia classica*, Bologna, Il Mulino, 1987, 332– 58; Engl. ver. Natural Laws and Economic Policy: Some Considerations on the Theoretical Foundations of the New Classical Macroeconomics, *Journal of Post Keynesian Economics,* 1985–86, **8**, 298–314.

L'equilibrio esterno; un vincolo allo sviluppo?, in *Moneta ed economia internazionale,* Cassa di Risparmio di Torino, *Piemonte Vivo Ricerche,* Special Number of *Piemonte Vivo,* 1985, 105–18.

Occupazione e sviluppo: un binomio inscindibile, in Ente per gli studi monetari, bancari e finanziari Luigi Einaudi, *Oltre la crisi. Le prospettive di sviluppo dell'economia italiana e il contributo del sistema finanziario,* Bologna, Il Mulino, 1986, 3–28.

La Questione Economica nella Società Italiana. Analisi e Proposte, 1987, Bologna, Il Mulino.

The Autonomy of Central Banks: Reflections and Comments, in G. Toniolo (ed.), *Central Banks Independence in Historical Perspective,* Berlin, Walter De Gruyter, 1988; It. ver. in S. Ristuccia and D. Masciandaro (eds),

L 'autonomia delle banche centrali, Milan, Comunità, 1988, 285–301.

On the Extension of Sraffa's Theory to a Growing Economy: Comment on P. Sylos Labini, *Sraffa's Critique of the Marshallian Theory of Prices,* Conference on Sraffa's Production of Commodities after Twenty-five Years, Florence, 24–27 August 1985; in J.A. Kregel (ed.), *Inflation and Income Distribution in Capitalist Crisis: Essays in Memory of Sidney Weintraub,* New York, Columbia University Press, 1989, 203–12; also in K. Baradwaj and B. Schefold (eds), *Essays on Piero Sraffa. Critical Perspectives on Revival of Classical Theory,* London, Unwin, 1990, 25–30.

Introduction

Ferruccio Marzano

When we settled to think about the international conference to be held in memory of Fausto Vicarelli, on the tenth anniversary of his death, those of us who had been entrusted with the organization of the conference had no hesitation in suggesting a 'general title' which would recall what Vicarelli saw as the two main aims of our professional work: first, an economic theory which would be strictly useful in the interpretation of reality, in particular that of capitalist economies, and second the economist's commitment to social justice.

On both issues all scholars who were invited to participate and read a paper in the conference gave us an immediate and positive answer. The conference, which was held under such a general title as 'The Economist between Theory, Reality and Social Commitment' in the Faculty of Economics of the University of Rome I 'La Sapienza' on 21–23 November 1996, was structured in four sessions. In each session two papers were included, one by a foreign economist and the other one by an Italian economist, each of whom had known Fausto and, particularly, had shared the 'core' of his analytical outlook on economics.

The four sessions were given the following titles: 1. Theoretical Analyses and Actual Economic Problems, 2. Present World Imbalances and the Need for a New International Economic Order; 3. Capital Accumulation: Real and Financial Aspects; 4. Social Choices, Economic Policy, and Moral Values.

As has already been said in the Preface, in the present volume the published material has been organized in much the same way in which it was delivered in the conference. In this Introduction my task will be that of signalling out what seem to me to be the main 'themes' of each of the eight papers, according to my recollection of the specific ways in which each author has seen the 'Economist's Stance' between 'Theory, Reality and Social Commitment'.

In the first Part on 'Theoretical Analyses and Actual Economic Problems', the aim of James Tobin's paper is to reaffirm the 'Old' Keynesian view held by American Keynesians that in market monetary economies involuntary unemployment depends on the labour and product markets being 'not instantaneously and continuously cleared by perfectly flexible prices' (see Tobin, 1993a b).

In this context, as to the meaning and role of the NAIRU concept versus the Natural Rate one, Tobin criticizes the effective significance of both concepts. In his words, 'The NAIRU is, like full employment, a barrier to expansion of demand and in some sense a boundary between regimes. But it need not be the best of all possible worlds, and departures from it need not have Friedman's dynamic consequences'. Hence, it is not a neutral concept, nor can it be regarded as a simple synonym for Natural Rate. First, since a NAIRU situation is to be interpreted as a stochastic macroeconomic equilibrium, it may well include substantial involuntary unemployment; second, owing to the possible existence of multiple equilibria, the adjustment process may actually be slow or perhaps non-existent, as wage stickiness but also the ineffectiveness of price and quantity adjustment by individual market participants prevail.

Actually, the NAIRU – unlike the Natural Rate – does not assume a Walrasian equilibrium, in which markets, in particular labour markets, are cleared by existing prices and wages. Instead it assumes an economy in which most markets are characterized at any time by excess demand or excess supply at prevailing prices. The weighted number of excess demand markets, relative to excess supply markets, will be greater the higher aggregate demand is, and vice versa. Then, the NAIRU is the unemployment rate at which the inflation-increasing effects of the excess-demand markets just balance the inflation-decreasing impact of the excess-supply markets.

Unlike the natural rate, there is a balance among disequilibrium markets, a stand-off between those in excess-demand and those in excess-supply. Unlike the natural rate, the NAIRU could not be modelled as a single economy-wide market or representative agent. At each moment in time any real economy can always be considered in terms of a multimarket disequilibrium model whereby some markets are characterized by a certain amount of vacancies and other markets by a certain amount of unemployment, both as percentages of the labour force.

For the economy as a whole vacancies are the sum of excess-demands over all excess-demand markets, and unemployment is the sum of excess-supplies over all excess-supply markets. Then, as aggregate demand rises from lower to higher levels, relative to potential supply, excess supplies fall, excess demands rise, and markets move from excess-supply to excess-demand status. Consequently, total vacancies increase and total unemployment decreases. The resulting relationship between a higher level of vacancies and a lower level of unemployment, as aggregate demand increases in an economy, and vice versa as aggregate demand decreases, is a downward sloping, and in practice concave, demand curve and is known as a Beveridge curve. Following Beveridge (1945), full employment can be defined as a situation in which unemployment is less than (or, at most, equal to; see Tobin, 1972) vacancies: as we move from right to left along a Beveridge curve, as aggregate demand increases, we can expect increasing wage and price pressures, whereas, as we move from left to right, as aggregate demand decreases, we can expect increasing stagnation pressures.

On the other hand, if we think in terms of a Phillips curve, full employment may be thought of as a situation in which vacancies and unemployment balance each other out at a specific 'equilibrium' rate of unemployment. In this case, if such a rate is actually lower than the 'equilibrium' one, there will be inflationary pressures, whereas there will be deflationary pressures if the actual rate is higher than the 'equilibrium' rate of unemployment. Phillips curves can be regarded as having been generated by the same model that generates Beveridge curves. Then, for each market there is a function that translates excess demand or supply into a market-specific wage change to which the common ongoing average wage change is added. However, the point is how the actual movement towards the 'equilibrium' situation is to be interpreted when positions away from 'equilibrium' are considered.

The traditional neoclassical view (on which the Phillips curve idea was also based) was that in each competitive market, prices and wages would rise or fall as a positive function of excess demand (regarding excess supply as negative excess demand). In particular, in the aggregate, the average wage increase would be the greater the more the distribution of labour markets was weighted in favour of excess-demand markets. In this respect the NAIRU would be the rate of unemployment that generates no change in the average wage rate.

But, Tobin stresses, things are different from a Keynesian point of view. Keynes was explicitly describing a monetary economy in which markets set nominal prices. Moreover Keynes considered it likely that adjustments of money wages to excess demand or supply would be sluggish, especially downward wage adjustments to excess supply of labour. This, though, should not be considered as due to money illusion at an individual level. Instead, such an imperfect flexibility may be given a much more elaborate interpretation. Each Phillips curve may be thought of as having the shape – in Tobin's words – of 'a reclining "S", with a long fairly flat middle, between sharp rises in inflation at low unemployment and falls at very high unemployment'. In terms of an 'insider-outsider workers model' we can say that, at very low levels of unemployment, firms tend to keep employed workers through substantial wage increases, whereas workers would accept relevant falls in nominal wages only at very high levels of unemployment. On the other hand, shifts from a 'higher' to a 'lower' curve represent a deterioration in labour markets, leading to greater frictional or structural unemployment, whereas shifts in the opposite direction represent a 'tightening' of labour markets.

Hence, in the actual conditions of a monetary market economy, we can speak of *temporary* nominal wage rigidity. In particular, a market's wage change $\hat{w}_i$ would be the ongoing average nominal change $\hat{w}$, to which is added or subtracted $\hat{w}_i^*$, a function of the present excess demand or supply in market 'i'. The average nominal wage change is dependent on the economy's overall status of aggregate demand, relative to potential supply, but indirectly on the monetary and fiscal policies which support it. Indeed, Tobin concludes that owing to such conditions of nominal wage 'stickiness', there appears the need for an active macro policy. In particular, in the presence of any process of persistent deflation, since there will be heavy costs in terms of loss of national product and of defaults as well as of deterioration of physical and human capital, there is both the need and the scope for activist monetary policies, as the recent comparative experiences of the United States and of both Europe and Japan do show.

Ignazio Musu's paper provides a thoughtful reappraisal of the relevance of Keynesian macroeconomics today. Starting with a synthesis of the causes and effects of the crisis of Keynesian economics at the end of the 1960s and of the success of monetarist and New Classical macroeconomics in the 1970s, Musu goes on to analyse the possible answers of Keynesian theorists to the resurgence of neoclassical economics.

Musu's thesis is that, since in contemporary market economies failures, imperfections and rigidities create difficulties and obstacles to the realization of macroeconomic conditions of efficient equilibria, there is a case for active policies in order that such equilibria may be reached and 'full' employment may prevail. Moreover, when the existence of such imperfections as increasing returns to scale, strategic interdependences, transition and search costs leads to multiple equilibria and coordination failures, the case for active macro policies of a Keynesian type is strengthened.

The point is how to interpret and explain failures, imperfections and rigidities in any actual situation of market economies. Musu recalls the present relevance of Keynes's ideas about the role of volatile entrepreneurs' expectations in bringing about cyclical fluctuations in investment spending and, hence, in overall economic activity. In particular, in the author's opinion, Keynes's central message concerns the inefficient way in which the market operates as a coordination mechanism among economic agents. Then, since 'traditional' Keynesian macroeconomics reduces the failure of such a coordination problem to the existence of sticky prices, there lies the root of the decline of Keynesian economics.

Instead, Keynes himself maintained that interaction and coordination among economic agents do not take place only through prices and that coordination through prices alone can sometimes lead to undesirable consequences. When markets are imperfect or incomplete, a situation which in all likelihood is accompanied by conditions of uncertainty and asymmetric information, the price mechanism will in any case encounter serious difficulties in performing its coordination task.

Musu also recalls that such a point has been strongly underlined in Vicarelli's own approach to Keynes's thought and seems to have been only recently accepted in the literature (see, in particular, Hahn and Solow, 1995). In this context, as Musu concludes, macroeconomic policy will have the crucial task of spurring the economic system on to overcome coordination failures by smoothing out spontaneous fluctuations of market forces and improving the efficiency of market institutions.

In the second Part on 'Present World Imbalances and the Need for a New International Economic Order', Paul Davidson's paper is, first of all, intended to underline that Fausto Vicarelli's insistence on the need 'to avoid a disembodied caricature to (Keynes's) contribution to economic theory' is 'even more apropos for mainstream open economy macro-models' as we enter the global economy of the twenty-first century. Therefore, in the present paper, Davidson sets himself the task of following 'Vicarelli's clarion call for an "alternative approach" that relies on Keynes's vision of capitalism to understand the role of speculation in the foreign exchange market and the international monetary system'.

Davidson refers to a recent paper by Eichengreen, Tobin and Wyplosz (1995) and fully subscribes to their position that 'volatility' in foreign exchange markets due to speculation has 'real economic consequences [which are] devastating for particular sectors and whole economies'. Actually, in today's global economy, more and more portfolio fund managers in search of yields and 'safe harbours' can move huge amounts of funds 'from one country to another in nanoseconds with a few clicks on their computer keyboard'. Even major central banks may not have sufficient resources to intervene effectively to extinguish any 'speculative currency fire'. The consequent panic may well bring about a cumulative worsening of the situation; then only a coordinated response could have the means and the credibility to stop the 'increasing *inferno*', but such a response is not always at hand.

Since such 'hot money' portfolio flows can have massive disruptive real economic effects, Tobin and his associates recommend a global *ad valorem* tax on all exchange transactions in order to discourage short term round-tripping without affecting long-term international portfolio investments.

However, Davidson's idea is that, on the basis of realistic values of the parameters involved in the usual calculations made by speculators, the usual suggested magnitude of a 'Tobin tax' or other similar 'opportunity cost' capital tax will only *marginally* increase the cost of speculating. Hence a Tobin tax would stop speculation only on relatively *small* movements in the exchange rate, while it could have a significantly larger impact on stemming real international trade. As a result of this conclusion and owing to the impossibility of creating any kind of a Supernational Central Bank (which is what Keynes would have suggested), Davidson's attention moves towards the 'modest goal' of obtaining an international agreement among the G7 nations with the aim of establishing a currency-speculation fire prevention institution and an alternative international payments system.

In short, the proposal is to establish an 'international clearing system' whereby an International Money Clearing Unit (IMCU) is created as a unit of account and ultimate reserve asset for international liquidity. All IMCU's would be held only by central banks and each central bank is committed to guarantee *one way* convertibility from IMCU deposits at the Clearing Union to its domestic currency while making available foreign moneys (through IMCU clearing transactions) to its own bankers and private sector residents. Ultimately, all major international transactions would be cleared between the central banks' accounts in the books of the International clearing institution.

Whereas the exchange rate between the domestic currency and the IMCU would be set *initially* so that a system of fixed exchange rates prevailed, it would change only to reflect variations in *efficiency wages* (which are related to money wages divided by the average product of labour, that is the unit labour costs modified by profit mark-up in domestic money terms of domestically produced GNP). By altering the exchange rate between local moneys and the IMCU to offset the rate of domestic inflation, the IMCU's purchasing power would bc stabilized. Then, if a country had a tendency towards persistent international deficits on its current accounts, there would be a *prima facie* evidence that it would not possess the productive capacity to maintain its current standard of living (and, if it is a poor country, it ought to be supported by rich nations). On the other hand, a 'trigger mechanism' should be established in order to encourage a creditor country to spend what is deemed (in advance) by agreement of the international community to be *'excessive' credit balances accumulated by running current account surpluses*.

Finally, Davidson's interesting proposal is completed by the proviso that, if any country objected to the idea of the limits that the IMCU system would be going to introduce into the free movement of capital funds, then any such nation is free to join other nations of similar attitudes in forming a Regional currency union and thereby assuring a free flow of funds among the residents of the union.

Giorgio Lunghini's paper deals with the crucial problem concerning the way in which the relationship between the production of commodities and employment of labour can be described nowadays, particularly in the case of capitalist or market economies. Whereas it is true that, if production declines, employment falls, the opposite is no longer true, to the effect that, if production recovers, then employment may *not* recover at all. Hence 'unemployment becomes crystallized through technological and organizational restructuring and tends to become irreversible'.

Actually, in capitalist economies, it is increasingly true that 'the consumer durables market has become progressively saturated, process innovation prevails over product innovation, the time horizons of investment decisions are shortened, while the geographical ones are widened'. More specifically, intensifying and lengthening production time and overtime inside the factories and contracting out overhead costs to the outside sections of the economy are more and more preferable to taking on more workers. Whereas in an open economy the problem of employment may be considered as one of competitiveness and of reduction in the cost of labour, such a recipe cannot be generalized. For, 'if one considers that the world is a closed system, a universal reduction of the cost of labour would be translated into a general crisis of overproduction'.

Even an overall reduction in the hours of work does not seem to be a 'practical' road towards solving the high and long-lasting unemployment problem, in so far as 'A policy of reducing the working week [for the same salary] nowadays arouses obvious and probably insuperable opposition from capitalists, but particularly it assumes that commodities can satisfy all needs'.

On the other hand, in a market economy in which an increased production of commodities goes hand in hand with a decreasing amount of wage-earning labour, the other side of increasing unemployment consists of 'unsatisfied social needs' which occur mainly in the production sphere of social services, that is in the direct production of 'use-values'. Then, 'if the correspondence between the dynamics of commodity production and the dynamics of employment disappears', it is clear that both 'too many commodities and too few jobs' and 'wasted labour and unsatisfied social needs' grow together.

Lunghini believes that the solution to be performed is 'to promote and organize socially useful jobs, whose nature is that of concrete labour [as opposed to abstract labour employed in the production of commodities]' and which 'must be jobs *immediately* directed at producing use-values' (instead of exchange-values) and 'must be capable of satisfying the social needs which commodity production does not satisfy'. Furthermore, Lunghini recognizes that 'Although conceptually simple, realizing this design is not. At least two problems must be mentioned: how to finance concrete labour and how to govern relations between the two sectors'. As to the first problem, in the present conditions of market economies, the choice cannot but fall on the taxation of rent, 'which nowadays is principally financial rent'.

As to the second problem, the idea put forward is that 'Setting up concrete labour requires intermediate government levels between the Market and the Dictator and different forms of society'. In particular, Lunghini refers to an idea suggested by Keynes (1926) when he writes: 'I believe that in many cases the ideal size for the unit of control and organization lies somewhere between the individual and the modern State. I suggest, therefore, that progress lies in the growth and the recognition of semi-autonomous bodies within the State-bodies. . . .'

In conclusion, Lunghini says that nowadays the problem of 'the explosive contrast between mass unemployment and the mass of unsatisfied social needs' is 'present all over the world, obviously to different degrees and in different forms'. In my opinion, though, the corresponding problem of 'too many commodities and a shortage of jobs' does *not* display the same features in poor countries as in rich ones. Instead, it seems to me that, in poor countries, there is still ample scope for increasing employment in the production of commodities; for there we are faced with acute problems of shortage of commodities and of unsatisfied commodity needs (particularly, food) as well as with unsatisfied social service needs. On the other hand, I entirely agree with Lunghini's further conclusion that in general 'The choice we are faced with . . . is not between welfare and austerity, it is between possible forms of austerity. Poverty awaits us if we let things take their course, a poverty predictably garbed in new forms of authoritarianism, or possibly a vigorous austerity'.

In the third Part on 'Capital Accumulation: Real and Financial Aspects', Jan Kregel's paper may well be thought of as a companion paper to Paul Davidson's in stressing the full relevance of Fausto Vicarelli's interpretation of the fundamental changes brought about by Keynes in economic theory (see, in particular, Vicarelli, 1977). Such changes have been overlooked not only by the so called 'neoclassical synthesis', but also by the more recent and inappropriately named 'New Keynesian economics', which 'seems to rely on the failure of the perfectly competitive market to allocate information efficiently'.

Actually, in both Vicarelli's and Kregel's positions, Keynes's explanation of the instability of capitalist economies was not based on the failure of the operation of the market's information mechanism, any more than on the existence of uncompetitive product or labour markets. Instead, Kregel writes, 'Keynes's analysis of instability was based on his belief that there was a basic difference in the way the price mechanism operated with respect to consumption goods and to capital or investment goods'.

In contrast to the acceptance of the assumption that short-term expectations were always realized, Keynes considered that it would be inappropriate to assume that long-term expectations could ever be realized. The reason for this difference is that 'it is the nature of long-term expectations that they cannot be checked at short intervals in the light of realized results' (Keynes, 1936, p. 51). If it was impossible to determine whether the expectations concerning an investment were satisfied, then the self-adjusting competitive market mechanism could not be applied to investment decisions. With reference to a 'monetary production economy' such as the capitalist economy, Kregel's point is that Keynes intended to 'rework' the theory of demand *and* supply in order to provide a 'new microtheory' which would consist in a reformulation of the theory of investment decisions to be based on such variables as the marginal efficiency of capital, the rate of interest (on the side of the demand prices for capital goods) *and* 'user costs' (as to the calculation of their supply prices).

Kregel's convincing position holds that 'It is necessary to calculate the appropriate supply price incurred in production of output and the present value of the net sum received per unit of output (the demand price or forward price) in order to identify the 'actual nature of the business decision' or the comparison of spot prices, current supply prices and forward prices', where – as may be seen – supply prices refer to 'future spot prices' of output. According to this interpretation, user costs play a central role in determining supply prices, but not so much in terms of maintenance costs, as of 'sacrifice', related to the decision to produce or not to produce. It is the present value of expected future returns that will determine the influence of the future on the present demand prices of capital goods, *while* user costs will determine the influence of the future on present supply prices.

Moreover, the rate of interest enters into the calculation of the demand prices through the specification of the rate of discount, *and* it enters into supply prices through the impact of the cost of carry on user costs. Kregel rightly adds to this the remark that it was for this reason that the *General Theory* (1936) differed from the *Treatise on Money* (1930) in the introduction of the distinction between the determinants of the marginal efficiency of capital and the rate of interest. Kregel's position is that liquidity preference and the concept of the 'liquidity premium' are a straightforward extension of the idea of user costs determining whether it is profitable to hold money for future use, rather than using it today to purchase consumption or investment goods.

Actually, the decision 'not to use' a commodity or capital equipment in production is the equivalent of retaining the privilege of doing so in the future. The instability of the system would be the result of the fact that it was impossible to compare expectations with results and there was no objective referent upon which expectations might be based. Entrepreneurial decisions would, therefore, need the calculation of present values which would require the specification of future returns prices discounted at the 'going' rate of interest. On the other hand, as future supply prices are given by spot prices plus the inclusion of carrying costs, there is no need to formulate expectations about future prices: *option values* instead will be used in order to make the needed calculation. More specifically, dividing the calculated future returns prices by the current interest rate will yield the calculated demand prices. But similar exercises would have to be made with reference to the calculation of future supply prices.

However, there is one crucial additional piece of information which is required in order to calculate the option values: the 'volatility' of product prices. This is *the only unknown* which we have to determine so that entrepreneurial decisions may be evaluated and made; but this is precisely what *is not*, and *cannot*, be known. If volatility cannot be predicted correctly, then option prices cannot be calculated correctly. This, as Kregel concludes, reflects Keynes's basic criticism of traditional theory. For we are thrown back to the problem that we do not know how changes in the state of expectations are produced and how they influence current business decisions. Anyhow it is the impact of changes in the state of expectations on price volatility which will determine whether or not the economy is inherently stable or unstable: volatility will then determine instability and with it the process of capital accumulation.

The title of Giangiacomo Nardozzi's paper – as well as that of Musu's paper – recalls the title of the book edited by Vicarelli in 1983 that collected a group of essays in honour of one of our unforgettable teachers, Federico Caffè. In agreement with both Vicarelli and Caffè, Nardozzi's point is that, if we want to understand and explain how financial markets work in the typical conditions of uncertainty in capitalist economies, and in particular in the present global markets, we cannot help but make reference to Keynes's analysis and especially to the Keynesian concept of uncertainty. In plain consonance with Davidson's and Kregel's positions, Nardozzi lists five points in favour of the relevance of Keynes's thought for the working of present financial markets.

The first point is the fact that more and more market economies have become monetary economies in Keynes's sense. In particular, in conditions in which uncertainty is mainly caused by the working of a 'monetary production economy', money specifically is a means of reserve value and of accumulation of financial wealth. In financial markets the Keynesian 'urge to action' fully displays itself in so far as it is meant to defeat uncertainty through a continuous interplaying of financial transactions.

Second, there can be little unsatisfaction in the way in which predominant theories set out to explain the very high levels of the rates of interest which prevail in present financial markets. In contrast to Keynes's thought, such theories concentrate on the relevance of the so-called 'fundamentals' which – according to neoclassical thought – are represented by a (lower) degree of thriftiness and a (higher) level of the marginal productivity of capital. Both phenomena, however, do *not* seem to have received satisfactory econometric support.

Third, it has become increasingly difficult to explain the recent large fluctuations in the 'prices' of financial assets in most capitalist economies on the basis of neoclassical theories. It seems that much more can be understood if we make reference to such Keynesian concepts as uncertainty, the irrationality of markets, animal spirits, the role of imitative behaviour. On the other hand, there is no point in pursuing explanations based on such positions as those taken by the so-called 'precarious psychology' of financial markets, for the answer must surely lie in a theory of the behaviour of such markets which we should try to develop on Keynesian foundations.

Fourth, and in close connection with the previous point, proper account must be taken of the fact that financial markets are not really 'moved' by the irrational behaviour of individual transactors, but rather by the overwhelming action of international institutional investors who can 'mobilize' enormous amount of funds. In such conditions our task is to try to put forward a theory based on Keynes's *objective* concept of probability which is not at all dependent on any 'subjective human fancy' but on individual rational assessment of all circumstances and information. In Nardozzi's penetrating words, 'this is the ground which should be ploughed most by economists nowadays'.

The fifth and final point refers to Nardozzi's remark that, in trying to do so, we should be guided by a Keynesian 'philosophy of praxis' more than by any pre-manufactured theory based on *a priori* assumptions. Then, in any given circumstance, the knowledge necessary for both action and the understanding of actions, will be based on information, experiences, and motivations, which are different in different conditions. Therefore, what is more likely to happen is what is more *reasonable*, and such a reasonableness of events remains the relevant one for action even if it may be 'disproved' by the outcome of individual events.

Finally, we must aim to put into practice the lessons which are to be learnt from any such point. Nardozzi concludes that a continuous attempt to understand and explain present and future trends in financial markets must pursue a *parallel* analysis of the actual behaviour of prices of different assets and of the interpretation of events which derives from the opinions of transactors, analysts and institutions, who daily operate in each market, both at the level of each relevant country and at the international market level.

In the fourth Part on 'Social Choices, Economic Policy and Moral Values', Anthony Atkinson's paper very interestingly outlines a proposal for a definite policy recommendation concerning the establishment of an official poverty line and the reduction of poverty as an explicit policy objective. More specifically, the proposal aims at the establishment of a Poverty Report by the British Government each year, along the lines of the publication of the quarterly Inflation Report which has recently been started by the Bank of England. Obviously this proposal may well have a more general application than that of the British case. Moreover, Atkinson draws a parallel between his proposal and those which several European Governments have made about the need for employment targets 'to be placed alongside those for government borrowing and debt'.

To start with, the author points out the ambiguity that seems to have characterized the British situation since the Beveridge Plan (1942), whereby while there are no official poverty standards, there exists a social security system with largely flat-rate benefit scales. In contrast, both the European Union Commission and the USA Federal Government have given a definition of a poverty standard and recently an official poverty line has been published in Italy too.

The point is, though, that the 'mere' publication of statistical poverty lines is not enough: what Atkinson strongly recommends is a 'statement of intent'. Essential to the proposal is that the official poverty line should be set *independently* of social security benefit scales. It is important to keep these separate, for the poverty target is an *objective*, while social security benefits are an *instrument*. Moreover, in terms of Tinbergen's theory of economic policy, Atkinson believes that the abolition of poverty is better to be a *flexible* rather than a *fixed* target, for a fixed target may prove to be a too rigid criterion (such is the case with the well-known Maastricht targets), whereas the attainment of such a flexible target may be limited on account of other constraints faced by the government.

Although the adoption of such a performance standard may seem entirely natural, some objections have been raised against it, each of which Atkinson intends to dismantle.

The first set of arguments is that there could be no agreement on the definition of a poverty line and on the contents of the Poverty Report. However, there are three considerations which will make the task of agreement easier: first, there is an important difference between agreeing on a criterion according to which benefits are to be paid and agreeing on a definition for purely statistical purposes; second, it may be possible to identify common ground even where there is not complete agreement; third, the Report should not concentrate on a single number, but present a range of information, as well as an informed commentary.

The second objection is that we can define an official line, but its adoption would not contribute to the reduction of poverty. It would be mere rhetoric and make no actual difference. However the answer depends on the model of behaviour which the government would be expected to follow. If viewed in principal/agent terms, there has to be a close link between policies and results, so that a commitment to specific policy measures may be more effective. The report may also provide grounds for raising the issue of combating poverty in all spheres of government policies.

The third objection is that it would make a difference but in the wrong direction, that is, it would be counter-productive. Atkinson points out, though, that any such risk can be moderated by a careful choice of the measure and by the use of multiple indicators.

Finally, there are those who can see no reason why a government should agree to a performance target. Why, for example, should politicians agree to a poverty target as part of the European project? The positive answer for an official poverty standard target lies in the same reason as in the case of the inflation policy target, that is, the search for credibility.

Atkinson's conclusion is that, even if there may be legitimate grounds for concern, particularly as to the fact 'that it would focus attention on the anti-poverty function of social transfers to the exclusion of other functions', on balance it seems that there is a good case for his proposal, both at a British and at a European level. This is especially so if the proposal is considered in the light of the 1995 Copenhagen Summit on Social Development when governments officially committed themselves to 'establish . . . strategies and affordable time-bound goals and targets for the substantial reduction of overall poverty and the eradication of absolute poverty'.

The final paper by Stefano Zamagni resumes the basic themes of Lunghini's paper, but it develops them in a rather different perspective. The starting point is an historical analysis of how the evolution of economic doctrines in modern times has seen the separation of economics from political theory and, therefore, the abandonment by economic theory of the analysis of civil society and of its 'status' as the theory of civil economy. But nowadays the urge is towards the ending of such a separation, a task that Zamagni believes should coincide with the rebuilding of 'the foundations of an economic constitution of civil society'. To this end proper account is to be taken of the fact that – in his words – 'civil society is the ideal-typical place to foster dispositions to trust; not so the private market which is instead a trust-consumer'.

Zamagni goes on to enlarge on the point and writes: 'The question is, therefore, how can one deal with the problem of extending trust to larger economic structures, having started from short-range relations (within families, small groups, . . . and so on)?' The author's answer to this question is that 'the winning strategy to generalize trust is to favour the creation of a new economic space, that of civil economy'. The civil economy consists in all those activities in which neither profit and self-interest (as in the private market sphere) nor coercion or compulsory action (as in the State or public sphere) are the *primum movens* of operation. In particular, whereas the principle of legitimization of economic decisions is represented, in private and public markets, by purchasing-power and by the right of citizenship respectively, in the civil economy it is represented by the *reciprocity principle*.

In terms of a recent formulation by S. Kolm (1994), the 'reciprocity relation' can be formalized 'as a series of bi-directional transfers, independent of one other, yet interconnected. Independence implies that each transfer is in itself voluntary which means free'; in other words, one transfer is never a pre-requisite for the occurrence of another. Moreover, we should recognize that reciprocity has a *strategic* dimension of its own. Unlike what happens with altruism, 'should the recipient of my transfer not reciprocate, at a later moment I will somehow put an end to our relationship'. In the economist's language, it may be said that 'reciprocity ties may modify the outcome of the economic game, whether by tending to stabilize cooperative behaviours by agents interacting within contexts of the prisoner's dilemma kind, or because the reciprocity practice tends to modify endogenously subjects' preferences themselves, that is to say the form of their objective functions'.

As to the question 'to what extent is reciprocity practised and how significant is it?', Zamagni indicates that one should look not only to practices within families, small informal groups, and associations of various kinds, but also to the transactions network which exists 'in all those enterprises that fill the variegated non-profit world, from cooperatives, in which reciprocity takes the form of mutuality, to voluntary organizations where reciprocity verges on . . . the free gift'. Moreover, as the Italian experience shows, 'the so-called model of the new competition' implies, to be practised, both the willingness to cooperate and a close-knitted transaction network with a structure very similar to that of reciprocity relations. The point is that, in this broader context, the market needs to be understood as consisting of both 'private exchanges' and 'reciprocal transfers'. Zamagni's conclusion on this point is that '*Free* competition between private economy and civil economy – placed on equal competition basis – will take care of decisions as to which (private) goods or services it is more appropriate or effective to provide according to the exchange of equivalents or reciprocity'. In my opinion, another point may be added to this conclusion: similar competition ought to be envisaged between the public economy and the civil economy, as to which *social* goods or services it is more appropriate to provide according to the coercion principle or to reciprocity.

Zamagni convincingly underlines the fact that 'unlike private goods that can be enjoyed alone, and unlike public goods that can be enjoyed jointly by more subjects', the reciprocity sector supplies *relational* goods, that is goods that produce utility to the consumer only if shared with other subjects. Unlike the case of the so-called 'positional' goods (see Hirsch, 1976), that is goods whose demand increases with economic growth but cannot be met by an increased supply, in the case of relational goods, as demand increases, supply may increase as well, since the latter and the former are linked together owing to the fact that the consumption of relational goods is commonly shared in the very process of transfer which is implied by the reciprocity principle.

Then, Zamagni (like Lunghini) refers to the specific feature of our post-industrial economies whereby there simultaneously prevail two-side affluence and two-side shortage. On the one hand, there exists overproduction of private goods (commodities and services) combined with high unemployment of labour. On the other hand, we face a situation of unsatisfied social needs combined with a want of resources needed to supply the appropriate social services. Moreover, an increase in the production of private goods no longer brings about increased employment, while the public sector is no longer able effectively and efficiently to supply those social services whose demand displays high increases in post-industrial societies. The crucial point, then, is that resources which are saved in the private sector, and most probably will not be directed into the public sector, may be utilized by the 'third sector' in order to supply those social services that are strongly and increasingly needed in post-industrial economies.

Zamagni's conclusion is that, in the present conditions of the post-industrial era, 'We need to build bridges spanning from a labour in quest of genuine significance to a consumption that cannot be an end in itself. That is where civil economics can offer a remarkable, perhaps unique, contribution in turning the consumer into a social actor well aware of the influential power he holds over what is produced and how it is produced'.

REFERENCES

Beveridge, W.H. (1942) *Social Insurance and Allied Services*, London, HMSO.

Beveridge, W.H. (1945) *Full Employment in a Free Society*, New York, Norton.

Eichengreen, B., Tobin, J. and Wyplosz, C. (1995) Two Cases for Sand in the Wheels of International Finance, *Economic Journal* **105**, 162–72 .

Hahn, F.H. and Solow, R. (1995) *A Critical Essay on Modern Macroeconomic Theory*, Oxford, Blackwell.

Hirsch, F. (1976) *The Social Limits to Growth*, Cambridge, Cambridge University Press.

Keynes, J.M. (1926) *The End of Laissez-faire*, London, Macmillan.

Keynes, J.M. (1930) *The Treatise on Money*, London, Macmillan.

Keynes, J.M. (1936) *The General Theory of Employment, Interest and Money*, London, Macmillan.

Kolm, S. (1994) The Theory of Reciprocity and the Choice of Economic Systems, *Investigaciones Economicas* **18**, 67–95.

Tobin, J. (1972) Inflation and Unemployment, *American Economic Review* **62**, 1–18.

Tobin, J. (1993a) Price Flexibility and Output Stability: An Old Keynesian View, *Journal of Economic Perspectives* **7**, 45–65.

Tobin, J. (1993b) An Old Keynesian Counterattacks, Yale University, *Cowles Foundation Discussion Paper* n. 1042.

Vicarelli, F. (1977) *Keynes. L'instabilità del Capitalismo*, Milano, Etas Libri; Engl. tr. Philadelphia, Univ. of Pennsylvania Press, 1984, and London, Macmillan, 1984.

Vicarelli, F. (ed.) (1983) *Attualità di Keynes*, Bari-Roma; Engl. tr. London, Macmillan, 1985.

Opening Address

Antonio Fazio

Fausto Vicarelli was an economist with solid theoretical foundations. His academic training began at the University of Rome in the mid-1950s, as a student of Volrico Travaglini, who acted as advisor for his degree thesis on 'Dynamic theory according to Hicks and the Swedish school'. Subsequently he was to win a Stringher scholarship and continue his studies at Harvard University.

As a teacher of economic theory and policy at the Universities of Ancona, Florence and Rome, he was always attentive to the needs of his students, always ready to give advice, clarify and explain. But at the same time bent on developing with his students a doctrine able to explain the economy starting from the practical problems of the particular historical moment.

A scholar deeply read in Keynes's works, he remained open to all the different currents of thought. He worked on international economics and finance, price theory and the allocation of resources, and development; in the last few years of his life he concentrated on labour and employment issues.

He provided the leading trade unions with disinterested advice in an exemplary manner, orienting them towards a policy that stressed stability and growth. In this field he worked with another economist and common friend, Ezio Tarantelli, who, like Fausto, was to die prematurely in tragic circumstances.

Fausto Vicarelli and Ezio Tarantelli carried out valuable research and advisory work at the Bank of Italy. My predecessors were the beneficiaries. I worked closely with them as head of the Bank's Research Department. Fausto's commitment was primarily towards the younger members of the staff; he was constantly and actively present in the Bank, and his involvement would increase during the preparation of the Annual Report.

Initially Fausto's work focused on the theory of value and some theoretical aspects of economic development. His participation in the activity of the Bank's Research Department led him to pay greater attention to the problems of finance and, in particular, to those connected with the international opening of the Italian financial system, which was just beginning.

His theoretical thinking and existential reflections, his awareness of the problems of employment led him increasingly to re-explore Keynes's ideas. His training in this field can be traced back to the courses he followed at Harvard and the academic discussions and debates on economic policy that animated the intellectual life of Boston in the early 1960s.

Vicarelli's reconstruction and exposition of Keynes's analysis show how its development was influenced by the tragic political and economic events of the Great Depression. In particular, he highlights Keynes's view of capitalism as a monetary economy, intrinsically based on credit and money; an economy characterized by the instability of demand and employment. Keynes's thinking, as reconstructed by Vicarelli, emphasizes the limits of the traditional approach of economic analysis, rooted in the notion of equilibrium.

The new element is first and foremost the historical moment: the Keynesian model starts out from the events and actual behaviour observed in the decades following the World War I, a period of upheaval offering a wealth of information on the relationships between economic agents, the main aggregates of the national accounts and metaeconomic and political factors.

Expectations, credit, money, financial markets and institutions become of decisive importance in the model – institutions in the sense both of 'norms and rules of the game' and of collective agents that pursue goals and objectives of general interest. Money is no longer superimposed, dichotomously, on the real variables, which, according to the classics, made the economy converge towards full employment equilibrium. The central issue that economists addressed in that period, and which perhaps they should continue to address, concerned the reasons that prevented the economy from returning to full employment. The analysis of the relationships between money and the real economy was later developed in masterly fashion by Patinkin.

Interest rates and developments in the financial markets are doubtless the result of rational behaviour, but market participants are influenced by expectations and metaeconomic events. Financial phenomena, in turn, affect investment, income and employment.

Starting from Fausto Vicarelli, from the concreteness of his analyses, I should like to examine with you some of the problems created by the behaviour of the international economy and the globalization of markets, in order to raise some questions. In classical theory, investment occurred as the result of saving; it was the material embodiment of saving. In a capitalist economy, such as that which emerged in the second half of the nineteenth century and the early decades of the twentieth, investment decisions are increasingly dissociated from those that determine the supply of saving. Credit, in all its forms, is the counterpart of investment within the economy and sustains it by providing the link with saving. The dissociation between the formation of saving and its use is now spreading to the international domain: investment projects and budget deficits are now financed to a significant extent in internationally integrated financial markets.

Under conditions of less than full employment, in Keynes, in contrast with classical economics, new investment leads to an increase in income and hence in saving.

The system is therefore controlled by demand. There are no forces, or only very weak ones, causing output to converge towards the level that guarantees full employment of the factors of production. The system is inherently unstable. The determination of interest rates, which is entrusted to the supply and demand for financial instruments, comes to depend decisively on conventions and expectations.

Keynes revives the distinction, well known to economists before Smith, between the profit rate and the rate of return on investment on the one hand and the money rate of interest on the other. The ancient laws on usury are revisited. In the present circumstances of the international economy, the comparison should be between the yield on securities in international markets and the growth rate of the economy.

In the early sixties Franco Modigliani – to whom I owe my introduction to the Keynesian model, to monetary theory and to the analysis of credit flows starting from Professor Tobin's *Manuscript* – pointed out to me that the development of Keynes's thinking by his followers had stressed the analysis of flows while neglecting that of stocks.

He invited me to study Friedman, with whom he none the less disagreed sharply on several issues. The equilibrium of stocks had been neglected above all in the conduct of monetary policy, although not in theoretical analysis: Tobin and his school again come to mind, as do the various attempts to include a demand function for stocks of financial assets in the Bank of Italy's econometric model.

From both a theoretical and a practical standpoint, it has always been difficult to include an overall equilibrium for financial assets in an analytically and empirically structured model in which the short-term equilibrium is determined by demand. Perhaps it is difficult to incorporate in such a model the changes of regime that take place in periods of crisis and the occurrence of rationing.

Monetarism in its contemporary guise was born with Friedman's *Restatement* of 1956, his Fordham lectures, the *Monetary History of the United States* and the simple and masterly *Role of Monetary Policy*.

After the period of stability in the 1960s, the growth in the budget in all the leading industrial countries tended to exceed the limits and distort the nature that Keynes had attributed to it. Rather than on investment, the emphasis was on social expenditure, which rose rapidly in relation to GDP. Nearly everywhere monetary policy was accommodating, the resistance it opposed to the inflationary pressures of domestic and international origin insufficient. The Volcker turning-point came in 1979: attention switched back from interest rates to the quantities of credit and money. Nominal and real interest rates rose sharply and their variability increased markedly.

All the industrial countries adopted the control of quantities. This had already happened on several occasions in Italy – at the end of 1947, in 1974 and again in 1977. On each occasion this entailed costs in terms of economic activity and employment, but the results in terms of exchange rate and price stability were satisfactory.

In the 1980s the money stock became the centre of attention everywhere. The rise in interest rates accelerated the growth in public debts and seriously aggravated the problem of the external debt of the developing countries, which was then further exacerbated by the appreciation of the dollar. At the international level there began to emerge what was later seen to be a global market in foreign currencies and securities. At a time of rising debt and restrictions on the quantity of money, real interest rates became positive everywhere – a new development compared with the experience of the preceding decades.

Monetary policies tamed inflation, but the trend growth rate of the industrial economies slowed significantly in comparison with the 1950s and 1960s. Signs emerged of the revival of a phenomenon that appeared to have been eliminated in the previous decades, a steady rise in unemployment.

In the second half of the 1980s, in response to technological innovation, and on analytical and ideological grounds, the liberalization of capital movements accelerated. One of the pillars of the

Bretton Woods system, the confining of banks' activity to their domestic markets, was eroded, thus giving additional impetus to the development of the global financial market. The measurement of many aspects of this market is still inadequate; we see their effects above all in exchange rates and securities markets, but we do not have a sufficient understanding of its working. I see the growth of the global market as having accelerated particularly in the last few years. The result has been a continuous conditioning of economies, even those of medium size.

In his research on the international opening of financial systems and floating exchange rates, Fausto Vicarelli foresaw the possibility of the external constraint reappearing in new forms. The fact that monetary policy was broadly effective in controlling inflation in the 1980s was also due to the return to a system of floating exchange rates between the main economic areas: the United States, Japan and Europe. Exchange rates were fixed within the EMS, but realigned on several occasions.

The process of disinflation entrusted to monetary policy was implemented in Italy, effectively, through the exchange rate link with countries with more stable currencies. Short-term interest rates in each country are under the control of the central bank, but especially in the last few years long-term rates have increasingly followed a cyclical path that is powerfully influenced by that of the leading monetary area.

Since the 1992 crisis Italy has had a floating rate regime. In our experience, a restrictive monetary policy appears able, by inducing particularly high short-term interest rates, in both nominal and real terms, to influence medium-term expectations regarding the exchange rate and prices and to lower long-term interest rates significantly.

Monetary policy has regained its effectiveness in controlling nominal quantities, exchange rates, prices and interest rates, but the situation of the real economy in Europe appears further and further away from that of the full utilization of available resources envisaged by classical theory. In the 1980s and the first half of the 1990s, the unemployment rate has continued to rise.

At the global level there are factors determining a reallocation of productive activity; there is the ever-fiercer competition of the new industrial economies, whose labour costs – and living standards – are much lower than those prevailing in Europe. The cost of labour in Latin America and Southeast Asia is not even one tenth of that in the older industrial countries. The demand that originates from the newcomers, where the rate of growth is extremely high, between 5 and 10 per cent a year, is sustaining production in the developed countries. In Europe, the rate of growth of some of the leading economies in recent years has been particularly unsatisfactory. The excessive rigidity of wages and terms of employment and the social security charges on labour are certainly among the principal causes of low growth and competitiveness.

There remains the problem of a shortage of effective demand. Monetary policies are effective and powerful in ensuring respect for the 'external constraint'; however, the 'internal constraint' of full utilization of available resources has still to be met. At the risk of overdrawing a theoretical analogy, the impression is that there is a new dichotomy between the real economy and the monetary economy. Only that now, unlike in neoclassical theory, the productive economy of the individual countries – which is the economic sphere with which we are basically concerned for the purposes of welfare – is somehow superimposed on a financial and monetary economy, in which the equilibria are determined in the international markets.

In systems that are open to international trade in goods and services, flexibility in the terms of the supply of labour can make an important contribution to the expansion of production and employment. But Keynesian theory teaches that flexibility alone is unable to impel the economy towards full employment; and, to a degree, we are verifying this proposition empirically. A sufficient level of aggregate demand is necessary. In the European economies the prospects for investment growth in particular appear deficient. I ask the economists who are assembled here to help us better understand the phenomena that we are experiencing; I ask them to help us to devise models in which the real economy, the level of economic activity and employment are functionally integrated with a monetary economy, which, I repeat, is expanding significantly and achieving equilibrium above all at the international level. Policymakers need to be able to rely on simple, comprehensible, workable models in order to overcome the problems that ultimately concern the population.

Your professional accomplishments and political and social awareness make me confident that you can contribute to progress in this direction.

Part I

Theoretical Analyses and Actual Economic Problems

1 Supply Constraints on Employment and Output: NAIRU Versus Natural Rate

James Tobin

'POTENTIAL OUTPUT' AND THE TWO REGIME MODEL

Every macroeconomic theory needs a concept of the economy's productive capacity, the overall constraint on the effectiveness of increasing aggregate demand in increasing actual output and employment. This is not a technocratic physical limit, such as could be relevant to a wartime emergency. In the United States in World War II the entire population was working overtime, unemployment was 1 per cent, plants were operating on shifts around the clock, and quantitative controls dictated by central government priorities displaced market prices and wages in allocating resources. This regime performed miracles. In 1944 nearly half the GNP was commandeered for war, and the remainder was greater than the entire prewar GNP. Clearly this kind of economy is not feasible in peacetime.

What we mean by potential GDP in peacetime is what a market economy without rationing and other quantitative controls, with households and businesses making most of the decisions affecting prices and resource allocations, can produce. Accordingly capacity *Net* Domestic Product is sustainable GDP minus allowance for the depreciation and depletion of productive resources. These are not unambiguous concepts, because there is generally no sharp dividing line beyond which additions to demand cease to induce response in increased production.

That is why it is natural to define the capacity constraint in terms of the effects of additional demand on prices (including nominal wage rates). In Keynes's *General Theory* (1936), potential output corresponds to *full employment* of labour, and the tell-tale symptom of excess demand is inflation. In the *General Theory* any stable level of aggregate demand and output short of full employment will be accompanied by stable prices. However, moving closer to full employment would raise prices. That is, the stable price level will be higher at a higher stable aggregate demand level. The picture is asymmetrical. Deflationary gaps in demand show up in shortfalls of actual output from full employment output but not in prices, whereas inflationary gaps of demand affect prices but not output. The notion that the economy can be in either of these two regimes demand-constrained or supply-constrained is an important and useful doctrine, central to Keynes's thought and to the meaning of the word 'general' in his title. Of course he believed that mature capitalist economies are usually demand-constrained.

COST-PUSH, DEMAND-PULL, AND PHILLIPS

In the middle 1950s American experience posed problems for this Keynesian model. Inflation arose and persisted at levels of GDP and employment that, on the basis of earlier observation, were thought to be well short of full employment. This inflation was dubbed cost-push in distinction to the inflation we economists thought we understood, demand-pull. Naming a phenomenon does not explain it, and there was no theory of cost-push inflation.[1]

Then came A.W. Phillips (1958) and his curve.[2] Stretched far beyond the author's intentions, this seemed to blur the distinction in a sensible way. The strength of cost-push depends on the pull of demand, as measured by the gap, positive or negative, between capacity output and actual output. That gap, in turn, is closely related to the unemployment rate, a relationship quantified by Arthur Okun for the Council of Economic Advisers in 1961 (*Economic Report of the President*, 1962, pp. 49–56; Okun, 1962). The Phillips curve provided a continuous relationship of wage inflation to unemployment. Assuming that prices of value added are normal labour costs per unit output marked up to cover fixed costs and capital costs, price inflation mirrors wage inflation less the trend of productivity growth.

One trouble with this development was that it left full employment undefined. Should it correspond to the unemployment rate at which wage inflation would just equal productivity growth, so that price inflation would be zero? This definition just revived the original problem: GDP at that unemployment rate didn't look and feel like full employment. But if full employment was further up the Phillips curve, how far? And wouldn't the Keynesian hypothesis that prices are stable when demand falls below full employment GNP have to be abandoned? Or alternatively the notion of a sharp dividing line between the two regimes, demand-determined and supply-determined, could be discarded in favour of the idea of a zone of more and less full employment.

THE PRICE-WAGE FEEDBACK

Phillips himself, Lipsey (1960), Samuelson and Solow (1960), and many other economists who adopted the Phillips curve recognized that wage inflation, a determinant of price inflation, would itself be affected by price inflation. There are two reasons for this reverse effect: workers seek compensation for increases in consumer prices, and employers are more willing to pay higher nominal wages when product prices are higher. In the early 1960s statistical Phillips curve fits on American post-war data were very good. When lagged price inflation was added as a regressor, its coefficient was significant but also significantly less than one. The notion of a long-run Phillips curve, the locus along which the dependent variable wage-change was the same as the independent variable price-change minus the productivity trend, was introduced. The long-run curve was steeper than the short-run Phillips curve, which assumed the inflation feedback term to be constant. As years passed and added observations in more inflationary environments, estimates of the feedback coefficient gravitated to one, making the long-run Phillips curve vertical and undermining the notion of a policy trade-off between unemployment and inflation popularized by Samuelson and Solow (1960).

THE NATURAL RATE

Then came the natural rate of unemployment. Phelps (1967) and Friedman (1968) maintained that rational behaviour precluded any long-run trade-off, a conclusion strengthened by regarding the inflation term on the right hand side of the Phillips wage equation as expectation rather than sluggish adjustment, and as rational rather than adaptive expectation. Thus was the sharp dividing line earlier provided by Keynes's concept of full employment restored, but in a new guise, with important differences. At Friedman's natural rate of unemployment, Friedman's full employment, it is not the price level but the inflation rate that is stable. The rate is determined by the growth in money supply and in nominal aggregate demand, possibly but not necessarily zero. Friedman's price dynamics are, unlike Keynes's, symmetric: when monetary policy produces unemployment less than the natural rate, inflation increases without limit, and when monetary policy produces unemployment unnaturally high, inflation decreases indefinitely.

Friedman describes the natural rate of unemployment as 'the level that would be ground out by the Walrasian system of general equilibrium equations, provided that there is embedded in them the actual structural characteristics of the labour and commodity markets, including market imperfections, stochastic variability in demands and supplies, the costs of getting information about job vacancies and labour availabilities, the costs of mobility, and so on'. By characterizing the natural rate as Walrasian Equilibrium, Friedman endows it with the usual optimal properties. The proviso is understandable, if not excusable. Without the non-Walrasian elements listed, the natural rate would be zero; if markets cleared, there would be no unemployment and no unfilled vacancies. But the proviso is a tall order. Generations of economists have not found an equilibrium system that embeds all those bothersome phenomena.

Keynes too recognized that there would be non-zero unemployment – frictional unemployment – at what he called full employment. He too finessed explanation of the size of frictional unemployment. He regarded full employment as optimal: 'I see no reason to suppose that the existing system seriously misemploys the factors of production which are in use . . . It is in determining the volume, not the direction, of actual employment that the existing system has broken down' (Keynes, 1936, p. 379). Keynes identified full employment with the 'classical' equilibrium of the aggregate labour market, defined as that volume of employment at which the marginal product of labour equals the real wage equals the marginal disutility of work. Unlike Friedman, of course, Keynes regarded involuntary unemployment, the demand-constrained regime, as the usual state of affairs.

Friedman was a short step away from the New Classical doctrine that markets are continuously clearing and grinding out optimal moving equilibrium solving the Walrasian equations. That leads to the conclusion that actual unemployment, whatever it is, is natural or 'full'. I recall seeing in 1962 a message on the blackboard in the economics graduate students' lounge at Stanford saying, 'The Bureau of Labour Statistics announced this morning that the natural rate of unemployment is now 9.4 percent'.

THE NAIRU

Franco Modigliani, I believe, originated the NAIRU concept – Non-Accelerating-Inflation Rate of Unemployment (Modigliani and Papademos, 1976). At first he called it simply NIRU, Non-Inflationary Rate of Unemployment. Somehow it got changed in common usage, presumably to reflect better the 'accelerationist' theory. I believe that the whole purpose of the concept was to escape the normative equilibrium connotations of the natural rate. The NAIRU is like full employment, a barrier to expansion of demand and in some sense a boundary between regimes. But it need not be the best of all possible worlds, and departures from it need not have Friedman's dynamic consequences. It is a mistake, I think to regard NIRU or NAIRU just as neutral synonyms of natural rate. My own interpretation of the difference between NAIRU and natural rate is as follows.

The NAIRU does not assume a Walrasian equilibrium, in which markets, in particular labour markets, are being cleared by existing prices and wages. Instead it assumes an economy in which at any time most markets are characterized by excess demand or excess supply at prevailing prices. Applied to labour markets, excess demand means a preponderance of job vacancies over unemployment, and excess supply means the opposite. The distribution of markets, weighted by the number of workers or jobs in them, depends systematically on the strength of aggregate demand relative to potential GDP. That is, the weighted number of excess demand markets, relative to excess supply markets, will be greater the higher is aggregate demand.

The NAIRU is the unemployment rate at which the inflation-increasing effects of the excess-demand markets just balances the inflation-decreasing impacts of the excess-supply markets. Unlike the natural rate, this is a balance among disequilibrium markets, a stand-off between those in excess demand and those in excess supply.

The existence of markets in diverse circumstances is essential for the NAIRU. Unlike the natural rate, the NAIRU could not be modelled as a single economy-wide market or representative agent.

The distribution of these markets as function of aggregate real demand I take to be a characteristic of an economy that remains fairly constant within the time span of a business cycle and indeed changes only slowly from cycle to cycle. However, this does not mean that the identities of the markets within the distribution is constant or slow-changing. Markets are always interchanging places, as a result of never-ceasing inter-sectoral flux of microeconomic demands and supplies. This flux is quite consistent with the maintenance of a fairly stable macroeconomic environment.

THE BEVERIDGE CURVE

A Beveridge curve plots, for the economy as a whole, Vacancies against Unemployment, both as percentages of labour force. Observed Beveridge curves can be thought to be generated by the multimarket disequilibrium model just described, in the following way. It is convenient to think of each market at a given time as characterized by either vacancies or unemployment (or by neither) but not by both at the same time. Indeed that might be the definition of an atomic market. Then for the economy as a whole vacancies are the sum of excess-demands over all excess-demand markets, and unemployment is the sum of excess-supplies over all excess-supply markets. As aggregate demand is hypothetically raised from low to high, relative to potential output, excess supplies fall, excess demands rise, and markets move from excess-supply to excess-demand status. Consequently total vacancies increase and total unemployment decreases. The resulting Beveridge Curve is downward sloping, and in practice concave (see Figure 1.1).

The coexistence of unemployment and vacancies is a sign of frictional unemployment, which could be measured in principle as the amount of unemployment at the point on the curve where V=U. Beveridge (1945) did not invent the curve that bears his name, but he did define full employment as a situation in which unemployment is less than vacancies.

A movement along a Beveridge curve up and left arises from expansion of aggregate demand. An outward and upward shift of the curve increases frictional unemployment and raises the rate of

Figure 1.1 Beveridge curves in theory

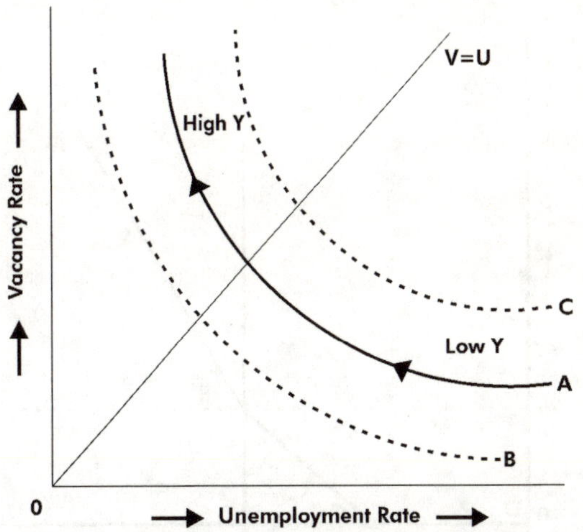

Note: Points above the U=V line are full employment by Beveridge's criterion. In practice, however, empirical measures of U and V are not commensurate. Indicated movement along curve A from low Y to high Y represents increase in aggregate real demand. Shift to curve C represents deterioration in labour market, leading to greater frictional or structural unemployment, likely also to an adverse shift in Phillips curve and NAIRU. Shift to curve B is benign.

vacancies associated with any given rate of unemployment. This might come about from an increase in the dispersion of excess demands and supplies across the markets, because of less efficient matching by labour markets or because of slower response of workers in moving from weak to strong markets. 'Structural unemployment', the label frequently given to unemployment not remediable by aggregate demand, might be an extreme case of frictional unemployment.

THE NAIRU AND THE PHILLIPS CURVE

A Phillips curve plots, for the economy as a whole, percentage increase in average wage rates against the economy-wide unemployment rate. Observed Phillips curves can be regarded as having been

Figure 1.2 Wage change as a function of excess demand or supply

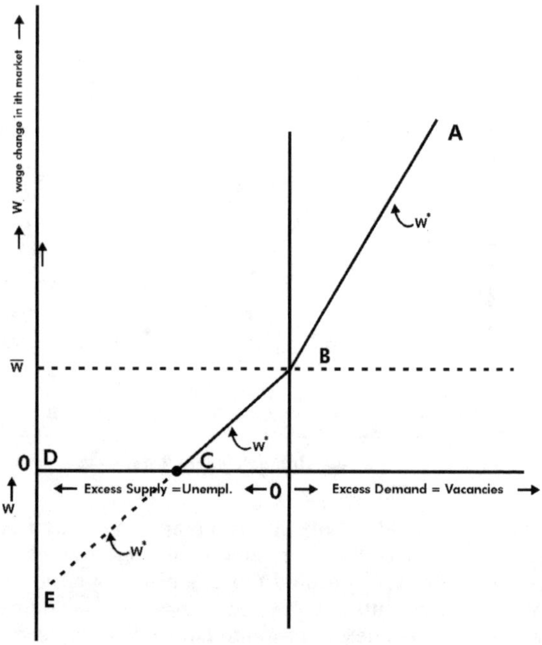

Note: $\bar{w}$ is the ongoing average nominal wage change of the economy. To this is added or subtracted w_i^*a function of Excess Demand or Supply in market i. As average wage-change rises or falls, point B moves with it. The function depicted is a broken line with steeper slope for Excess Demand than for Excess Supply. This is realistic but inessential. Temporary resistance to negative w_i is indicated by substitution of ABCD for ABCE as the wage-change function.

generated by the same model that generates the Beveridge curve. For each market there is a function that translates excess demand or supply into a market-specific wage change to which is added the common ongoing average wage change.

Figure 1.2 shows wage change in a single market as a function of excess demand or supply in that market. For each level of aggregate demand there is a point on the Beveridge curve and also a corresponding average wage change, which can be plotted either against the aggregate unemployment rate, as does the Phillips curve, or against aggregate vacancies. Since vacancies and unemployment are symmetric indicators of disequilibrium, it is logical to associate wage pressures with both of them. Just as unemployment might be expected to induce workers, individually or collectively, to moderate the terms on which they are willing to work, so vacancies might be expected to induce employers to bid higher for labour. (See Baily and Tobin (1977) for statistical wage-change regressions on both vacancies and unemployment.) An upward shift in the Beveridge curve, signifying an increase in frictional unemployment, should mean an increase in the wage inflation associated with a given rate of unemployment.

The old-fashioned neoclassical view of the mechanics of adjustment to excess supply or demand in individual markets was simply that prices would rise or fall as a positive function of excess demand (regarding excess supply as negative excess demand). Traditionally, this was just assumed to be a plausible characteristic of competitive markets, but it is also a likely implication of models of optimal price and quantity adjustments by individual market participants. In any case, the average wage increase would be greater the more the distribution of labour market was weighted in favour of excess-demand markets. Phillips (1958) and Lipsey (1960) took this approach as the obvious logic of the Phillips curve.

In addition, there would usually be in each market a non-zero wage increase or decrease related to the growth of productivity in that market and to the ongoing economy-wide pattern and expectation of wage and price inflation or deflation. This would occur in the absence of excess demand or supply.

The NAIRU is the rate of unemployment that generates no change in the average wage change. At the NAIRU the excess-demand and excess-supply markets' components of wage change average to zero. Does this model imply that the 'long-run' Phillips curve is vertical at the NAIRU, just as it is vertical at the natural rate in the Friedman-Phelps model? The answer is 'not always'. The multi-market stochastic macro-equilibrium model allows for a different possibility, about to be explained.

NOMINAL WAGE STICKINESS AND THE COSTS OF ZERO INFLATION

An important difference of Keynesian from neoclassical economics is that Keynes was explicitly describing a monetary economy, in which markets set nominal prices. Neoclassical economics is a theory of real or relative prices, essentially multilateral barter. Dudley Dillard (1988) convicted it of 'barter illusion'. Keynes considered it likely that adjustments of money wages to excess demand or supply would be sluggish, especially downward wage adjustments to excess supply of labour. This should not be considered as money illusion or as a characteristic of market-clearing equilibrium in any individual market or of Walrasian equilibrium in the whole economy.

Empirical evidence for downward wage stickiness is overwhelming. Availability of replacement workers outside the factory gate is almost never an occasion for employers to cut wages. At the same time, there is evidence that nominal wages will give way to save insiders' jobs when the employing company can convincingly claim financial distress and can threaten imminent shutdown. Perhaps the Phillips curve is a reclining 'S' with a long fairly flat middle, between sharp rises in inflation at low unemployment and falls at very high unemployment.

In Tobin (1972) I set forth a model of temporary downward nominal wage rigidity, namely that a market's wage change would be the maximum of 0 and w^*, where w^* is calculated from the formula above, shown in Figure 2, the sum of the change related to excess supply or demand and the common economy-wide pattern, but could be zero continuously for only a finite time. Thus if a market remained in a situation of large excess supply and w^* were negative, eventually the money wage would fall and this source of unemployment–inflation trade-off would cease. However, if microeconomic flux always puts another market into a similar excess-supply situation, some element of downward rigidity is always there, enabling an increment of aggregate demand to reduce unemployment permanently while increasing inflation permanently, or making a permanent increase of unemployment a cost of lowering the ongoing inflation trend.

This curvature in the long-run Phillips curve exists only at low inflation rates. If the economy's average wage inflation is high enough, there will never be any real wage adjustments in any markets that cannot be made without negative wage change, simply by falling behind the general pattern.

A recent paper at the Brookings Institution (Akerlof *et al.*, 1996) presents a similar model, and estimates and tests it empirically, finding that the model even explains the combination of rising unemployment and galloping deflation in the Great Depression in the United States. The authors estimate that at present pushing the price inflation trend in the United States to zero from 3 per cent would cost an additional full point of unemployment every year. By Okun's law, this is a permanent 2 or 2.5 per cent loss of GDP. This Brookings paper seems to be tempering the enthusiasm for literal price stability in the United States.

UNCERTAINTY ABOUT NAIRU AND POLICY TRADE-OFFs

Where the NAIRU is at any given time is quite uncertain. Evidently it rose in the United States after the 1960s, when 4 per cent seemed a good guess. NAIRU was widely estimated as 6 per cent at the beginning of the 1990s. This was the Federal Reserve's belief. But the Fed has allowed unemployment to decline almost to 5 per cent during the present recovery without hitting the monetary brakes. No significant inflationary consequences have followed. It seems that NAIRU has declined. Other indicators of labour market tightness – a low help wanted index, a proxy for vacancies, and a low ratio of job leavers to job losers – suggest that the current environment is like that of 1960, when the NAIRU was 5 per cent or less.

Natural rate theory implied that there is no durable policy trade-off between unemployment and inflation. New Classical Macroeconomics and Real Business Cycle Theory went one step further, asserting there is no temporary trade-off either. Nominal stickiness is, as argued above, a reason for curvature of the long-run Phillips curve at low rates of inflation. In any case, the uncertainty of the location of the NAIRU, whether it is a constant or a function of the unemployment rate, is an independent source of policy trade-off.

This trade-off is between two risks. Associated with any actual unemployment rate and thus indirectly with the monetary policy that supports it, are a range of possible discrepancies of actual unemployment from the unknown NAIRU. If the NAIRU is higher than the actual rate, the cost is higher inflation. If the NAIRU is lower than the actual rate, the costs are the jobs and output unnecessarily forgone. The lower the actual unemployment rate chosen, the more likely the first kind of error and the less likely the second kind. The central bank has to balance the probability-weighted disutilities of the two kinds of errors.

Figure 1.3 Empirical Beveridge curve points: US 1956–95

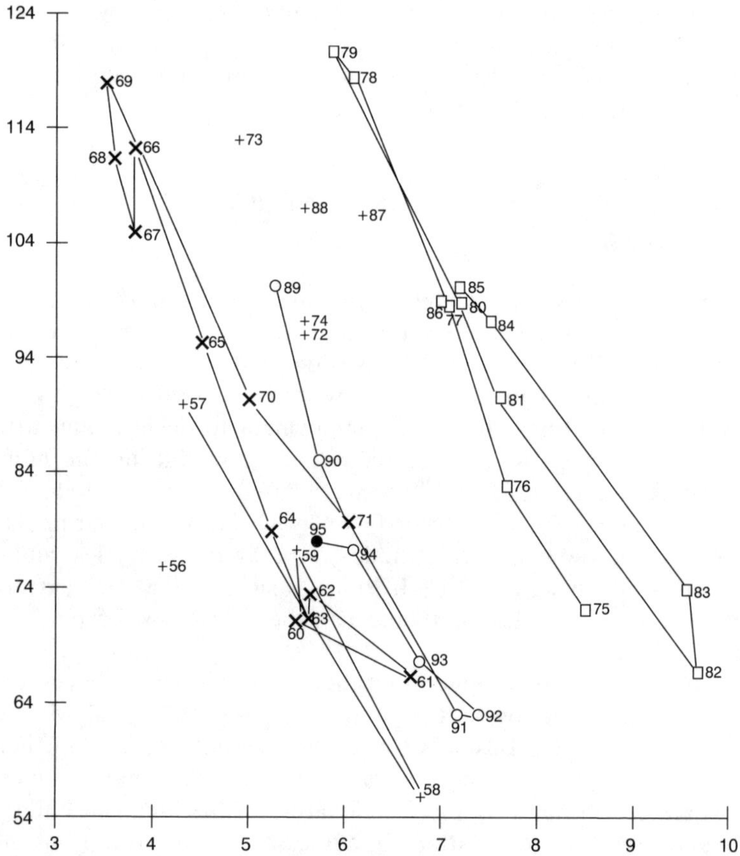

Note: The proxy of the vacancies is the Help-wanted index relative to the labour force. The curve for the 1950s and 1960s was favourable for combining low vacancies with low unemployment and low inflation. The situation deteriorated in the 1970s, and the curve for the 1980s was unfavourable. However, in the 90s the curve appears to have shifted back to the benign curve of the 1960s.

Events will provide information for a new policy decision. If, for example, more inflation occurs than the central bank bargained for, the policy-makers will presumably decide to aim for a higher unemployment rate. Some commentators appear to regard NAIRU as a threshold to a burst of wage-price spiral exceedingly difficult

Figure 1.4 Job leavers/losers ratio and Help-wanted index: US 1967–95

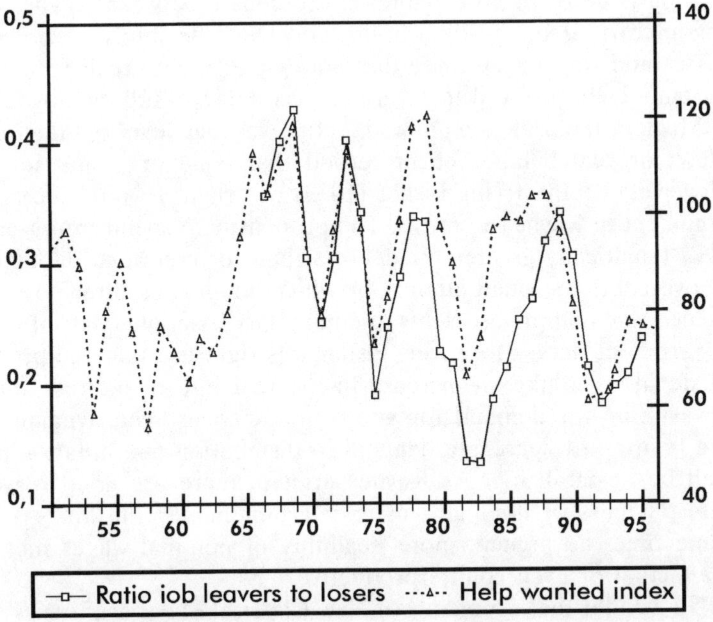

Note: Unemployed workers are either leavers, who quit jobs voluntarily, or losers, who were laid off. When the labour markets are tight, the leavers/losers ratio could be expected to be high because workers can quit with reasonable expectation of finding another job. The figure shows that this ratio confirms the message of Figure 3. The ratio has recently been rising but is still in 1995 quite low considering how low unemployment is.

and costly to reverse. Worse yet, it may be like the virus of a dread disease, which doesn't break out for a long time. Accordingly they counsel a very conservative policy. But there is no convincing evidence of that kind of asymmetric discontinuity as between the two types of error.

THE NEED FOR ACTIVE MACRO POLICY

Do we need policy to stay at the NAIRU, that is to return to it promptly whenever an aggregate demand shock pushes the economy away from it? Or, if you prefer, is the natural rate equilibrium stable without the help of active monetary or fiscal policy? This is the big issue of macroeconomics, the debate between Keynes and Pigou, carried on by their followers. Does flexibility of nominal prices and wages guarantee that enough aggregate real demand is automatically restored to return the economy to full employment?

Much of the profession nowadays believes that years ago the Pigou effect or real balance effect settled that issue once and for all. However, I think Irving Fisher (1933) was right. I would recast his argument in Keynesian terms. The propensity to spend from wealth is systematically greater for debtors than for creditors, enough so to overcome the small amount by which nominal creditor positions exceed nominal private debts, the monetary base, plus part of other government debt. Moreover, Fisher was right too that the process of deflation is like an increase in the real rate of interest and is devastating for demand for goods and services. The dynamics of the relation of aggregate demand to disinflation and inflation may well be destabilizing. As Keynes argued, there are good reasons for stickiness of nominal wages; it is not money illusion. At the same time, he argued, more flexibility of nominal wages may be ineffectual or even counterproductive.

No wonder that exponents of New Classical Macroeconomics and Real Business Cycle Theory evade the problem by assuming perfect flexibility in the sense of continuous instantaneous market clearing, so that excess demands and supplies never occur for even a second of real time. Actual is always Potential. Real demand shocks never occur, that is, incipient shocks are instantaneously absorbed by market-clearing price settings.

Since 1962 the Federal Reserve has fine-tuned its monetary policy, expressed in the Federal Funds rate on base money. As a result the US economy recovered from the deep 1981–82 recession and a shallow 1990–91 setback, and achieved virtually full employment with low inflation, a macroeconomic performance much superior to that of Europe or Japan, where monetary policies are much less activist and much more subservient to monetarism and New Classical theories, and much more dedicated to price stability to the exclusion of high employment and output. Actually the United States passes all the Maastricht tests, which no EU member save Luxembourg can meet.

NOTES

1. C.L. Schultze (1959) examined the supposed two kinds of inflation and concluded that the problem was the sensitivity of key industrial sectors to increases in demand when the economy as a whole was not at full employment, plus the asymmetrical insensitivity of prices and wages to decrease in demand.
2. I. Fisher (1925, 1926) anticipated Phillips, showing with American data that the price changes and either the volume of trade or the volume of employment were negatively correlated. These articles were scarcely noticed, while Phillips's article came at a time when the subject was at the forefront of professional and political attention.

REFERENCES

Akerlof, G., Dickens, W.T. and Perry, G. (1996) The Macroeconomics of Low Inflation, *Brookings Papers on Economic Activity*, 1–76.

Baily, M.N. and Tobin, J. (1977) Macroeconomic Effects of Selective Public Employment and Subsidies, *Brookings Papers on Economic Activity*, 511–41.

Beveridge, W.H. (1945) *Full Employment in a Free Society*, New York, W.W. Norton.

Dillard, D. (1988) The Barter Illusion in Classical and Neoclassical Economics, *Eastern Economic Journal* **14**, 299–318.

Economic Report of the President 1962, Washington, US Government Printing Office.

Fisher, I. (1925) Our Unstable Dollar and So-called Business Cycle, *Journal of the American Statistical Association*, 179–202.

Fisher, I. (1926) A Statistical Relationship between Unemployment and Price Changes, *International Labour Review*, 785–92.

Fisher, I. (1933) The Debt-Deflation Theory of Great Depressions, *Econometrica* **1**, 337–57.

Friedman, M. (1968) The Role of Monetary Policy, *American Economic Review* **58**, 1–17.

Keynes, J.M. (1936) *The General Theory of Employment, Interest and Money*, New York, Harcourt Brace.

Lipsey, R.G. (1960) The Relation between Unemployment and the Rate of Change of Money Wage Rates in the U.K., 1862–1957: Further Analysis, *Economica* **XXVII**, 1–61.

Modigliani, F. and Papademos, L. (1976) Monetary Policy for the Coming Quarters: The Conflicting Views, *The New England Economic Review* **76**, 2–35.

Okun, A.M. (1962) Potential GNP: Its Measurement and Significance, *Proceedings of the Business and Economic Section, American Statistical Association 1962*, 145–58.

Phelps, E.S. (1967) Expectations of Inflation and Optimal Unemployment Over Time, *Economica* **XXXIV**, 254–81.

Phillips, A.W. (1958) The Relation between Unemployment and the Rate of Change of Money Wage Rates in the U.K., 1861–1957, *Economica* **XXV**, 283–99.

Samuelson, P.A. and Solow, R.M. (1960) Analytical Aspects of Anti-Inflation Policy, *American Economic Review* **50**, 177–94.

Schultze, C.L. (1959) Recent Inflation in the United States, *Study Paper n. 1 for Joint Economic Committee, Congress of United States*, Washington, US Government Printing Office.

Tobin, J. (1972) Inflation and Unemployment, *American Economic Review* **62**, 1–18.

Comment

Sergio Parrinello

My comment will focus on the part of Professor Tobin's paper which deals with the non-accelerating inflation rate of unemployment. Instead of this long expression and in order to avoid the acronym NAIRU, I will use the term *non-inflationary rate of unemployment* or *non-inflationary rate tout court* to indicate the same concept.

It should be noticed that the structural relation at issue, consistent with the empirical evidence, involves acceleration rates, whereas the level of inflation and the level of unemployment do not enter that relation in a structural way. This characterization is important for the underlying assumption of accommodating monetary policy.

Let us turn now to the two basic issues in which there is a substantial convergence between the positions held by Tobin and by many contemporary New Keynesians. First, the point that the non-inflationary rate includes involuntary unemployment. Second, the question that the adjustment process towards a given non-inflationary rate can be slow or even non-existent.

Let us examine Tobin's position on the second proposition. In his 1975 (pp. 195–6) article we read: 'The real issue is not the existence of a long-run static equilibrium with unemployment, but the possibility of protracted unemployment which the natural adjustments of a market economy remedy very slowly if at all.'

It can be observed that Tobin's notion of non-inflationary rate does not necessarily reflect the New Keynesian motto 'The NAIRU brings peace in the battle of the mark-up' (Layard, *et al.*, 1991, p. 378); which means prices as a mark-up on expected wages, wages as a mark-up on expected prices, and wages of certain wage earners as a mark-up on wages of other groups in the battle of their relative positions.

The above quotation from Tobin suggests instead that, independently of the presence of monopolistic competition in some markets, the existence of competitive market equilibria, which should hold simultaneously and which are unique and 'stable', is an exceptional case, rather than the rule. On the basis of this presumption, Tobin argues that the concept of a non-inflationary rate of unemployment possesses two important features: (a) it must be interpreted as a stochastic macroeconomic equilibrium; and (b) in general, instead of a unique non-inflationary rate, a whole range of these rates exists and this range is represented by a horizontal segment of the typical trade-off curve.

I am sympathetic towards a stochastic-macroeconomic equilibrium interpretation of the non-inflationary rate. Incidentally, I do present a similar concept – that is, the notion of statistical macroeconomic equilibrium taken from statistical mechanics – in my contribution (Parrinello, 1996) to a volume in honour of Fausto Vicarelli. In another article (Tobin, 1972, p. 9) Tobin argued that the non-inflationary rate is 'stochastic because random intersectoral shocks keep individual labor markets in diverse states of disequilibrium; macroeconomic, because the perpetual flux of particular markets produces fairly definite aggregate outcomes of unemployment and wages'.

Tobin's statistical interpretation of the non-inflationary rate reflects frictions related to a non-synchronized adjustment of different labour markets. However, it is not clear how close his approach is to the statistical equilibrium concept adopted by Boltzmann and other physicists. In the economics of unemployment the adoption of that notion of equilibrium should overcome some serious limitations of the traditional aggregate economic models, founded on the concept of representative agents and characterized by deterministic microfoundations. In fact, these aggregate models cannot explain a persistent state of unemployment as a probability distribution of unemployed workers, distinguished in terms of social groups and geographical areas. It should be clear that the characteristic values of this distribution, for instance its dispersion, is crucial for an economic policy for employment. The 1996 Nobel laureate, William Vickrey, has strongly emphasized this last point in his 1993 Presidential address.

> While 5 percent unemployment might be barely tolerable if it meant that everyone would be taking an additional two weeks of vacation every year without pay, it is totally unacceptable as a social goal when it means unemployment rates of 10, 20, or even 40 percent among disadvantaged groups. . . . Yet the hard political fact is that at such a NAIRU the great majority of the voting population, including most of the politically active upper and middle classes, will have relatively little personal experience of

severe unemployment, while nearly everyone will have some direct experience of inflation.

(Vickrey, 1993, p. 2)

Let us examine now the second feature attributed by Tobin to the non-inflationary rate of unemployment: the non-uniqueness of this rate. Once again Tobin's position is not founded on the existence of multiple equilibria associated with monopolistic competition (although this assumption is not inconsistent with his approach). Analytically Tobin's idea is close to the notion of hysteresis interpreted in the appropriate sense. In a narrow sense hysteresis has been identified by some economists as the special case of a linear and stable dynamic model, in which at least one eigenvalue is equal to unity in discrete time (or equal to zero in continuous time). For example, Blanchard and Summers (1986) and Gordon (1988) seem to adopt this unit-root interpretation. However, the relevant property, from a policy perspective, is not the 'unit-root case', but either the case of *permanence* without hysteresis or the case of general hysteresis in the sense used in physics (Cross, 1995).

In the permanence case we encounter a slow speed of convergence towards an equilibrium and, if it is slow enough, the very assumption of a fixed structure of the model becomes precarious. General hysteresis is met in non-linear models and, as Cross (1995) has already pointed out, it is not compatible with the notion of a 'determinate' non-inflationary rate of unemployment. In this case the non-inflationary rate will exhibit a drift: its value at a certain time becomes dependent on past shocks, therefore on the past rates of unemployment related to the changes in nominal magnitudes. Hence, a whole range of non-inflationary rates will exist, each of which represents a possible stationary position with respect to a certain history of the economy. In Solow's words 'a natural rate that hops around from one triennium to another under the influence of unspecified forces, including past unemployment rates, is not "natural" at all . . . epiphenomenal would be a better adjective' (1987, p. 533).

There is an extensive literature which analyses the sources of the state of affairs illustrated above. Among these sources we can find, besides the distinction between the 'insider' and 'outsider' behaviours, those costs and legacies of disinflation illustrated by Tobin in his 1982 essay.

> Protracted high unemployment destroys human capital, . . . prolonged excess capacity likewise deters physical capital formation; . . . Recession and stagnation also squeeze public-sector budgets; in the United States, the overhead capital . . . is not even being maintained and replaced. . . . These are the irreversible and durable costs incident to the hundreds of billions of dollars of lost production during the war to subdue inflation.
>
> (Tobin, 1982, p. 21)

These irreversible or slowly reversible externalities, such as the erosion of the labour skills of unemployed workers, become pervasive in the presence of certain contractionary shocks. The same features lead us to deny the role of a classical attractor to the non-inflationary rate of unemployment, for the sake of economic policy in general and of a policy to fight unemployment in particular. Of course, we should not exaggerate the scope of these phenomena related to prolonged unemployment. In the historical experience of the US, after 1939, many of those legacies (especially the shortage of physical capital stock) were rapidly overcome through an expansionary policy of aggregate demand management. After the recovery of the US economy in 1982, the existing bottlenecks have been removed, although interspersed with certain relapses, without triggering serious inflationary processes.

However, even if they should not be exaggerated, the kind of irreversibilities mentioned above must be taken into account in order to assess the social costs of unemployment, which should not consist only of losses of percentage points in the GDP.

In the title of his 1982 essay, Tobin raised a provocative question for the USA: *After disinflation, Then What?* The same query has been re-examined by Tobin in his recent collection of essays (Tobin, 1996). In the light of the theoretical debate about the non-inflationary rate of unemployment, the same question should be addressed to the European Monetary Union (EMU), and the full costs of the deflationary policy to achieve that target should be properly assessed.

Most representatives of Italian economic policy prefer to avoid a direct answer to that question. Instead they tend to 'answer' by raising another question: What would be the consequences if the Italian economy were to postpone its membership to the EMU, if only by a couple of years? The tone of their answer to the latter question is apocalyptic, although the arguments advanced are rather thin indeed. So they prefer to talk about the costly losses from remaining outside instead of the accruing benefits from entering the Monetary Union. I believe that facing the problem of economic expansion in Europe, after the legacy of that deflationary policy, can be a useful way of commemorating the social aspects of the theoretical contribution of Fausto Vicarelli (Vicarelli, 1987). I will just introduce this theme for further discussion.

On the basis of the theoretical issues examined above, the lesson learnt from the recent history of deflation experienced by the countries which endorsed the Maastricht Treaty, confirms the following conjecture: the effects of a deflationary economic policy are not only the traditional macroeconomic effects, but also structural effects, some of which were supposed to be brought about by means of orthodox *ad hoc* microeconomic policies. From the point of view of positive economics, this amounts to the kind of methodological inversion which some like to call macrofoundations of microeconomics. It should hardly be surprising, therefore, if the astuteness of reason prescribes macroeconomic policies – in this case policies founded on fixed financial rules – to achieve some structural changes, which would be otherwise politically unfeasible if pursued by direct micro-structural interventions.

Admittedly these results are still in progress, but Tobin's question 'After disinflation, then what?' leads us to another kind of question: What scope will there be for a feasible expansionary policy in the EMU?

This question involves the problem of policy coordination among European national states, which are still so diverse in terms of culture, life-style, political orientation and, in particular, their different sensitiveness towards the problem of inflation as opposed to unemployment. While we wait for the solution to this puzzle, the serious arguments put forward to demonstrate the benefits of 'after disinflation' boil down to the expected impact of a decrease in the nominal and real interest rates on private investments. Outside the ideology of 'private is beautiful', it is dubious whether a sufficient stimulus to private investment will accrue only from lower interest rates and in the presence of an unconstrained international mobility of financial capital. Public investment, especially in infrastructure, can indeed play the role of an essential complementary force. On these grounds a new Keynesianism for Europe should carefully re-examine the traditional separation between the public versus the private sector of the economy in the light of the emergence of the so called 'third sector'. We can expect the public sector to be associated less and less with national government expenditure, following the gradual extension of supernational and subnational institutions. Furthermore the concept of private might encompass a sphere of new types of consumption and new working activities directed to social aims. In our country this process seems to run the risk of displacing the social State without any public regulation but with the support of public resources. I am well aware that it is easy to slip into sterile rhetoric on this issue and experts of other disciplines outside economics may offer a more comprehensive contribution which should take into account the historical and cultural dimensions of the problem.

But returning to the narrower ground of economics for a concluding remark, it can be stressed that the criticism raised by Tobin and by other 'non-reconstructed' Keynesians against the notion of non-inflationary rate of unemployment, adds to the doubts about the two-stage tactics that are currently being adopted to achieve the EMU: the stage of prolonged disinflation first; the stage of recovery and development, hopefully, afterwards.

REFERENCES

Blanchard, O.J. and Summers, L. (1986) Hysteresis and the European Unemployment, in O.J. Blanchard and S. Fischer (eds), *NBER Macroeconomics Annual*, Cambridge, MA, MIT Press.

Cross, R. (1995) Is the Natural Rate Hypothesis Consistent With Hysteresis? in R. Cross (ed.), *The Natural Rate of Unemployment: Reflections on 25 Years of the Hypothesis*, Cambridge, Cambridge University Press.

Gordon, R. (1988) Back to the Future: European Unemployment Today Viewed from America in 1939, *Brookings Papers on Economic Activity*, 271–304.

Layard, R., Nickell, S.J. and Jackman, R. (1991) *Unemployment: Macroeconomic Performance and the Labour Market*, Oxford, Oxford University Press.

Parrinello, S. (1996) Equilibri Statistici e Nuovi Microfondamenti della Macroeconomia, in C. Gnesutta (ed.), *Incertezza, Moneta, Aspettative, Equilibrio*, Bologna, Il Mulino.

Solow, R. (1987) Unemployment: Getting the Question Right, *Economica* **53**, 523–34.

Tobin , J. (1972) Inflation and Unemployment, *American Economic Review* **62**, 1–18.

Tobin, J. (1975) Keynesian Models of Recession and Depression, *American Economic Review* **65**, 195–202.
Tobin, J. (1982) After Disinflation, Then What? in J. Cornwall (ed.), *After Stagflation, Alternatives to Economic Decline,* Oxford, Blackwell.
Tobin, J. (1996) *Full Employment and Growth*, Cambridge, Cambridge University Press.
Vicarelli, F. (1987) *La Questione Economica nella Società Italiana*, Bologna, Il Mulino.
Vickrey, W. (1993) Today's Task for Economists, *American Economic Review* **83**, 1–10.

Comment

Paolo Sylos Labini

The criticism that Tobin makes of the Natural Rate of Unemployment and of its twin concept, the long-run vertical Phillips curve, can be fully endorsed – including his witty and amusing remarks. The NAIRU concept is not so misleading, but it is also open to serious criticism.

The equation of the Phillips curve, that originates from the article by Samuelson and Solow of 1960, is the following:

$$\hat{P} = a\hat{W} - b\hat{\pi}$$

where $\hat{W} = a'U^{-1}$ which is a simplified version of the Phillips curve, and where $\hat{\pi}$ is the trend of productivity growth, assumed to be constant. (P represents the general price level, W the wage rate, U unemployment and the circumflex accent indicates the rate of change). Tobin points out that Phillips himself, as well as Samuelson and Solow and many other economists who adopted the Phillips curve recognized that wage inflation, a determinant of price inflation, would itself be affected by price inflation. For simplicity, however, he reasons as if wage were the only variable that matters. In fact, he writes: 'Assuming that prices of value added are normal labour cost per unit of output marked up to cover fixed and capital costs, price inflation mirrors wage inflation less the trend of productivity growth'. Now, this extreme simplification could be justified only by conceiving the economy as a homogeneous system and by neglecting foreign relations; but such an extreme simplification cannot be admitted, since prices behave differently in different sectors and foreign relations cannot be neglected, not even when considering the American economy.

Strictly speaking, the cost plus models apply only to industry and the retail trade and the mark up refers, not simply to labour cost, but also to direct costs, that in the case of industry include, apart from labour, also raw materials and energy, a part or a large part of which in industrialized economies is imported as a rule; on the other hand, the prices of imported finished goods operate as a moving upper limit to the increases of internal prices. Both the prices of imported raw materials and of imported finished goods depend on both the prices in the markets of origin and exchange rates.

Of course, James Tobin knows all this; but clearly he thinks that in a first approximation the said simplification can be helpful, whereas I am convinced that it is not so, both from the standpoint of theoretical analysis and of policy prescriptions.

In the analysis, instead of the two equations mentioned above, we have to consider at the very least the following system:

$$\hat{W} = cU^{-1} + d\hat{P}_r + eTUP$$

$$U^{-1} = qY = q(fI)$$

$$\hat{P}_f = g\hat{W} - h\hat{\pi} + i\hat{R}_m + l\hat{P}_{imp}$$

$$\hat{P}_r = m\hat{W} + n\hat{\pi}_r + o\hat{T}$$

where $\hat{P}_r$ is the consumer price index, *TUP* trade union pressure (that can be quantified in a way that I have suggested elsewhere), *Y* aggregate real product, *I* aggregate investment, $\hat{P}_f$ and $\hat{P}_{imp}$ represent the prices of internal and imported finished goods at the wholesale level (corrected for the exchange rates in the latter case), $\hat{\pi}$ and $\hat{\pi}_r$ indicate labour productivity in industry and retail trade, $\hat{R}_m$ is the price of raw materials and of energy (corrected, when imported, for the exchange rates) and $\hat{T}$ indicates tariffs.

If it is true that the above system, though simple, contains all the relevant variables, then the prescriptions of economic policy based on NAIRU can be misleading for various reasons. First, wages depend not only on unemployment, but also on the prices of consumer goods; and such prices depend not only or mainly on wages, but also – among other variables – on the prices of imported goods. Thus, a policy aiming at stabilizing the exchange rates, in order to prevent 'imported inflation', is to be recommended.

Second, among the variables affecting wages we cannot neglect trade union pressure, that in certain periods and in certain countries, like Italy, has played an important role either in accelerating or in slowing down wage increases. Trade union pressure can in turn be conditioned by laws and by measures constituting the so-called incomes policy. It is true that the economists of the Keynesian tradition, among whom we find Tobin, do not by any means exclude the utility of an incomes policy; but it is also true that an oversimplification of the kind discussed here tends to belittle the role of such a policy.

Third, when trade unions are not willing to agree on an incomes policy and insist in claiming high wage increases that are likely to contribute to a process of inflation, then the central bank can announce its intention to raise the discount rate, which, if carried out, tends to reduce investment and to increase unemployment, with a consequent downward pressure on wages. Such an announcement is meant to persuade trade union leaders to moderate their claims and to encourage industrialists to strengthen their resistance, and thus prevent price increases that would probably be introduced, through the mark up, to recoup the higher costs.

Fourth, the view that unemployment depends principally on aggregate investment is typically Keynesian. Monetarists attribute unemployment mainly to wages being too high and to their downwards inflexibility. The monetarist approach, however, which is strictly connected with the Walrasian approach, is unsatisfactory, owing to its static character. The trouble with wages is not that they are too high or that they are rigid downward; the main trouble is that in certain periods wages increase too quickly, in other words, more than productivity. Wage cuts are always open to the criticism made by Keynes about the effect they have on aggregate demand – many economists seem to forget this criticism. It is true, however, that in an expanding economy the additional employment at lower wages manages to avoid this criticism. On the other hand, there are other kinds of flexibility other than wage flexibility in the labour market that are relevant for the level of employment. The view that the various types of flexibilities in the labour market are important for employment, especially in the long run, does not contradict the Keynesian view that aggregate investment is the main determinant of the level of employment: the two views are complementary.

While there is some truth in the monetarists' position on the question of flexibility, they have very little, or nothing, to say about trade union pressure, which they consider irrelevant or even harmful, or about the policy of stabilization of exchange rates. With their unconditional trust in the automatism of all kinds of markets, they have no recommendations to make about exchange rates, except to make these markets completely free and not to worry about speculation.

The NAIRU, then, is not a wrong concept; it suffers from an

oversimplified use of the Phillips curve. Phillips himself – by taking the long period 1861–1913 as the reference curve and by pointing out that the data for the period 1949–57 (when his analysis ends) are also consistent with the 1861–1913 curve (the data for the interwar period perform badly, but, of course, this is no wonder) – has in a sense justified the oversimplifications of the kind discussed here.

A further justification has arisen from the empirical analyses carried out by other economists for the following years, until 1969. The breakdown of the Phillips curve, which appears in the years following 1970, was not due, as Friedman and Phelps have suggested, to the learning process of firms and workers during a period of inflation, but on several factors, among which a primary importance should be attributed to the abandonment of the Bretton Woods Agreements: since then, both the prices of raw materials and exchange rates have undergone violent fluctuations, which had nothing to do with the relations between unemployment and wages and indirectly affected wages by pushing up the prices of finished goods and consumer prices. Empirical estimates of the four equations above, as well as of the equations of a broader model in which they are included, give good or very good results; and since there is more than one explanatory variable of both wages and prices, we cannot see in the diagrams which variables can explain the breakdown of the simplified (and modified) version of the Phillips curve. By inspection, however, we see clearly that the Phillips curve breaks down after the abandonment of the Bretton Woods Agreements, that is after 1971; and this is true not only for the United States, but also for Italy, the only other country for which I have found estimates of that curve. The violent fluctuations in raw material prices lasted until the beginning of the 1980s; but the fluctuations in the exchange rates lasted even longer.

In the last four or five years in the United States only both raw material prices and exchange rates have fluctuated much more mildly and unemployment has fallen, with low inflation, as Tobin observes towards the end of his paper. To be sure, raw materials and exchange rates are only two of several factors to be considered, among which we find trade union pressure, that in the United States has, as a rule, been much weaker than in Italy. And in Italy in 1993 there was an agreement between the government and trade unions in the spirit of an incomes policy; most economists as well as the association of industrialists recognize that the ensuing diminution of inflation owes much to that agreement – the very few monetarists available in Italy have been silent on this question. But, I repeat, there are several factors at play and even those considered in the said equations are not all. I believe, however, that they are the most important.

2 On the Relevance of Keynesian Macroeconomics: A Reappraisal

Ignazio Musu

THE CRISIS OF KEYNESIAN MACROECONOMICS

Fausto Vicarelli's interest in Keynes in the 1970s stemmed from his passion for economic policy, from his conviction that macroeconomic policy was important and had a lot more to accomplish than the minor role it was assigned by the emerging new classical macroeconomics, which he strongly opposed. In particularly he stressed the stabilizing function of macroeconomic policy, as he was convinced that Keynes was right in denouncing that the spontaneous dynamics of flexible prices had an inherently destabilizing nature in the capitalist system. Because of this conviction, Vicarelli was very reluctant toward the neoclassical synthesis, according to which unemployment was basically due to inadequate price flexibility.

During the ten years which separate us from Fausto's untimely death, we have witnessed the hegemony of new classical macroeconomics in theory and policy and the decline of Keynesian economics. The present state of macroeconomics, however, is far from clear. The early enthusiasm for new classical macroeconomics is calming down, but its influence still persists; the objection that Keynesian theory neglected the microeconomic foundation of its own macroeconomic propositions has made its mark.

On the other hand, microeconomic theory is also evolving. The growing interest of microeconomics in strategic interdependency, uncertainty and asymmetric information re-opens a space for economic policy, giving new perspectives also to macroeconomic policy. New classical macroeconomics has confined the task of macroeconomic policy to avoiding inflation and maintaining general price stability. However, recession and real instability have not disappeared from the economic stage; hence the typical question of the Keynesian approach periodically arises: is the market, left to its spontaneous working, able to manage such kinds of situation without the support of some macroeconomic policy strategy? Today aggregate demand policy, under the influence of the new classical message, is not considered a reliable instrument to promote economic expansion, particularly because of the danger of spurring inflation. But we are not told which strategy should be followed to successfully lead an economic system successfully out of a recession.

Sixty years from the publication of the General Theory, it seems reasonable to look into the current perspectives of Keynesian macroeconomic theory and policy, moving on from recent research in this field. At the same time it must be taken into account that time does not pass in vain, so that we cannot ignore the crisis of public intervention in the economy, which is, in turn, linked to the ways Keynesian economic policy has been implemented.

The crisis in the relation between market and state intervention in the economy forces a discussion of the validity of an assumption, typical of the welfarist approach which the Keynesian vision also shared, that public intervention can be seen as automatically correcting any market failure, neglecting incentive compatibility issues and transaction costs entailed by the implementation of any policy action.

It is also worth keeping in mind the negative effects of the ways Keynesian policies have been enforced: aggregate demand policies have increasingly acted by means of transfers which stress the redistributive over the expansionist role of public expenditure; too little attention has been given to investments and to the entrepreneurs' 'animal spirits'; structural public deficits have been tolerated and even promoted, forgetting that Keynes himself viewed them as a sign of failure of expansionist policies as they meant that real income was not able to grow enough to produce the taxes required to absorb the deficit and to make it a purely transient event.

From the theoretical point of view, any reappraisal of Keynesian macroeconomics must change the perspective from that of the neoclassical synthesis or even that of the fix price general equilibrium models whose main concern was of integrating Keynes within the Walrasian analytical framework. While accepting market interdependence, it is clear that problems of interest for the Keynesian approach are typical of a non-Walrasian microeconomic reality, where the term 'non-Walrasian' refers to market imperfections and incompleteness, relevance of the costs of organizing markets and coordinating individuals' interaction.

In the following sections I will reconsider critically the traditional Keynesian approach and compare it with the various theoretical positions which currently refer to a neokeynesian inspiration; I will take side with those positions that stress the importance of coordination and coordination failure not only because I am convinced that they, more than others, reflect the essence of the Keynesian message, but above all because they are a good starting point on which to found an effective macroeconomic policy, assigning a defensible role to aggregate demand management.

TRADITIONAL KEYNESIAN MACROECONOMICS AND THE NEW CLASSICAL MACROECONOMICS

In the period where Keynesian theory exerted an hegemonic role in macroeconomics, the bases were laid for it to be overcome by the new classical theory. The scope of traditional Keynesian theory in the 1950s and 1960s was to integrate Keynes within the Walrasian general equilibrium framework. In this framework, one or more nominal rigidities are assumed to obtain unemployment equilibrium. The neoclassical synthesis (Hicks, 1937; Modigliani, 1944) assumed nominal wage rigidity; fix price equilibrium models (Patinkin, 1955; Clower, 1965; Barro and Grossman, 1976; Malinvaud, 1977; Benassy, 1982) extended nominal rigidity to all prices.

If rigid nominal wages and prices are assumed, agents will perceive quantity rationing and adjustment to general economic equilibrium will take place through quantities. If firms are rationed on the goods market and households are rationed on the labour market, the interaction between the two will generate an adjustment process towards an equilibrium characterized by production below capacity and unemployment due to a lack of effective demand. The adjustment process is exactly the one described by the Keynesian multiplier so that the resulting excess supply fix price general equilibrium has been christened 'Keynesian unemployment'.

This equilibrium is different both from that of the neoclassical synthesis, where only wage is rigid and equilibrium has excess supply only in the labour market, and from the so called 'classical unemployment equilibrium', where the real wage is too high and there is excess supply in the labour market but excess demand in the goods market. In Keynesian unemployment, reducing the real wage is likely to worsen unemployment because it induces a lower demand for goods and this is reflected on a lower demand for labour. This is clearly a result in line with the Keynesian inspiration and with the empirical evidence in recession periods. However, it comes from a theoretically weak model both because of the institutional framework assumed and because of the superficial way it treats markets' organization.

In fix price general equilibrium models, the rigidity of monetary wages and prices is assumed and lacks an explanation. The assumption of fix prices, made independently to any other qualification about the institutional structure of the markets, can easily be objected to in the name of agents' rationality, another assumption which the fix price models do not dispute. If the adjustment through quantities, maintaining prices unchanged, leads the economy to an inefficient equilibrium, why do rational agents not act in order to make prices flexible which would allow for an efficient equilibrium? Once Keynesian theory had been reduced to representing a general economic equilibrium with assumed fixed prices and quantity rationing, it is no wonder that the monetarist and new classical theories were the winners.

The initial reaction of monetarists to Keynesianism was not radical opposition. They were writing in an atmosphere deeply influenced by the Keynesian 'revolution' and perceived the tactical unproductiveness of a head-on clash. They revived the idea of the important role of expectations which had been stressed in Keynes's thought, but they used it rather differently from Keynes. For Keynes, expectations had the power to permanently move the economy out of the full employment equilibrium and to be confirmed in involuntary unemployment equilibrium without any further need of change. For the monetarists, expectations themselves would change in order to let the economy move toward a long-run full employment equilibrium.

The full employment equilibrium derived from the Walrasian general equilibrium model (christened the 'natural rate of unemployment equilibrium') could be considered as a long run steady state of the economy, from which temporary 'Keynesian' equilibria could deviate because of the role played by expectations. However temporary underemployment equilibria were not properly Keynesian as unemployment was only voluntary. The deviation could be only transitory as expectations would adjust in the long run in such a way as to make temporary Keynesian equilibria tend to the long run natural rate of unemployment equilibrium.

In the monetarist approach (Friedman, 1968; Phelps, 1968; Lucas, 1972) temporary equilibria are determined by the expectations of the general price level prevailing at any moment. They can differ from the long run equilibrium because agents confuse changes in the general price level with changes in some relative prices. Starting from long-run equilibrium, when demand grows, firms see increases in their own product prices as a decline in real wages and hence they increase employment and output; expectations adjust to the higher general price level, firms correct their mistakes and the system returns to its natural rate of unemployment equilibrium.

Perfectly rational agents however would rather have rational expectations (Muth, 1961). Rational agents cannot accept an expectations model leading them to make systematic mistakes. These mistakes could be avoided by a learning process of the fundamental factors determining the economic structure (technology and preferences). With rational expectations exploiting this learning process and using the maximum amount of information available, we would have only stochastic errors, which cannot be foreseen. Only unpredicted aggregate demand policies can have provisional real effects: on average these effects disappear. The economy is always in a natural rate of unemployment equilibrium, except for casual perturbations that are not serially correlated.

In the rational expectations world there is no longer room for Keynesian macroeconomics: it has been definitely displaced by new classical macroeconomics.

NEOKEYNESIAN THEORY AND IMPERFECT MARKETS

One possible answer put forward by the Keynesian theorists to the challenge of new classical macroeconomics has been to give a foundation to nominal rigidities rather than simply assuming them. Assuming market imperfection instead of assuming nominal or real rigidities and setting an imperfect market as the foundations of such rigidities would do the job. However, this only seems to move the problem to a different level.

Why should rational agents accept market imperfections when they know that they produce inefficient equilibria? The answer could be that, while conceding that institutional microeconomic policy should try to reduce market imperfection to a minimum, there are difficulties and sometimes structural obstacles (such as increasing returns to scale) to the success of this attempt. In any case, while market imperfections exist, rational agents should follow maximizing behaviour under such an institutional constraint, and macroeconomic policy should act to improve efficiency given the existing market imperfection.

Some scholars have tried to establish a link between the assumption of imperfect markets and Keynesian results in a direct way, without passing through the explanation of any nominal or real price rigidity. Hart (1982), Benassy (1987), D'Aspremont *et al.* (1990), Silvestre (1993) have mainly been concerned with flexible price adjustments in imperfect markets where some market power exists. They have found that involuntary unemployment emerges when market power exists not only in the labour market, but either in the goods market alone or in both markets (Silvestre, 1993). In particular D'Aspremont *et al.* (1990) have been able to show that involuntary unemployment at any real wage can be an equilibrium outcome with oligopoly in the goods market and perfect competition in the labour market.

American neokeynesian economists (Mankiw, 1985; Rotemberg, 1987; Ball *et al.*, 1988; Dixon, 1991; Romer, 1993; Dixon and Rankin, 1994) have focused their research on explaining nominal rigidities in a context of imperfect competition where firms determine prices and decide if and how to change them once they are faced with a demand shock. The object of their analysis is to explain price rigidity and quantity adjustment to a demand shock through the interaction of imperfect competition with price adjustment costs (menu costs) and the externality entailed by a generalized decline in prices after an aggregate demand fall (Akerlof and Yellen, 1985; Blanchard and Kiyotaki, 1987).

Interaction of imperfect competition with menu costs is enough to produce nominal price rigidity and quantity adjustment to a demand shock. When an imperfect competitive firm, faced with a leftward shift of its demand curve, reduces prices, there is a gain from the higher quantity sold but a loss from the lower price. The net gain is positive without adjustment costs; but even with low menu costs, the gain, net of these costs, may not be positive so that price adjustment may not be profitable.

Introducing the externality effect of a generalized price reduction after an aggregate demand fall reinforces these conclusions.

Assume a lower nominal money supply without price adjustment: the aggregate demand is lower and the individual firms' demand curves shift leftwards, entailing lower profits for firms. If prices adjust, the real money stock turns out to be unchanged and each firm has a net gain measured by the avoided profit loss. Why then do firms not reduce prices when nominal money supply is reduced? The answer lies in their perception that the generalized price reduction acts as an externality: this public good is not necessarily supplied voluntarily. We are in a typical 'prisoners' dilemma' game: if, faced with a lower demand, a firm does not reduce its own price, while the others reduce theirs, the firm gains the benefit of the unchanged aggregate demand without paying any costs. It is clear that if any firm has an incentive to behave in this way, there will be no price reduction to respond to the monetary shock, and this will imply a high social loss in terms of output and employment.

Neokeynesian economists' research has produced an interesting result showing that real rigidities have a role in determining nominal rigidities. The meaning of real rigidity here is that a relative price (for instance a firm's price relative to the aggregate price level) is insensitive to a change in aggregate demand (Romer, 1996). The higher the degree of real rigidity, the lower the incentive to adjust nominal prices once faced with an exogenous demand shock. A flat marginal cost curve is a sign of real rigidity because, even without menu costs, it means that a fall in demand, given that other firms maintain their prices unaltered, will have only a minor effect on the individual firm's price (Ardeni *et al.*, 1996; Romer, 1996).

Special attention is given by neokeynesians to the cyclical insensitivity or the mildly procyclical behavior of real wages. To give account for these stylized facts, they have had to explain a certain amount of cyclical real wage stickiness. If firms do not find it convenient to see real wages reduced when there is excess supply in the labour market, we may conclude that unemployment is involuntary in nature.

Basically three lines of thought have been followed which can interact in many ways. The first refers to a labour market characterized by a bilateral monopoly between a firms' union and a workers' union (McDonald and Solow, 1981). A workers' union alone is enough to explain real wage rigidity if it has to bear costs to adjust real wages. If a union is considered as a monopolist selling labour, it has the same problems in adjusting its selling price (nominal wage, and hence, given the price level, real wage) as an imperfect competitive firm with menu costs; in this case menu costs may relate to the reliability relation between the union and its members. In a bilateral monopoly model, the workers' union maximizes the utility of the employed with the real wage constrained to be higher than a reservation level, while the firms' union maximizes firms' profit: the contract curve gives an increasing relation between real wages and employment, while any profit-sharing rule between the two parts gives a decreasing relation between the two variables. The fact that a demand shock moves the two curves in an opposite direction explains cyclical real wage stickiness.

The second line of thought refers to the insider-outsider model (Lindbeck and Snower, 1988). In this model high substitution costs of the insiders and high training costs of the outsiders give the insiders a monopoly power which prevent outsiders from being hired even if they would be willing to accept lower real wages: hence outsiders can be defined as involuntary unemployed.

The third explanation of real wage stickiness is the efficiency wage theory. It does not require labour market imperfections; it rather requires an increasing relation between real wage and the efficiency of the individual worker. This relation may be justified in various ways: among them, by the need of avoiding shirking when asymmetric information against firms creates a problem of moral hazard (Shapiro and Stiglitz, 1984; Akerlof and Yellen, 1985). In this model firms may face a conflict between lowering real wages and a negative effect caused by this decision, such as lower productivity or lower workers' effort. To avoid this conflict firms refrain from reducing the real wage; hence the unemployed can be defined involuntary because they would have been willing to work for a lower wage but that was prevented by the firms' optimal decisions.

An interesting explanation of real wage rigidity has been recently provided by integrating the insider-outsider approach with the idea of a social norm which individuals accept to solve a coordination problem (Hahn and Solow, 1995). In Hahn and Solow's proposal, this social convention is a Rawlsian contract under the veil of ignorance. The idea is that individuals can be in a favourable state of nature and be employed, or they can be in an unfavourable state of nature and be unemployed. There exist two equilibrium real wages, the first determined by bargaining among the insiders alone, the second determined after opening the bargaining process to both insiders and outsiders.

Assuming there is no utility in being unemployed, the expected utility when outsiders do not bargain is the product of the probability of being employed and the utility provided by the equilibrium real wage among insiders. This expected utility will be higher than that provided by the equilibrium real wage when everybody is allowed to participate in the bargaining process, if the probability of being employed is sufficiently high. In other words, if all know that they will most probably be employed, no outsider will assume a non-cooperative behaviour leading him or her to enter the bargaining process at a lower wage, so that the universal bargaining process leading to the equilibrium with full wage flexibility will be prevented from functioning. Only when the probability of being employed is very low, does the convention break down and outsiders enter the bargaining process with wage flexibility. Given that the probability of being employed is determined by demand factors, this model provides a whole range of demand-determined employment levels associated with involuntary unemployed outsiders and rigid real wages.

From the analysis of imperfect product and labour markets, neokeynesian economists have derived the concept of a non-accelerating inflation rate of unemployment (NAIRU), which has been opposed to the natural rate of unemployment of the monetarist and new classical macroeconomics schools. NAIRU is the rate of unemployment generating consistency between a real wage acceptable to firms, determined by the labour productivity and firms' markup, and a target real wage for workers. In hysteresis theories NAIRU is not independent from the actual unemployment rate; on the contrary they make the latter act as a magnet, pulling the former in the same direction. This happens basically for two reasons: duration, linked to depreciation of the unemployed human capital which make them increasingly unemployable; and insider-outsider reasons, because outsiders are made less and less able to enter the bargaining process (Layard *et al.*, 1991).

Some neokeynesian economists have stressed the role of imperfection in financial markets by explaining real effects of aggregate demand shocks; financial markets imperfections can work together with imperfections in the labour and goods markets (Stiglitz and Weiss, 1981; Greenwald and Stiglitz, 1993a, b). The theoretical importance of this contribution lies in its stressing the role of uncertainty and asymmetric information to obtain Keynesian results.

The analysis considers imperfections both in equity and in the credit markets. Equity market imperfections (equity rationing) may arise because of adverse selection reasons, from the fact that under asymmetric information the market may interpret the decision of issuing new shares as a negative signal, or because of moral hazard reasons, from the fact that fixed debt obligations may be a sign of stronger managerial incentives. Firms that do not have easy access to external finance through equity issues and have to move to debt finance may be forced into bankruptcy and are likely to become risk averse. The overall state of the economy will influence the perception of risks by a risk averse firm; profits and the liquid assets position will also be influenced. If firms want to maintain their level of activity with a reduced cash flow from lower profits when the economy goes into a recession, they have to increase their debt position: the marginal bankruptcy costs then increase and the aggregate supply curve shifts to the left together with the aggregate demand curve. Price rigidity may result, the adjustment being made through output reduction, but this price rigidity is not assumed *a priori*.

Effects through the credit market may worsen the negative real consequences of an aggregate demand fall. Under asymmetric information, banks have an incentive to respond to an increased credit demand by firms, not by raising the interest rate but by credit rationing. Adverse selection and moral hazard reasons are behind this strategy because increasing interest rates may worsen the quality of borrowers and give them incentives to undertake risky activities (Stiglitz and Weiss, 1981). If banks themselves are risk averse, they will respond to bad conditions of the economy by investing in safer activities than loans to private firms, such as government bonds (Greenwald and Stiglitz, 1990).

The risk averse nature of firms will increase the likelihood of efficiency wage factors acting to produce wage rigidity and involuntary unemployment when there is a recession: not only does the demand for labour curve shift leftwards, but the uncertainty about possible negative effects of lower wages on effort, quality and turnover of labour is also likely to increase under firms' risk aversion.

SELF-FULFILLING EXPECTATIONS, IMPERFECT MARKETS AND MULTIPLE EQUILIBRIA

In Keynes's General Theory cyclical fluctuations in business activity are determined by fluctuations in investment spending which in turn are determined by volatile entrepreneurs' expectations (what Keynes called 'animal spirits'). After Keynes, in the positivist approach taken by economic theory, objections have been made to assigning changes in expectations a determinant role in explaining economic fluctuations: expectations were considered too subjective factors while it was felt that science should be concerned solely with objective factors. Moreover, resorting to instability of expectations was considered an easy way of explaining practically everything, making statements of the economic discipline arbitrary and giving them too little predictive power.

Recently, expectations have found their place again in macroeconomics, but this revival has linked them to the concept of equilibrium, which plays a crucial role in all the modern economic theorizing. As seen above, the concept of rational expectations made popular by new classical macroeconomics generally requires expectations to be confirmed in equilibrium according to the fundamentals of the true economic model. It must however be noticed that the main result of new classical macroeconomics – that macroeconomic equilibrium is a market clearing one without involuntary unemployment – cannot be explained by referring to rational expectations alone. Basically it depends on the assumption of perfect and complete markets where market clearing is ensured by perfect price flexibility. If the institutional structure of the economy is different, if markets are imperfect and perhaps with asymmetric information, rational expectations can still be used but they have to be consistent with the different true model of the economy. We then may well have a macroeconomic equilibrium with sticky prices and quantity adjustment that is perfectly consistent with the theory of rational expectations.

The point made by new classical macroeconomics about the role of expectations is slightly different however. It is claimed that, if expectations change without any change in the fundamentals of the true model, this cannot lead to a new self-fulfilled rational expectations equilibrium. This claim amounts to stating that expectations concerning, for instance, entrepreneurs' 'animal spirits' cannot be rational in the sense that they can be self-fulfilled in a new rational expectations equilibrium. Moreover it implies stating that no movement to a different rational expectations equilibrium is possible if the change in the expectations comes from a causal event that is exogenous to fundamentals.

Recent research on 'sunspot equilibria' (Cass and Shell, 1983) has shown that this claim is not well grounded. Randomizing among the many non-stochastic non-stationary equilibria which lead to one (or more) non-stochastic stationary equilibrium, it is possible to have a sequence of probability distributions converge to an invariant stationary probability distribution which defines a continuum of rational expectations equilibria (Farmer, 1994). If imperfect markets are assumed, sunspot equilibria with involuntary unemployment may be obtained with self-fulfilling expectations: if, for example, there is a sunspot on the rate of return on capital, one can solve for the stock of capital and investment demand required to bring about the *ex-post* rate of return after the sunspot has occurred, obtaining a stochastic difference equation representing a stationary Markov process followed by the capital stock. From this the desired capital stock in each period is derived as a function of the sunspot history. The belief that investment will respond in the future to the sunspot history according to this function makes the belief correct also in the present according to the same function (Woodford, 1991).

In this kind of model endogenous fluctuations are not generated as a response to exogenous shocks to economic fundamentals as in real business cycle theory (Long and Plosser, 1983), but they are due to self-fulfilling revisions of expectations. It can be shown (Woodford, 1991) that stabilizing policies may be successful in preventing such fluctuations. However, when the basic model is one of an economy with market imperfections, there is no reason to assume that stabilizing policies are exhaustive. Deterministic steady states are not efficient and there can even be multiple steady state equilibria in a deterministic sense, produced by market imperfections or by structural conditions inherently linked to market imperfections, such as increasing returns to scale, which can be ordered with respect to their efficiency.

COORDINATION FAILURES

When multiple equilibria can be ordered according to their efficiency, two kinds of problems have to be solved: the first concerns the reasons why an economy may settle down to the less efficient equilibrium; the second concerns how to promote the kind of coordination which makes it possible for the economy to settle down to a higher efficiency level. Assume for simplicity only two equilibria; when the less efficient equilibrium prevails we have a 'coordination failure': the way market interaction operates does not permit the coordination required to achieve the efficient equilibrium. The first problem is to explain why market interaction fails, and the second is a typical economic policy issue: how to improve coordination in order to move from a less efficient to a more efficient equilibrium.

Increasing returns to scale in imperfect competition is one important source of multiple equilibria (Weitzman, 1983; Kiyotaki, 1988; Manning, 1990; Hahn and Solow, 1995). In these models an upward-sloping labour demand curve is obtained which, together with an upward-sloping wage-setting curve, allows for multiple equilibria in the real wage-employment space. With two such equilibria, the high wage-high employment one is more efficient. Optimistic expectations can lead to a high level of investment and through increasing returns to scale to the more efficient equilibrium, while pessimistic expectations and low investment lead to the less efficient one. Both kind of expectations are self-fulfilling (Kiyotaki, 1988).

Another source of multiplicity of equilibria in imperfect markets is strategic interdependence. Multiple equilibria can be obtained in this setting with a condition known as 'strategic complementarity' (Cooper and John, 1988). This condition entails that, with two firms, the marginal profit of each firm depends positively on an action to expand production of the other. In this case reaction functions are increasing and can cross more than once. The equilibrium with a high level of action is more efficient than that with a low level of action.

Multiple equilibria and coordination failures can also be obtained because of the existence of transaction and search costs (Diamond, 1982; Howitt, 1985). This approach explicitly exposes the limitations of the Walrasian model, which assumes zero transaction and search costs, using the artificial device of the auctioneer whose job is not only that of finding equilibrium prices, but also that of solving the problem of how to match sellers and buyers. In this way the Walrasian approach ignores the issues of market organization and related costs which are the true source of problems in market economies. If, in their spontaneous working, markets automatically solved these problems, no coordination failure would exist and multiple equilibria would all be efficient. But as it is precisely this that is questioned in market economies of the real world, the problem arises of finding the most appropriate kind of economic policy and of deciding the space to be given to macroeconomic demand policy.

Costs related to the organization of market exchanges create positive and negative externalities: an agent using resources to buy a good reduces the costs of those who are trying to sell it, but at the same time creates problems for other potential buyers (Howitt, 1990). The higher the number of the agents taking part in the exchange process, the more likely the matching of buyers and sellers and the lower the weight of market organization costs. The higher the transaction level, the more likely the success of the transaction process and the more desirable it is to engage in this process. If the size of the market is too small, it may not be advisable for the individual agents to engage in a search process to find possible profitable exchange opportunities.

When firms expect a high level of aggregate demand, their transaction costs are lower and this will encourage higher production levels. This in turn will lead to an equilibrium where expectations are self-fulfilled. For the same reason, the expectation of a lower level of demand may be self-fulfilling because too thin markets and high transaction costs will discourage production.

Yet another factor of multiplicity of equilibria and potential coordination failure is the inadequacy of economic institutions. Mention can be made of two: market incompleteness and lack of coordinating mechanisms. In chapter XIV of his *General Theory* Keynes clearly uses an incomplete market argument. Accepting the scheme of an investment demand inversely related to the rate of interest and of a saving supply positively depending on the rate of interest, he analyzes the effects of a negative shock on investment demand. 'Classical' theory would simply see an intertemporal substitution between present and future consumption made possible by excess saving, and would deny any aggregate real effect, merely forecasting a crowding-out effect on investments and a change in demand composition favouring consumption. Keynes objected to this conclusion claiming that firms would not see present lower sales as perfectly compensated by future ones because of an incompleteness of intertemporal markets which make them perceive the excess saving simply as lower current demand. Hence they would reduce production and a real aggregate effect would be lower output and employment (Keynes, 1936).

Recent research (Heller and Starrett, 1976; Bryant, 1983; Murphy *et al.*, 1989a, b) has shown that with market incompleteness, equilibria can be different according to the number of markets: equilibria with a larger number of markets are more efficient but they are not reached because of the lack of signals due to market absence.

The lack of coordination mechanisms can lead to inefficient subgame perfect non-cooperative equilibria with involuntary unemployment. This point has been made by John Roberts (1987, 1989). Individuals who do not expect to be hired will constrain their product demand; firms, knowing this, will not hire workers: pessimistic expectations will be confirmed and the resulting unemployment is involuntary. Each firm knows that a hiring decision would benefit any other firm but the lack of reliable coordinating mechanisms makes this decision highly unlikely, so that the economy remains trapped in the involuntary unemployment equilibrium.

COORDINATION, MARKETS AND ECONOMIC POLICY

There is a clear interaction and sometimes an overlapping among the different factors determining coordination failures. A common feature is the possibility for the economy to eventually settle down to an undesirable equilibrium so that an economic policy problem arises of how to move the economy to a more desirable equilibrium. This makes the coordination failure approach the most interesting and promising in the revival of Keynesian macroeconomics, linking it to an extensively debated issue of our time, the relative role of the market and of public intervention in the performance of an economic system.

Keynes's central message concerns the way the market operates as a coordination mechanism among economic agents. In the Walrasian model and in its macroeconomic prototype, the new classical macroeconomics model, the only source of coordination among economic agents is the price mechanism. Traditional Keynesian macroeconomics followed the general equilibrium approach on the same ground, reducing the coordination problem to the existence of sticky prices: there lies the root of the decline of Keynesian economics. Of course Keynes did not deny the importance of the price mechanism; he noticed, however, that interaction and coordination among economic agents do not take place only through prices and that coordination only through prices can sometimes lead to undesirable consequences.

In his *General Theory* Keynes questioned the success of full price flexibility. He did not consider deflation a cure to unemployment. In chapter XIX of the *General Theory* he made it clear that downward flexibility of wages and prices following a negative demand shock could worsen instability through its effects on expected future wages and prices and perhaps delay the adjustment to a new full employment equilibrium almost indefinitely. A compensating stabilizing aggregate demand policy would reduce the negative welfare effects of instability and allow for a quicker adjustment to a full employment equilibrium (Keynes, 1936).

Keynes's idea has been taken up by some authors who have been able to give a more rigorous analytical treatment and explanation to the intuition formulated in the *General Theory* (Hicks, 1939; Vicarelli, 1977; Grandmont, 1982; Medio and Musu, 1983; Hahn and Solow, 1995). However it has not found the right place in Keynesian macroeconomics. The issue raised by Keynes is important in a time where a new positive attitude toward the benefits of a dynamic free competition process is gaining ground. It may be worthwhile to take into account that this process can also entail destabilizing consequences, mainly through excessive price flexibility, which may be rather costly in terms of lost welfare and which may possibly be reduced by a macroeconomic policy that does not impair the benefits of the competitive process itself.

When markets are imperfect or incomplete, a situation which in all likelihood goes together with conditions of uncertainty and asymmetric information, the price mechanism encounters serious difficulties in performing its coordination function. All this is ignored in the abstract market vision of the Walrasian parable and of the new classical macroeconomics, while the Keynesian vision considers the market in a more problematic way as an institution in which there are organization and transaction costs. The Keynesian approach recognizes that the market has been one of the most successful interaction mechanisms to provide coordination among agents in the economy; but from this acknowledgment it does not follow that the coordinating mechanism is a perfect one.

Hence in the Keynesian approach, because of the organizational and institutional complexity of markets, adjustment of quantities operates together with adjustment of prices. There is not a dichotomy as in the Walrasian world, where agents send quantity signals and the market, personified by the auctioneer, makes these quantity signals compatible through price signals. The artificial simplicity of the Walrasian model persists in the new classical macroeconomics with its assumptions regarding the representative agent and perfect and complete markets.

New classical macroeconomics has broken any link with the recent interesting results of microeconomics research in industrial organization theory whereas the Keynesian approach did not. Now it should recover these links more explicitly and deepen their implication for macroeconomic theory and policy.

In this framework macroeconomic policy has two tasks. The first is to help improving coordination by smoothing fluctuations due to the spontaneous working of market forces and entailing high welfare costs. The Keynesian message is that this is not merely done by a credible and constant rule of monetary policy, as suggested by the new classical macroeconomics, but by active policies. Historical experience in market economies seems to show an asymmetry in the working of monetary and fiscal policies, the first being more appropriate to fight inflationary pressures and the second to move a system out of a recession.

The second task is to help the system overcome coordination failures. This requires a credible strategy which includes measures to improve the efficiency of market institutions, to increase their transparency by reducing information asymmetries, to widen the size and number of markets, and to convince economic agents to have optimistic coordinated beliefs from which coordinated behaviours will follow. This strategy is more, and more complex, than a pure macroeconomic demand policy; it may require a combination of demand and supply policies and a microeconomic policy to provide economic agents with the appropriate incentives.

With respect to both tasks, the success of macroeconomic policy depends on the degree of information and of efficiency of the public institutions deputized to intervene. Moreover the costs and benefits of any policy action must be balanced in an intertemporal horizon. For example, risks of structural deficits and of inflationary pressures should be avoided when using aggregate demand expansion to help an economy come out of a recession; risks of adverse selection and moral hazard should be considered when implementing policies to sustain economic activity.

Awareness of the complexity of any macroeconomic policy decision does not justify a vision requiring a minimum resort to policy intervention when this minimalist approach is based upon theoretical premises such as those of perfect and complete markets and of certainty and perfect information, which are so distant from the basic facts characterizing the organization of market economies in the real world.

REFERENCES

Akerlof, G. and Yellen, J. (1985) A Near-Rational Model of the Business Cycle with Wage and Price Inertia, *Quarterly Journal of Economics* **100**, 823–38.

Ardeni, P.G., Boitani, A., Delli Gatti D. and Gallegati, M. (1996) La Nuova Economia Keynesiana: risultati e problemi, in M. Messori (ed.), *La Nuova Economia Keynesiana*, Bologna, Il Mulino, 49–144.

Ball, L., Mankiw, G. and Romer, D. (1988) The New Keynesian Economics and the Output-Inflation Trade-off, *Brookings Papers of Economic Activity*, 1–65.

Barro, R. and Grossman, H. (1976) *Money, Employment and Inflation*, Cambridge, Cambridge University Press.

Benassy, J.P. (1982) *The Economics of Market Disequilibrium*, London, Academic Press.

Benassy, J.P. (1987) Imperfect Competition, Unemployment and Policy, *European Economic Review* **XXXI**, 417–26.

Blanchard, O. and Kiyotaki, N. (1987) Monopolistic Competition and the Effects on Aggregate Demand, *American Economic Review* **77**, 647–66.

Bryant, J. (1983) A Simple Rational-Expectations Keynes-Type Model, *Quarterly Journal of Economics* **XCVIII**, 525–8.

Cass, D. and Shell, K. (1983) Do Sunspots Matter?, *Journal of Political Economy* **91**, 193–227.

Clower, R. (1965) The Keynesian Counter-Revolution, in F. Hahn and F. Brechling (eds.), *The Theory of Interest Rates*, London, Macmillan, 103–25.

Cooper, J. and John, A. (1988) Coordinating Coordination Failures in Keynesian Models, *Quarterly Journal of Economics* **CIII**, 441–63.

D'Aspremont, C., Dos Santos Ferreira, R. and Gerard Varet, L. (1990) On Monopolistic Competition and Involuntary Unemployment, *Quarterly Journal of Economics* **CV**, 895–919.

Diamond, P. (1982) Aggregate Demand Management in Search Equilibrium, *Journal of Political Economy* **90**, 881–94.

Dixon, H. (1991) Macroeconomic Equilibrium and Policy in a Large Unionized Economy, *European Economic Review* **XXXV**, 1427–48.

Dixon, H. and Rankin, N. (1994) Imperfect Competition and Macroeconomics: A Survey, *Oxford Economic Papers* **XLVI**, 171–99.

Farmer, R. (1994) *The Macroeconomics of Self-Fulfilling Prophecies*, Cambridge, Cambridge University Press.

Friedman, M. (1968) The Role of Monetary Policy, *American Economic Review* **58**, 1–17.

Grandmont, J.M. (1982) *Money and Value*, Cambridge, Cambridge University Press.

Greenwald, B. and Stiglitz, J. (1990) Macroeconomic Models with Equity and Credit Rationing, in R.G. Hubbard (ed.), *Information, Capital Markets and Investments*, Chicago, University of Chicago Press, 15–42.

Greenwald, B. and Stiglitz, J. (1993a) Financial Market Imperfections and Business Cycles, *Quarterly Journal of Economics* **CVIII**, 77–114.

Greenwald, B. and Stiglitz, J. (1993b) New and Old Keynesians, *Journal of Economic Perspectives* **VII**, 23–44.

Hahn F. and Solow R. (1995) *A Critical Essay on Modern Macroeconomic Theory*, Oxford, Blackwell.
Hart, O. (1982) A Model of Imperfect Competition with Keynesian Features, *Quarterly Journal of Economics* **XCVII**, 109–38.
Heller, W. and Starrett, D. (1976) On the Nature of Externalities, in S. Lin (ed.), *The Theory and Measurement of Economic Externalities*, New York, 9–22.
Hicks, J. (1937) Mr. Keynes and the Classics, *Econometrica* **V**, 147–59.
Hicks, J. (1939) *Value and Capital*, Oxford, Clarendon Press.
Howitt, P. (1985) Transaction Costs in the Theory of Unemployment, *American Economic Review* **75**, 88–100.
Howitt, P. (1990) *The Keynesian Recovery*, New York, Philip Allan.
Keynes, J.M. (1936) *The General Theory of Employment, Interest and Money*, London, Macmillan.
Kiyotaki, N. (1988) Multiple Expectational Equilibria under Monopolistic Competition, *Quarterly Journal of Economics* **CIII**, 695–713.
Layard, R., Nickell, S. and Jackman, R. (1991) *Unemployment: Macroeconomic Performance and the Labor Market*, Oxford, Oxford University Press.
Lindbeck, A. and Snower, D.J. (1988) *The Insider-Ousider Theory of Employment and Unemployment*, Cambridge, MA, MIT Press.
Long, J. and Plosser, C. (1983) Real Business Cycles, *Journal of Political Economy* **91**, 39–69.
Lucas, R. (1972) Expectations and the Neutrality of Money, *Journal of Economic Theory* **IV**, 103–24.
Malinvaud, E. (1977) *The Theory of Unemployment Reconsidered*, Oxford, Blackwell.
Mankiw, G. (1985) Small Menu Costs and Large Business Cycles: a Macroeconomic Model of Monopoly, *Quarterly Journal of Economics* **C**, 529–39.
Manning, A. (1990) Imperfect Competition, Multiple Equilibria and Unemployment Policy, *Economic Journal* **100**, 151–62.
McDonald, I. and Solow, R. (1981) Wage Bargaining and Employment, *American Economic Review* **71**, 896–908.
Medio, A. and Musu, I. (1983) Changes in Money Wages and Employment in a Keynesian Analysis, *Economic Notes* **12**, 6–21.
Modigliani, F. (1944) Liquidity Preference and the Theory of Interest and Money, *Econometrica* **XII**, 45–88.
Murphy, K., Shleifer, A. and Vishny, R. (1989a) Income Distribution, Market Size and Industrialization, *Quarterly Journal of Economics* **CIV**, 537–64.
Murphy, K., Shleifer, A. and Vishny, R. (1989b) Industrialization and the Big Push, *Journal of Political Economy* **97**, 1003–26.
Muth, J. (1961) Rational Expectations and the Theory of Price Movements, *Econometrica* **XXIX**, 325–35.
Patinkin, D. (1955) *Money, Interest and Prices*, New York, Harper and Row.
Phelps, E. (1968) Money-Wage Dynamics and Labor Market Equilibrium, *Journal of Political Economy* **76**, 687–711.
Roberts, J. (1987) An Equilibrium Model with Unvoluntary Unemployment at Flexible Competitive Prices and Wages, *American Economic Review* **77**, 856–74.

Roberts, J. (1989) Unvoluntary Unemployment and Imperfect Competition: a Game Theoretical Macromodel, in G. Feiwel (ed.), *The Economics of Imperfect Competition: Joan Robinson and Beyond*, London, Macmillan, 146–65.
Romer, D. (1993) The New Keynesian Synthesis, *Journal of Economic Perspectives* **VII**, 5–22.
Romer, D. (1996) *Advanced Macroeconomics*, New York, McGraw Hill.
Rotemberg, J. (1987) The New Keynesian Foundations, *NBER Macroeconomics Annual*, **II**, 69–104.
Shapiro, C. and Stiglitz, J. (1984) Equilibrium Unemployment as a Worker Discipline Device, *American Economic Review* **74**, 433–44.
Silvestre, J. (1993) The Market-Power Foundations of Macroeconomic Policy, *Journal of Economic Literature* **XXXI**, 105–41.
Stiglitz, J. and Weiss, A. (1981) Credit Rationing in Markets with Imperfect Information, *American Economic Review* **71**, 393–410.
Vicarelli, F. (1977) *Keynes. L'instabilità del capitalismo*, Milan, ETAS Libri.
Weitzman, M. (1983) Increasing Returns and the Foundations of Unemployment Theory, *Economic Journal* **92**, 787–804.
Woodford, M. (1991) Self-Fulfilling Expectations and Fluctuations in Aggregate Demand, in G. Mankiw and D. Romer (eds), *New Keynesian Economics*, vol. II, Cambridge MA, MIT Press, 77–110.

Comment

Antonio Pedone

Ignazio Musu has done an excellent job in reviewing the most important contributions and debates in the field of macroeconomics from Keynes on. He points out clearly the differences between Keynesian unemployment, the equilibrium of the neoclassical synthesis, the classical unemployment equilibrium, and the monetarist natural rate of unemployment equilibrium. He also shows how in the rational expectations world Keynesian macroeconomics has been definitely displaced by new classical macroeconomics. But, even in the world of natural expectations, market imperfections of various sources may produce multiple equilibria, and many factors may determine market coordination failures that lead the economy to eventually settle down to an undesirable equilibrium. In such situations, which are likely to arise in a world of uncertainty and asymmetric information, the price mechanism encounters serious difficulties in performing its coordination function, and a new opportunity for economic policy opens up. Musu thus vindicates Vicarelli's belief that pure-market coordination has an inherently destabilizing nature in the capitalist system and that there is scope for an effective macroeconomic policy, assigning a defensible role to aggregate demand management. Of course, it is not just a question of the old simple arithmetic of the budget multiplier. As Musu points out, it requires a more complex strategy than a pure macroeconomic demand policy. The complexity of the task raises the problem of possible policy coordination failures, also in the light of past experiences.

In fact, the rise and fall of fiscal policy can be explained not only by the changing ideological attitudes towards the extent of public intervention in the economy, and by analytical controversies about the (micro and macro) economic foundations of stabilization policies. The changing fortunes of fiscal policy can also be attributed to constraints imposed on the implementation of countercyclical policies due to the growing difficulties connected with the internal and external coordination of fiscal and monetary policies followed in industrial countries, in addition to the traditional forecasting problems, time-lags in operation, and the lack of control on some budgetary items (for example, entitlements).

As regards the internal coordination of fiscal and monetary policies, many things have changed since the mid-1950s, when it was a widely shared view that 'a community can have full employment, can at the same time have the rate of capital formation it wants, and can accomplish all this compatibly with the degree of income-redistributing taxation it ethically desires'. Monetary and fiscal policies were thought of as independent and effective instruments of economic policy; by the principle of effective market classification, fiscal policy was assigned to internal equilibrium and monetary policy to external equilibrium (assuming capital flows to be responsive to interest rate differentials), thereby insuring internal and external equilibrium at the same time. Elaborating on the assumption of independence and effectiveness, a large number of analytical and econometric models were then developed to take into account capital flows and stocks, fixed and fluctuating exchange rates, expectations about future income and prices. The independence and effectiveness of monetary and fiscal policy was assumed on the basis of the institutional arrangements defining the actions of the different authorities in charge of fiscal policy (taxing, spending, borrowing) or of monetary policy (controlling the magnitude of some monetary aggregate). 'Pure' fiscal and monetary policies were regarded as appropriate tools of economic analysis and as a sufficient basis for economic policy. But the economic effects of each kind of pure fiscal or monetary policy instrument assumed implicitly a given response by the authorities in charge of the other kind of fiscal or monetary policy instrument. This interconnection (not interdependence) of fiscal and monetary policies was very soon acknowledged as very important in determining the different effects of each policy instrument.

In the 1970s, the many changes in the external economic environment and the evident failure of economic policies pursued in most industrialized countries to attain full employment, growth, price stability and external equilibrium shifted the emphasis towards the interdependence and ineffectiveness of monetary and fiscal policies and away from their independence or interconnection. The growing size of nominal public sector deficits along with high inflation (not necessarily caused by government deficits) made the interdependence of monetary and fiscal policies clear. Their interdependence emerges clearly when we consider the government budget constraint. Under the government budget constraint, any decision about today's deficit and its financing influences the feasible set of fiscal-monetary combinations in future periods. Today's fiscal (monetary) policy is largely influenced by yesterday's monetary (fiscal) policies and, in turn, affects tomorrow's policies. Thus, intertemporal interdependence of fiscal and monetary policies depends on expectations about future budgetary and monetary policy induced by today's decisions. The interdependence and relative effectiveness of fiscal and monetary policies in influencing nominal income may vary over a broad range according to the expectations which we assume actually to be realized.

The ineffectiveness of large government deficits (especially when the deficit depends on high real interest payments) to support aggregate demand and national income has become more and more evident. The upward trend of the public debt/GDP ratio in most industrial countries since the mid-1970s has limited the opportunity for an active counter-cyclical fiscal policy. In fact, since the 1980s, in most countries discretionary rises in tax revenues have exceeded the increase in primary expenditure even during a recession, while most of the increase in the debt ratio took place in non-recessionary periods. This apparently incongruous behaviour can be explained in many ways which involve credibility games, the influence of the initial conditions of public finances, the political costs of budgetary decisions, and many institutional aspects.

A similar evolution (or involution) has characterized the constraint on the use and effectiveness of fiscal policy originating from international economic integration. In the still largely closed economies of the 1950s, the effectiveness of autonomous national fiscal policy was restricted only by leakages due to the intensity of foreign trade relations, with prevailing stable exchange rates and strict controls on capital movements. From the 1970s onwards, the autonomy and effectiveness of national fiscal policy has been progressively eroded by the fluctuations in exchange rates (and in exchange rate regimes), by the drastic reductions in transport and communication costs and by the deregulation and liberalization of capital movements. The increasing interdependence of national economies has influenced the allocation of resources, and imbalances in the saving-investment ratios have taken on very large dimensions, with corresponding surpluses and deficits in the balance of payments current accounts. These imbalances have been accompanied (and to some degree caused) by uncoordinated fiscal and monetary policies.

The adoption of uncoordinated measures or unilateral action on the part of each single country has often done more harm than good to stabilization policies. Some kind of international economic cooperation in various fields of economic policy has been pursued in an attempt to achieve high economic growth with low inflation, while preserving free trade and free capital movements, and relatively stable exchange rates. The push toward international economic cooperation has varied according to the perceived intensity of the constraints created by the trade-off between the different objectives, and of the nature and extent of the costs of their partial attainment. In any case, the process of international economic cooperation implies a self-restraint on the autonomous use of national fiscal policy, as compared with the complete loss of autonomy in domestic policies in a world of national economies made interdependent and footloose by technological developments and deregulation.

Through international economic cooperation the role and effectiveness of national fiscal policy may be restored, but it would be foolhardy to expect international economic cooperation to obtain much more than the often disappointing results of the coordination of economic policies within each single country. Here too, the limits and the problems of international economic policy coordination arise not only from different views about the theoretical foundations of economic management, but from organizational, procedural and institutional matters. A solution to the market coordination problems (or failures) pointed out by Musu and to policy coordination problems (or failures) can be found only by combining sound economic theory, empirical research and the analysis of institutions, as Fausto Vicarelli did in most of his scientific work.

Part II

Present World Imbalances and the Need for a New International Economic Order

3 Vicarelli, Keynes's Vision of Capitalism, and Currency Speculation

Paul Davidson

INTRODUCTION

In his book *Keynes: The Instability of Capitalism*, (1984) Fausto Vicarelli argues that to understand Keynes's analysis one must recognize Keynes's 'Vision of Capitalism'. According to Vicarelli (1984, p. 3): 'Keynes displayed an enviable ability to identify basic causes and themes to draw conclusions of general validity for the understanding of capitalism. Compared to traditional economic theory, permeated with its abstract concepts and cautions engendered by "marginalist" economics, this was a revolutionary way of attacking reality'.

Vicarelli (1984, p. 4) warns that the massive interpretative literature that has formed the basis of mainstream Keynesian economics in the decades since Keynes wrote has generally been compromised by imposing, in the name of a hard-headed scientific basis, a marginalist microfoundation on Keynes's analytical framework. In so doing, mainstream economists have disembowelled Keynes's analytical framework 'from the earthly context in which it was generated. An alternative approach is the only way to avoid a disembodied caricature of his contribution to economic theory'. Although Vicarelli was criticizing the closed economy models of mainstream economics that had been developed in the first four decades since *The General Theory* was written, Vicarelli's comments are even more a propos for mainstream open economy macromodels.[1] As we enter the 'global economy' of the twenty-first century, it is more essential than ever that we revert back to the 'earthly context' of Keynes's vision of capitalism if we are to develop practical real world policies to resolve present world imbalances and provide for a new and stable international monetary-economic order.

Vicarelli (1984, p. 19) notes that as early as 1913, 'although Keynes had acquired a degree of wisdom about the non-neutrality of financial institutions and money *vis-à-vis* the interests directly engaged in the organization of a capitalist economy, his steadfast rationale was to improve the efficiency of these institutions'. In Keynes's writings on how to establish a new international order after World War II, Keynes clearly saw the need to limit financial market domination of international economic relationships. Yet, today, we see pragmatic politicians and practical central bankers attempting to organize a capitalist international economic order on the basis of leaving important speculative (portfolio) financial market and exchange rate determination decision to a laissez-faire marketplace – in the name of efficiency. This micro-marginalist based view is likely to give capitalism the same bad name it had before Keynes (1936, p. 372) set out to tame the 'outstanding faults of the economic system in which we live'.

With the technological improvements in our communicative transmission of information (and misinformation) these practical politicians and central bankers in authority are typically the slaves not of defunct economists (as Keynes (1936, p. 283) pictured such practical men in his day), but of wrong-headed Nobel Prize winners in economics whose analytical thought are 'permeated' with exactly the 'abstract concepts and cautions engendered by "marginalist" economics' that Vicarelli so correctly condemned. Accordingly, in this paper, we follow Vicarelli's clarion call for 'an alternative approach' that relies on Keynes's vision of capitalism to understand the role of speculation in the foreign exchange market and the international monetary system.

WHOSE VISION ON SPECULATION IS REALISTIC?

In the classical model, where agents know the future with perfect certainty or, at least, can form statistically reliable predictions without persistent errors (that is, rational expectations), speculative market activities can be justified as stabilizing. When, on the other hand, the economic future is uncertain (non-ergodic), today's agents 'know' they cannot reliably predict future outcomes. Hicks (1979, p. vii) has argued that if economists are to build models which reflect real-world behaviour, then the agents in these models must 'know that they just don't know' what is going to happen in the future.

In the uncertain world we live in, therefore, people cannot rely on historical or current market data to, in a statistical sense, reliably forecast future prices. In the absence of strong institutions that assure orderly spot financial markets, there can be no reliable existing anchor to future spotmarket prices of liquid assets. In such a world without institutions that guarantee orderly markets for liquid assets, speculative activities can not only be highly destabilizing in terms of future market prices, but the volatility of these future spot prices can have costly real consequences to the aggregate real income of the community. Nowhere has this been made more obvious than in the machinations of the foreign exchange markets since the end of the Bretton Woods era of fixed exchange rates.

Tobin and his associates, that is, Eichengreeen and Wyplosz, (hereafter ETW) (1995, p. 164) have recognized that volatility in foreign exchange markets due to speculation has 'real economic consequences devastating for particular sectors and whole economies'. At approximately the same time the ETW article appeared in print, the Winter 1994–95 Mexican peso crisis exploded and spilled over into a US dollar problem. In international financial markets, where image is often more important than reality, the dollar was dragged down by the peso during the late Winter and early Spring of 1995 while the German mark and Japanese yen appeared to be the only safe harbours for portfolio fund managers.

Portfolio fund managers in search of yields and 'safe harbours' can move funds from one country to another in nanoseconds with a few clicks on their computer keyboard. In today's global economy any whiff of currency weakness becomes a conflagration spread along the information highway. Federal Reserve Chairman Alan Greenspan was quoted in *The New York Times* as testifying that 'Mexico became the first casualty . . . of the new international financial system' that permits hot portfolio money to slosh around the world 'much more quickly'. Can the real economies of the twenty-first century afford to suffer many more casualties in this new international financial system?

If initially the major central banks do not dispatch sufficient resources to intervene effectively to extinguish any speculative currency fire, then the resultant publicity is equivalent to shouting 'fire' in a theatre. The consequent panic worsens the situation and central banks whose currencies are seen as safe havens may lose any interest in a coordinated response to the increasing inferno.

What Tobin and his associates are worried about is that with electronically linked international financial markets and an interconnected global economy there is a strong possibility, which even advocates of free international capital markets have begun to admit, that 'hot money' portfolio flows can have massive disruptive real economic effects. Accordingly ETW recommend a global ad valorem tax on all exchange transactions to discourage short-term round tripping without affecting long-term international portfolio investments.

In the real world in which we live, pragmatists such as Tobin and his associates are implicitly arguing that, because of the possibility of speculative portfolio changes, the social costs of freely flexible exchange rates far exceed the social benefits. Accordingly, there is a role for some form of government intervention in the foreign exchange market. In contrast, orthodox economic theory traditionally argues that government interference imposes real costs while unfettered exchange rate markets, like all efficient markets, provide real benefits. For mainstream theorists all speculative activities in efficient markets are stabilizing. They typically reach this conclusion because they conflate the concept of speculation with the concept of arbitrage. Since the latter is always a stabilizing force, orthodoxy insists that the former is also always a stabilizing factor.[2]

If the social costs of free exchange markets do exceed the social benefits as pragmatists such as Tobin imply, then what is required in this global economy with computer-linked financial markets is not a system of *ad hoc* central bank interventions while what Greenspan calls the 'new international financial system' burns the real economy. What is necessary is to build into the international system permanent fireproofing rules and structures that prevent imagery-induced currency fires. *Crisis prevention rather than crisis rescues must be the primary long-term objective*. If the developed nations do not hang together on a currency-fire prevention system, then they will all hang separately in a replay of the international financial market crisis of the Great Depression.

Reasonable people do not think it is a violation of civil liberties to prohibit people from boarding an aeroplane with a gun. Moreover, no one would think we are impinging on individual rights if the society prohibits anyone from entering a movie theatre with a Molotov cocktail in one hand and a book of matches in the other – even if the person indicates no desire to burn down the theatre. Yet, in the name of free markets, fund managers can imagine an exploding Molotov cocktail and then yell 'fire' in the crowded international financial markets any time the 'image' of a possible profitable fire moves them.

Fifty years ago, Keynes recognized what the best and the brightest economists are only beginning to recognize today, namely that 'there is not a country which can . . . safely allow the flight of funds (hot money) . . . Equally there is no country that can safely receive . . . [these portfolio] funds which cannot safely be used for fixed investment (Keynes, 1980, p. 25).'

Tobin has taken up this Keynesian theme and argued for fire prevention in the form of 'sand in the wheels of foreign exchange markets', that is, to levy a tax on moving funds from one currency to another. (This is equivalent to taxing, rather than banning, the Molotov cocktail member of the theatre audience). ETW have also explored the possibility of imposing compulsory interest-free deposits or other capital requirements (therefore creating an 'opportunity cost' tax) to 'discourage short-term round tripping, but not long-term investment' (Greenway, 1995, p. 160).

A published discussion between ETW (1995), Garber and Taylor (1995) and Kenen (1995) did not focus on the economic rational in terms for a Tobin tax (or any other form of government intervention). Rather Garber and Taylor raised the issue of the institutional feasibility of a foreign exchange transaction tax, while Kenen concentrated specifically on capital controls and why he perceives the impossibility of such controls at this time. Little discussion of the theoretical rational for any controls was provided.

Keynes, on the other hand, who distinguished the speculative motive for liquidity preference from the marginal efficiency demand for real investment analysed this problem in some detail in the 1940s and concluded, as the citation above suggests, that a system of outright prohibition of international hot money flows would be required. With the help of the formula developed below, it is easy to see why Keynes reached this conclusion.

CAPITAL UNCERTAINTY AND SPECULATIVE FLOWS

In order for any asset to be considered as a liquid store of value over time, that asset must be readily resalable in a well organized, orderly spot market. The institution of 'market-maker' is a necessary condition for the existence of well-organized, orderly spot markets

(Davidson, 1972, pp. 64–71). Since the spot market price of any liquid asset in such a market can change over time, savers who are storing claims on resources must contemplate the possibility of an appreciation or depreciation in the asset's spot market price at a future date when the holder wishes to liquidate his or her holdings. This potential capital gain or loss is obtained by subtracting today's spot price ($p_s^{t_0}$) from the expected spot price at a future date ($p_s^{t_1}$) when the asset will be resold. If $(p_s^{t_1} - p_s^{t_0}) > 0$, a capital gain is expected from holding the asset till t_1; if $(p_s^{t_1} - p_s^{t_0}) < 0$, a capital loss will be expected. Offsetting the possible capital loss on choosing any liquid asset is the future earnings (q) that can be obtained from owning the asset during a period of time net of carrying costs (c) incurred by holding this asset. Both q and c tend to increase with the time period the asset is held. There are also transactions costs (T_s) incurred in both buying and reselling a liquid asset. These transactions costs are usually independent of the time interval that the liquid asset is held. These transactions costs, however, normally increase at a decreasing rate as the value of the asset increases.

If an unforeseen liability should come due in the immediate future, then the transactions cost of taking a position and then liquidating it can easily swamp any net income flow (q − c) received from holding the asset for such a short time while the capital gain (or loss) is likely to be negligible. It is, therefore, normal to prefer to hold some saving in the form of the money in which near-term contractual obligations will come due to cover planned and some possible unforeseen obligations (Hicks, 1967).

The more uncertain the future appears, the more unforeseeable liabilities may come due. The more desirable, therefore, it will be to minimize transactions costs by storing saving in the form of money or other safe short-term assets denominated in terms of the currency of contractual settlement. This smoothes our fears of becoming illiquid if anything unpredictable occurs during the period.[3]

Savers find a capital loss repugnant but the lure of capital gains seductive. Let q be the future expected income to be received from holding a financial security over a period of time, and c be the carrying costs, where both q and c are denominated in terms of the specific currency of the issuer of the financial asset. Let us allow foreign currencies and stocks and bonds denominated in foreign currencies be included in the choice of assets to be held in any portfolio. If, for a specific liquid asset the portfolio manager expects

$$(q - c) + (p_s^{t_1} - p_s^{t_0}) - T_s > 0, \quad (1)$$

then the manager is a 'bull'. If it is expected that

$$(q - c) + (p_s^{t_1} - p_s^{t_0}) - T_s < 0, \quad (2)$$

then the fund manager is a 'bear'. In the simplest case, for example, if $(q - c)$ minus T_s equals zero, then if

$$[p_s^{t_1} / p_s^{t_0}] > 1, \quad (3)$$

then the person is a bull, while if

$$[p_s^{t_1} / p_s^{t_0}] < 1, \quad (4)$$

the person is a bear.

If one holds one's own domestic money there is no future net income $[(q - c) = 0]$, no capital gain or loss $[(p_s^{t_1} + p_s^{t_0}) = 0]$, and no transactions costs $[T_s = 0]$.

In a flexible exchange rate system, fund managers will estimate the expected future income plus capital gain or loss on all domestic and foreign liquid securities. For ease of exposition in analysing portfolio decisions in a multination open economy context, let us include the fund manager's expected capital gains and losses for each security (in terms of the currency the security is denominated in) in the magnitude of $(q - c)$. Accordingly, the term $(p_s^{t_1} - p_s^{t_0})$ can be reserved for the *ceteris paribus* effect of an expected change in the spot exchange rate. Thus, besides expected capital gains (or losses) and all the transactions costs (T_s) associated with the purchase and sale of a liquid asset including the usual cost of converting currencies, expected changes in the exchange rate must also be factored in the decision as to which international liquid assets to hold.

Obviously, the portfolio manager will choose to move money into those assets that are expected to yield the highest positive values as in inequality (1) and sell those assets that have negative perspective yields as in inequality (2).

In orthodox economic theory when interest rates are equalized, if similar financial assets denominated in different currencies are perfect substitutes, then the $(q - c)$ term for these securities is assumed to be equal given the state of expectations about future exchange rates *vis-à-vis* today's rate. Under these stylized circumstances, international speculative hot money flows will occur whenever there is, *ceteris paribus*, a sudden change in sentiment involving the expected value of the future spot exchange rate relative to the current rate, that is, the portfolio managers' evaluation of the $(p_s^{t_1} - p_s^{t_0})$ term changes.

If one or more portfolio managers who control significant portfolio sums suddenly change their expectations regarding future exchange rates, then there can be a massive movement in funds from one country to another. Once a significant international flow of funds occurs, this can encourage other fund managers to change their expectations of $(p_s^{t_1} - p_s^{t_0})$ until either:

1. The foreign reserves of the central bank of the nation suffering the outflow of hot money are nearly exhausted.[4] Then the nation cannot maintain an orderly exchange rate market. Consequently fund managers who are late-comers cannot readily convert their holdings into foreign assets.
2. Or the country being drained of reserves increases its interest rate (the $q - c$ term) sufficiently to offset the expected potential capital gain $(p_s^{t_1} - p_s^{t_0})$.
3. Or central banks deliberately intervene in the exchange market in an attempt to change private sector expectations regarding $(p_s^{t_1} - p_s^{t_0})$.
4. Or some form of taxation is added to increase the value of the T_s term to offset the expected increase in capital gains from an exchange rate change.
5. Or some form of outright prohibition of hot money portfolio-flows are successfully introduced.

The Tobin tax falls under the fourth item where governments use taxation in an attempt to stop speculative flows of hot money. The belief behind the Tobin tax is that adding a marginal tax will increase social costs until they coincide with social benefits, so that private decisions will become socially optimum. By using the above equational relationships, however, it can be shown that the usual suggested magnitude of a 'Tobin tax' or other similar 'opportunity cost' capital tax will only marginally increase the cost of speculating. Consequently a Tobin tax will stop speculation on relatively *small* movements in the exchange rate (independent of the time horizon of the fund manager) while it will have a significantly larger impact on stemming real international trade. In other words, the Tobin tax is not able solve the problem whenever speculative portfolio flows become significant large conflagrations, while simultaneously they induce large and permanent private costs (in excess of social costs) on real international trade flows.

The 'half percent tax' used by ETW (1995, p. 164) as an illustration is equal to 1 per cent of a round-trip transaction. Thus the relationship for determining one's bullishness (or bearishness) requires evaluating the following terms:

$$(q - c) + (p_s^{t_1} - p_s^{t_0}) - (x)(p_s^{t_1} + p_s^{t_0}) - T_s,$$

where (x) equals the magnitude of the Tobin tax rate. If

$$(q - c) + (p_s^{t_1} - p_s^{t_0}) - (x)(p_s^{t_1} + p_s^{t_0}) - T_s > 0, \quad (5)$$

the person is a bull, while if

$$(q - c) + (p_s^{t_1} - p_s^{t_0}) - (x)(p_s^{t_1} + p_s^{t_0}) - T_s < 0, \quad (6)$$

the portfolio manager is bearish. When

$$(q - c) + (p_s^{t_1} - p_s^{t_0}) - (x)(p_s^{t_1} + p_s^{t_0}) - T_s = 0, \quad (7)$$

the agent is neither bullish or bearish and will not engage in any speculative activities.

Equations (5) to (7) show that given the values of $(q - c)$ and T_s, the Tobin tax merely increases slightly the differential between expected future spot price and the current spot price before speculative bull or bear responses are induced.

If we assume the simplest case that $(q - c) = T$, then if

$$[p_s^{t_1} / p_s^{t_0}] > [(1 + x) / (1 - x)], \quad (8)$$

then the person is a bull, while no bullish speculative flows will be induced even if expected $p_s^{t_1}$ was greater than $p_s^{t_0}$ up to the point where

$$[p_s^{t_1} / p_s^{t_0}] = [(1 + x) / (1 - x)]. \quad (9)$$

Thus, for example, if the magnitude of the Tobin tax is 0.5 per cent, then the expected future spot price must be at least 1.01 per cent higher than the current spot exchange rate[5] to make the agent willing to speculate on any foreign currency.

Comparing inequality (8) and equation (9) with inequalities (3) and (4) provides us with a measure of the magnitude of the minimum expected changes in the exchange rate that must occur to induce bullishness or bearishness in the presence of a Tobin tax compared to the no tax case. For example, if the magnitude of the Tobin tax is 0.5 per cent, then, *ceteris paribus*, the expected future spot price must increase only by more than 1.01 per cent more than it would have had to increase in the absence of the tax to induce a bullish sentiment. In other words, even though the negative annual rate of return on a one-day round-trip is 365 per cent when there is a 0.5 per cent Tobin tax, any increase in the spot price of more than an additional 1.01 per cent compared to the no tax situation can still spawn significant speculative flows. As long as the spot price is expected to change, *ceteris paribus*, by more than 1.01 per cent during any period where there is a 0.5 per cent Tobin tax, speculative flows still have a significant positive payoff. Consequently any Tobin tax less than 100 per cent *of the expected capital gain* (on a round-trip) is unlikely to stop the sloshing around of hot money.

Whenever there is a speculative run on a currency, one expects dramatic changes in the currency. For example, the Mexican peso fell by approximately 60 per cent in the Winter of 1994–95. A Tobin tax of over 23 per cent would have been required to stop the speculative surge that created the peso crisis. At best, the Tobin tax might slow down the speculative fever when small exchange rate changes are expected.

The grains of sand of a Tobin tax might be the straw that breaks the speculative back of very small portfolio managers, since normal transactions costs (T_s) of foreign transactions are essentially regressive. An additional proportional (Tobin) tax on top of a large regressive transactions cost might keep very small speculators out of the market. For movements of larger sums, however, the normal transactions costs quickly shrink to a negligible proportion of the total transaction. In today's free-wheeling financial markets, individuals with even small portfolio sums can join mutual funds that can speculate on foreign currencies, therefore, a Tobin tax is unlikely to constrain even small investors – who can always join a large mutual fund to reduce the impact of total transactions costs sufficiently to reduce the remaining Tobin tax to relative insignificance whenever speculative fever runs high.

Finally, there is a rule of thumb that suggests that under the current flexible exchange rate system, there are five normal hedging trade transactions in every real final goods trade compared to two for every speculative flow in international finance. If this ratio is anywhere near correct, then a 0.5 per cent Tobin tax could imply levying up to a 2.5 per cent tax on normal real trade flow transactions compared to a 1 per cent round-trip speculative tax. It would appear then that a Tobin transaction tax might throw larger grains of sand into the wheels of international real commerce than it does into speculative hot money flows. A 0.5 per cent Tobin tax could be equivalent to instituting a 2.5 per cent universal tariff on all goods and services traded in the global economy.[6]

Independent of questions of the political and economic feasibility of instituting a ubiquitous Tobin tax, therefore, proposals to increase marginal transactions costs in foreign exchange by either a Tobin tax or a small feasible opportunity cost tax on capital is unlikely to prevent speculative feeding frenzies that lead to attacks on major currencies and their economic neighbours while it may inflict greater damage on international trading in goods and services.

It is such considerations that led Keynes to suggest an outright prohibition of all significant international portfolio flows through the creation of a supranational central bank and his 'bancor' plan. At this stage of economic development and global economic integration, however, a supranational central bank is not politically feasible. Accordingly, what should be aimed for is a more modest goal of obtaining an international agreement among the G7 nations. To be economically effective and politically feasible, this agreement, while incorporating the economic principles that Keynes laid down in his bancor plan, should not require any nation to surrender control of local banking systems and fiscal policies. Keynes introduced an ingenious method of direct prohibition of hot money flows by a 'bancor' system with fixed (but adjustable) exchange rates and a trigger mechanism to put more of the onus of resolving current account deficits on surplus nations. It is possible to update Keynes's prohibition proposal to meet twenty-first century circumstances. In the next section such a system will be proposed. Moreover, this system will be in the best interests of all nations for it will make it easier to achieve global full employment without the danger of importing inflationary pressures from one's trading partners.

There is not enough space in this paper to debate all possible alternative proposals for fire prevention of currency speculation. Instead I hope to raise the public consciousness for the potential tremendous real benefits that can accrue by establishing currency-speculation fire prevention institutions rather than merely relying on either fire fighting intervention such as the suggested Emergency Fund financed by contributions of the G7 nations and managed by the IMF, or a laissez-faire policy on international capital markets that can produce currency fires to burn the free world's real economies. We must recognize the very real possibility that there can be no safe harbour when a major currency is attacked.

THE GOLDEN AGE OF ECONOMIC DEVELOPMENT

The Bretton Woods years were an era of unsurpassed economic global prosperity. Economist Irma Adelman of the University of California has characterized the Bretton Woods period as a 'Golden Age of Economic Development . . . an era of unprecedented sustained economic growth in both developed and developing countries'. Table 3.1 provides the statistical evidence that Adelman used in reaching her conclusion about our economic golden age.

Although we do not possess reliable statistics on GDP per capita before 1700, it is probably true that from biblical times until the Renaissance the average standard of living in the world showed little improvement from year to year or even generation to generation. Improvement in global economic living standards began with the development of merchant capitalism during the Renaissance period in Europe. Between 1700 and 1820 (see Table 3.1) the per capita slice of the economic pie was increasing at an average annual rate of 0.2 per cent. Thus if the average person lived approximately 45 years, the person's standard of living increased less than 10 per cent from the time of birth to death.

Living standards started to increase substantially early in the nineteenth century. The Industrial Revolution period was truly revolutionary. During the years 1820–1913, annual living standards improved ten times faster than in the previous century, an annual growth rate of 1.2 per cent compounded year after year. The average increase in labour productivity was almost 7 times greater than during the previous 100 years. The per capita income of the advanced nations of the world more than trebled in less than 100 years. No wonder this period is often portrayed in Western literature as the era of growth of the common man.

During this 1820–1913 period the volume of world exports grew

Table 3.1 Real GDP (Annualized growth rate (%))

Years	*Real GDP per capita OECD nations*		
1700–1820	0.2		
1820–1913	1.2		
1919–1940	1.9		
1950–1973	4.9		
1973–1981	1.3		
	Major industrial nations	*New industrializing nations*	*Developing nations*
1973–1990	2.5	3.5	–0.1
	Total real GDP		
	OECD nations	*Developing nations*	
1950–1973	5.9	5.5	
	Real GDP per capita		
	OECD nations	*Developing nations*	
1950–1973	4.9	3.3	

thirty fold as a global economy and financial system were created with a fixed exchange rate under a gold-sterling standard. The growth rate during the Golden Age of Bretton Woods, however, was almost double the previous peak annual growth rate of the industrializing nations during the Industrial Revolution (from 1820 to 1913). Annual labour productivity growth between 1950 and 1973 was more than triple that of the Industrial Revolution. Moreover, between 1950 and 1973, real GDP per capita in the developed (or OECD) nations grew 2.6 times faster than between the wars.

The resulting prosperity of the industrialized world was transmitted to the less developed nations through world trade, aid, and direct foreign investment. From 1950–73, annual growth in per capita GDP for *all* developing nations was 3.3 per cent, almost triple the growth experienced by the industrializing nations during the Industrial Revolution. The total GDP pie of the less developed countries (LDCs) increased at almost the same rate as that of the developed nations, 5.5 per cent and 5.9 per cent respectively, but the higher population growth of the LDCs caused the lower per capita income growth.

By comparison, the economic record of the flexible rate systems between the world wars and since 1973 is dismal. The growth rate of the major developed nations since 1973 is approximately half of what it was during Bretton Woods, not much better than the experience of the nineteenth and early twentieth centuries. Moreover the OECD nations have suffered through persistently higher rates of unemployment and, especially during the 1970s, recurrent bouts of inflation. The contrast for the LDCs since 1973 is even more startling with annual real income per capita declining. The best performances since 1973 have been turned in by the newly developing nations along the Pacific rim, but even with their 'economic miracle' the per capita improvements are significantly lower than those experienced by the industrial nations between 1950 and 1973.

Finally it should be noted that during the Bretton Woods period there was a better overall record of price level stability than either during the post-1973 period, or between the wars, or even under the international gold standard.

THE LESSON THAT SHOULD HAVE BEEN LEARNED

What can we conclude from these facts? First, fixed exchange rate systems are associated with better global economic performance than flexible systems. Second, during the post-war period until 1973, global economic performance was nothing short of spectacular. It exceeded the remarkable performance of the Industrial Revolution and the gold standard fixed exchange rate system. This unparalleled 'golden age' experience required combining a fixed exchange rate system with another civilizing principle; namely that the creditor nations must accept a major share of the responsibility for solving persistent international payments imbalances that may develop. Third, the Bretton Woods period was a remarkably crisis-free economic era.

Since the breakdown of Bretton Woods, on the other hand, the global economy has stumbled from one global economic crisis to another. Economic growth around the world has slowed significantly while the growing global population threatens to reduce standards of living. The number of mouths to be fed are threatening to increase at a faster rate than global GDP. Economics has once more become the dismal science with its Malthusian overtones.

Instead of bringing the utopian benefits promised by conservative economics, the post Bretton Woods system has generated a growing international monetary crisis. As early as 1986 *New York Times* columnist Flora Lewis noted that government and business leaders recognize that 'the issues of trade, debt, and currency exchange rates are intertwined'. Lewis warned that the world is on a course leading to an economic calamity, yet 'nobody wants to speak out and be accused of setting off a panic . . . the most sober judgement is that the best thing that can be done now is to buy more time for adjustments to head off a crash . . . decision makers aren't going to take sensible measures until they are forced to by crisis'.

The current international payments system does not serve the emerging global economy well. The *Financial Times* of London and the *Economist*, both previously strong advocates of today's floating rate system, have acknowledged that this system is a failure and was sold to the public and the politicians under false advertising claims.[7] Yet no leader is calling for a complete overhaul of a system that is far worse than the one we abandoned in 1973. No one has the courage to speak out in public forums and suggest that the conservative philosophy that has governed our economic affairs in recent decades is a formula for economic disaster.

THE RESPONSIBILITY FOR RESOLVING INTERNATIONAL TRADE IMBALANCES IN A CIVIL GLOBAL COMMUNITY: THE MARSHALL PLAN EXAMPLE

During World War II, Europe's productive capacity was ravaged. Immediately after the war, Europeans required huge quantities of imports to feed themselves and to rebuild their factories and cities. During 1946 and 1947 European nations used up almost all of their pre-war savings (their foreign reserves) to pay for imports from the United States, the only nation that had available productive capacity.

Under any conventional conservative international monetary system, once their reserves were exhausted the Europeans would have to either accept the burden of adjustment by 'tightening their belts', that is by reducing demand for imports to the negligible amount they could earn from exports, or to borrow dollars to pay for imports. The Catch 22 of these alternatives was:

1. Europeans could not produce enough to feed their population. To tell a starving person to tighten one's belt is not only an uncivilized suggestion but it imposes an impossible condition. Had the necessary 'belt tightening' been undertaken, the result

would have been to depress further the war-torn standard of living of Western Europeans. This would have induced political revolutions in Europe, not to mention recession in the USA's export industries.

2. During the Great Depression, European export earnings were so low that they defaulted on most of their international debts. Given this experience and the fact that their post-war industries were in shambles and could not produce enough in exports to service their debt, American banks would not make the massive loans needed by Europeans. It was also obvious that any direct US government loans could not be repaid.

As a civilized strategy to avoid the political and economic chaos that would probably have occurred in Europe, the United States offered to pay for the European potential trade deficits (of imports over exports) necessary to rebuild Europe through the Marshall Plan and other aid programmes. In essence, the Marshall Plan permitted foreigners to buy United States exports without either drawing down their last pennies of foreign reserve savings or by going into debt that could not be repaid in the foreseeable future. Through the Marshall plan and other aid programmes, the United States was demonstrating a civilized attitude to the entire global community.[8]

If the United States had left deficit nations to adjust to the vast looming trade imbalance by reducing imports, then (a) the standard of living of European and Asian residents would have been substantially lower; and (b) the United States would have slipped into a great recession as there would have been too little international demand for the products of her surplus industrial capacity.

The Marshall Plan and large scale foreign military and economic aid programmes *gave* foreigners large sums of American dollars, *as a gift*, so that they could buy American products. The result was that:

1. huge benefits accrued to both foreigners and US citizens. Foreigners used these gifts to buy the American goods necessary to rebuild their economies and to feed their people. Americans obtained additional jobs and earned more income by selling exports to these foreigners; and,
2. by its generosity the United States invigorated, enriched and strengthened the international community to the immense economic gain of all nations outside the Iron Curtain.

The Marshall Plan gave away a total of $13 billion in four years. (In 1994 dollars this is equivalent to $139 billion.) This 'give away' represented 2 per cent per annum of the United States GDP. Nevertheless, American consumers experienced no real pain. During the first year of the Marshall Plan, US real GDP per capita was 25 per cent greater than in 1940 (the last peacetime year). Employment and per capita GDP grew continuously between 1947 and 1957 as these foreign aid funds financed additional demand for US exports. These were exports produced by employing what otherwise would have been idle American workers and factories created jobs and incomes for millions of Americans. For the first time in its history, the United States did not suffer from a severe recession immediately after the cessation of a major war.

The entire free world experienced an economic 'free lunch' as both the debtor and the creditor nations gained from this United States 'give away'. The Bretton Woods system in tandem with the Marshall Plan, where the United States took deliberate steps to prevent others from depleting their foreign reserves and become overindebted internationally, resulted in a global golden age of economic development.

By 1958, however, the US international position of being able to export more than it imported was coming to an end. Foreign aid grants exceeded the United States' trade surplus of demand for US exports over US imports. Unfortunately, the Bretton Woods system had no mechanism for automatically encouraging emerging trade surplus (creditor) nations to step into the civilizing adjustment role the US had been playing since 1947. Instead these creditor nations converted a portion of their annual dollar export earnings into calls on the gold reserves of the United States. In 1958 alone, the US lost over $2 billion of its gold reserves. In the 1960s, increased US military and financial aid responses to the Berlin Wall and Vietnam accelerated this trend.

The seeds of destruction of the Bretton Woods system were sown and the golden age of global economic development ended as the trade surplus nations continually drained gold reserves from the United States. When the US closed the gold window in 1971 in order to avoid a continuing reduction in its foreign reserves and then in 1973 unilaterally withdrew from Bretton Woods, the last vestige of a potentially enlightened international monetary approach was lost – apparently without regret or regard as to how well it had served the global economy.

COMPARING THE MARSHALL PLAN AND THE TREATY OF VERSAILLES

This civilized historical episode enhancing a post-War international civil community can be compared to the barbaric policy and the resulting fragmented international system that followed World War I. Under the 1919 Treaty of Versailles, the victorious Allies imposed a harsh settlement on the defeated nations. Massive reparations were imposed on Germany as the European Allies attempted to obtain compensation for the costs of the war that they had incurred.

In his book *Economic Consequences of the Peace*, John Maynard Keynes spoke out against the uncivilized policy of imposing reparations on these war-torn nations. Perhaps the victorious European nations whose citizens had suffered through years of war cannot be blamed for mistrusting Keynes's civilized economic arguments or the political ideals of President Woodrow Wilson. The evils of waging war may have eroded the civilized values of the European Allies to the point where they felt compelled to demand a barbaric financial retribution.

The result of this Allied barbarism may have been initially satisfying to the warlike passion for revenge by humiliating a former enemy. But barbaric treatment can breed more barbarism, as the evils imposed by the oppressor shape the values of the oppressed. Although the primary responsibility for Nazi Germany does not lie with the British and French economic policies after the War, to the extent that they helped shape German society's values of the 1920s and 1930s, the harsh Allied terms for peace did have a significant role in the outcome that occurred in the 1930s and 1940s in Europe.

The United States was the only victorious nation that pursued a civilized policy of not claiming reparations. The United States developed a loan plan (the Dawes Plan) for aiding the Germans to meet the Allied claims. Unlike the other victorious Allies, the United States enjoyed an economic boom in the 1920s as the Allies bought American goods with these Dawes Plan dollars. The European victors, even with the boost of war reparations, experienced much tougher economic times.

USING KEYNES'S VISION TO DEVELOP AN ALTERNATIVE INTERNATIONAL PAYMENTS SYSTEM

Fifty years ago, Keynes (1980, p. 168) provided a clear outline of what is needed when he wrote:

> We need an instrument of international currency having general acceptability between nations . . . We need an orderly and agreed upon method of determining the relative exchange values of national currency units. . . . We need a quantum of international currency. . . . [which] is governed by the actual current [liquidity] requirements of world commerce, and is capable of deliberate expansion . . . We need a method by which the surplus credit balances arising from international trade, which the recipient does not wish to employ can be set to work . . . without detriment to the liquidity of these balances.

What is required is a *closed*, double-entry bookkeeping clearing institution to keep the payments 'score' among the various trading regions plus some mutually agreed upon rules to create and reflux liquidity while maintaining the international purchasing power of the international currency. The eight provisions of the clearing system suggested in this section meet the criteria laid down by Keynes. The rules of this Post Keynesian proposed system are designed

1. to prevent a lack of global effective demand[9] due to any nation(s) either holding excessive idle reserves or draining reserves from the system;
2. to provide an automatic mechanism for placing a major burden of payments adjustments on the surplus nations;
3. to provide each nation with the ability to monitor and, if desired, to put boulders into the movement of international portfolio funds in order to control movements of flight capital;[10] and finally
4. to expand the quantity of the liquid asset of ultimate international redemption as global capacity warrants.

Some elements of such a clearing system would include:

1. The unit of account and ultimate reserve asset for international liquidity is the International Money Clearing Unit (IMCU). All IMCU's are held *only* by central banks, not by the public.

2. Each nation's or UMS's central bank is committed to guarantee one way convertibility from IMCU deposits at the clearing union to its domestic money. Each central bank will set its own rules regarding making available foreign monies (through IMCU clearing transactions) to its own bankers and private sector residents.[11]

Since central banks agree to sell their own liabilities (one-way convertibility) against the IMCU only to other central bankers and the International Clearing Agency while they simultaneously hold only IMCUs as liquid reserve assets for international financial transactions, there can be no draining of reserves from the system. Ultimately, all major private international transactions clear between central banks' accounts in the books of the international clearing institution.

3. The exchange rate between the domestic currency and the IMCU is set *initially* by each nation – just as it would be if one instituted an international gold standard. Since enterprises that are already engaged in trade have international contractual commitments that would span the change-over interval, then, as a practical matter, one would expect that the existing exchange rate structure (with perhaps minor modifications) would provide the basis for initial rate setting.

Provisions 7 and 8 *infra* indicate when and how this nominal exchange rate between the national currency and the IMCU would be changed in the future.

4. Contracts between private individuals will continue to be denominated into whatever domestic currency permitted by local laws and agreed upon by the contracting parties. Contracts to be settled in terms of a foreign currency will, therefore, require some announced commitment from the central bank (through private sector bankers) of the availability of foreign funds to meet such private contractual obligations.

5. An overdraft system to make available short-term unused creditor balances at the Clearing House to finance the productive international transactions of others who need short-term credit. The terms will be determined by the *pro bono* clearing managers.

6. A trigger mechanism to encourage a creditor nation to spend what is deemed (in advance) by agreement of the international community to be *'excessive' credit balances accumulated by running current account surpluses*. These excessive credits can be spent in

three ways: on the products of any other member of the clearing union; on new direct foreign investment projects; and/or to provide unilateral transfers (foreign aid) to deficit members. Spending on imports forces the surplus nation to make the adjustment directly through the balance on goods and services. Spending by way of unilateral transfers permits adjustment directly by the current account balance; while direct foreign investment provides adjustment by the capital accounts (without setting up a contractual debt that will *require* reverse current account flows in the future).

Provision 6 provides the surplus country with considerable discretion in deciding how to accept the 'onus' of adjustment in the way it believes is in its residents' best interests. It does not permit the surplus nation to shift the burden to the deficit nation(s) through contractual requirements for debt service charges independent of what the deficit nation can afford.[12] The important thing is to make sure that continual oversaving[13] by surplus nations cannot unleash depressionary forces and/or a building up of international debts so encumbering as to impoverish the global economy of the twenty-first century.

In the unlikely event that the surplus nation does not spend or give away these credits within a specified time, then the clearing agency would confiscate (and redistribute to debtor members) the portion of credits deemed excessive.[14] This last resort confiscatory action by the managers of the clearing agency would make a payments adjustment through unilateral transfer payments in the current accounts.

Under either a fixed or a flexible rate system, nations may experience persistent trade deficits merely because trading partners are not living up to their means – that is because other nations are continually hoarding a portion of their foreign export earnings (plus net unilateral transfers). By so doing, these oversavers are creating a lack of global effective demand. Under provision 6, deficit countries would no longer have to deflate their real economy merely to adjust payment imbalances because others are oversaving. Instead, the system would seek to remedy the payment deficit by increasing opportunities for deficit nations to sell abroad and thereby earn their way out of the deficit.

7. A system to stabilize the long-term purchasing power of the IMCU (in terms of each member nation's domestically produced market basket of goods) can be developed. This requires a system of fixed

exchange rates between the local currency and the IMCU that changes only to reflect permanent increases in efficiency wages.[15] This assures each central bank that its holdings of IMCUs as the nation's foreign reserves will never lose purchasing power in terms of foreign produced goods, even if a foreign government permits wage-price inflation to occur within its borders. The rate between the local currency and the IMCU would change with inflation in the local money price of the domestic commodity basket.

If increases in productivity lead to declining nominal production costs, then the nation with this decline in efficiency wages (say of 5 per cent) would have the option of choosing either (a) to permit the IMCU to buy (up to 5 per cent) less units of domestic currency, thereby capturing all (or most of) the gains from productivity for its residents while maintaining the purchasing power of the IMCU, or (b) to keep the nominal exchange rate constant. In the latter case, the gain in productivity is shared with all trading partners. In exchange, the export industries in this productive nation will receive an increased relative share of the world market.

By altering the exchange rate between local monies and the IMCU to offset the rate of domestic inflation, the IMCU's purchasing power is stabilized. By restricting use of IMCUs to central banks, private speculation regarding IMCUs as a hedge against inflation is avoided. Each nation's rate of inflation of the goods and services it produces is determined solely by the local government's policy towards the level of domestic money wages and profit margins *vis-à-vis* productivity gains, that is, the nation's efficiency wage. Each nation is, therefore, free to experiment with policies for stabilizing its efficiency wage to prevent inflation. Whether the nation is successful or not, the IMCU will never lose its international purchasing power. Moreover, the IMCU has the promise of gaining in purchasing power over time if productivity grows more rapidly than money wages and each nation is willing to share any reduction in real production costs with its trading partners.

Provision 7 produces a system designed to maintain the relative efficiency wage parities among nations. In such a system, the adjustability of nominal exchange rates will be primarily (but not always, see Provision 8) to offset changes in efficiency wages among trading partners. A beneficial effect that follows from this proviso is that it eliminates the possibility of a specific industry in any nation put at a competitive disadvantage secure a competitive advantage against foreign producers solely because the nominal exchange rate was changed independently of changes in efficiency wages and the real costs of production in each nation.

Nominal exchange rate variability will no longer create the problem of a loss of competitiveness due solely to the overvaluing of a currency as, for example, experienced by the industries in the American 'rust belt' during the period 1982–85. Even if temporary, currency appreciation can have significant permanent real costs, for example, industries may abandon markets and the resulting idle existing plant and equipment may be cast aside as too costly to maintain.

Provision 7 also prevents any nation from engaging in a beggar-thy-neighbor, export-thy-unemployment policy by pursuing a real exchange rate devaluation that does not reflect changes in efficiency wages. Once the initial exchange rates are chosen and relative efficiency wages are locked in, reductions in real production costs that are associated with a relative decline in efficiency wages is the main factor (with the exception of provision 8) justifying an adjustment in the real exchange rate.

Although provision 6 prevents any country from piling up persistent excessive surpluses this does not mean that it is impossible for one or more nations to run persistent deficits. Proposal 8 infra provides a programme for addressing the problem of persistent export-import deficits in any one nation.

8. If a country is at *full employment* and still has a tendency towards persistent international deficits on its current account, then this is *prima facie* evidence that it does not possess the productive capacity to maintain its current standard of living. If the deficit nation is a poor one, then surely there is a case for the richer nations who are in surplus to transfer some of their excess credit balances to support the poor nation.[16] If it is a relatively rich country, then the deficit nation must alter its standard of living by reducing the relative terms of trade with major trading partners. Rules, agreed upon in advance, would require the trade deficit rich nation to devalue its exchange rate by stipulated increments per period until evidence becomes available to indicate that the export-import imbalance is eliminated without unleashing significant recessionary forces.[17]

If on the other hand, the payment deficit persists despite a continuous positive balance of trade in goods and services, then there is evidence that the deficit nation might be carrying too heavy an international debt service obligation. The *pro bono officials* of the clearing union should bring the debtor and creditors into negotiations to reduce annual debt service payments by: (1) lengthening the payments period; (2) reducing the interest charges; and/or (3) debt forgiveness.[18]

If any government objects to the idea that the IMCU provisions provide governments with the ability to limit the free movement of 'capital' funds, then this nation is free to join other nations of similar attitude in forming a regional currency union [UMS] and thereby assuring a free flow of funds among the residents of the currency union.

CONCLUSION

In normal times with free capital markets 'speculators may do no harm as bubbles on a steady stream of enterprise. But the position is serious when enterprise becomes the bubbles on a whirlpool of speculation' (Keynes, 1936, p. 159). The grains of sand of a Tobin tax may prick the small bubbles of speculation, but the sand is likely to significantly restrict the flow of real trade. On the other hand, the sands of the Tobin tax will be merely swept away in whirlpools of speculation. Boulders are needed to stop the destructive currency speculation from destroying global enterprise patterns, for 'it is enterprise which builds and improves the world's possessions' (Keynes, 1930, p. 148).

NOTES

1. In an open economy context, according to Keynes, the Law of Comparative Advantage could be just as misleading as a policy guide as Say's Law was to a closed economy.
2. Some mainstream economists will consider '*ad hoc*' central bank interventions as an acceptable short-run palliative if disruptive exogenous shocks create short-run disorderly markets.
3. Transactions costs (of holding alternative liquid assets) in the broadest sense – that is including the *fear* of rapid *unpredictable* changes in spot prices, or operating in a thin spot market where no financial institution will act as a residual buyer and seller – are basic to determining the magnitude of transactions, precautionary and speculative demands for money in the current income period. If all assets were instantaneously resalable without any costs, there would never be a

need to hold 'barren money' rather than a productive asset, except for the necessary nanosecond before it was necessary to meet a contractual commitment that came due. In the real world, the magnitude of actual costs of moving between liquid assets and the medium of contractual settlement is related to the degree of spot market organization and the existence of financial institutions that 'make' spot markets and that thereby assure reasonable moment-to-moment stickiness in spot prices.

4. In flexible exchange rate markets, the central bank typically provides foreign exchange support for private (commercial) banks who make the market in foreign exchange.
5. Or 1.01 per cent higher than the agent's expectation of the future spot exchange rate in the absence of the tax, if the agent requires a risk premium.
6. Even if the 5 to 1 ratio overestimates the number of real trade transactions compared to speculative flows, as long as there is some multiple, the Tobin tax is likely to impact trade flows more than speculative flows.
7. The *Economist* magazine (6 January 1990) indicated that the decade of the 1980s will be noted as one in which 'the experiment with floating currencies failed'. Almost three years earlier (17 February 1987), the *Financial Times* admitted that 'floating exchange rates, it is now clear, were sold on a false prospectus . . . they held out a quite illusory promise of greater national autonomy. . . . [but] when macropolicies are inconsistent and when capital is globally mobile, floating rates cannot be relied upon to keep the current accounts roughly in balance'.
8. The Marshall Plan was even offered to the Soviet Union who refused it.
9. Williamson (1987, p. 200) recognizes that when balance of payments 'disequilibrium is due purely to excess or deficient demand', flexible exchange rates *per se* cannot facilitate international payments adjustments.
10. This provides *as* an added bonus by making tax-avoidance and profits from illegal trade more difficult to conceal.
11. Correspondent banking will have to operate through the International Clearing Agency, with each central bank regulating the international relations and operations of its domestic banking firms. Small scale smuggling of currency across borders, and so on, can never be completely eliminated. But such movements are merely a flea on a dog's back – a minor, but not debilitating, irritation. If, however, most of the residents of a nation hold and use (in violation of legal tender laws) a foreign currency for domestic transactions and as a store of value (for example, it is estimated that Argentineans hold close to $5 billion US dollars), this is evidence of a lack of confidence in the government and its monetary authority. Unless confidence is restored, all attempts to restore economic prosperity will fail.
12. Some may fear that if a surplus nation is close to the trigger point it could short circuit the system by making loans to reduce its credit balance *prior* to setting off the trigger. Since preventing unreasonable debt service obligations is an important objective of this proposal, a

mechanism which monitors and can restrict such pretrigger lending activities may be required.

One possible way of eliminating this trigger avoidance lending loophole is as follows: An initial agreement as to what constitutes sensible and flexible criteria for judging when debt servicing burdens become unreasonable is established. Given these criteria, the clearing union managers would have the responsibility for preventing additional loans which push debt burdens beyond reasonable servicing levels. In other words, loans that push debt burdens too far, could not be cleared through the clearing union, that is, the managers would refuse to release the IMCU's for loan purposes from the surplus country's account. (I am indebted to Robert Blecker for suggesting this point.)

The managers would also be required to make periodic public reports on the level of credits being accumulated by surplus nations and to indicate how close these surpluses are to the trigger point. Such reports would provide an informational edge for debtor nations permitting them to bargain more successively regarding the terms of refinancing existing loans and/or new loans. All loans would still have to meet the clearing union's guidelines for reasonableness.

I do not discount the difficulties involved in setting up and getting agreement on criteria for establishing unreasonable debt service burdens. (For some suggestions, however, see the second paragraph of provision 8.) In the absence of cooperation and a spirit of goodwill that is necessary for the clearing union to provide a mechanism assuring the economic prosperity of all members, however, no progress can ever be made.

Moreover, as the current international debt problem of African and Latin American nations clearly demonstrates, creditors ultimately have to forgive some debt when they previously encourage excessive debt burdens. Under the current system, however, debt forgiveness is a last resort solution acceptable only after both debtor and creditor nations suffer from faltering economic growth. Surely a more intelligent option is to develop an institutional arrangement which prevents excessive debt servicing burdens from ever occurring.

13. Oversaving is defined as a nation persistently spending less on imports plus direct equity foreign investment than the nation's export earnings plus net unilateral transfers.
14. Whatever 'excessive' credit balances that are redistributed shall be apportioned among the debtor nations (perhaps based on a formula which is inversely related to each debtor's per capita income and directly related to the size of its international debt) to be used to reduce debit balances at the clearing union.
15. The efficiency wage is related to the money wage divided by the average product of labour, it is the unit labour cost modified by the profit mark-up in domestic money terms of domestically produced GNP. At this preliminary stage of this proposal, it would serve no useful purpose to decide whether the domestic market basket should include both tradable and non-tradeable goods and services. (With the growth of tourism more and more nontradeable goods become potentially

tradable.) I personally prefer the wider concept of the domestic market basket, but it is not obvious that any essential principle is lost if a tradable only concept is used, or if some nations use the wider concept while others the narrower one.

16. This is equivalent to a negative income tax for poor fully employed families within a nation.
17. Although relative prices of imports and exports would be altered by the change in the terms of trade, the adjustment is due to the resulting income effect, not a substitution effect. The deficit nation's real income will fall until its import surplus disappears.
18. The actual programme adopted for debt service reduction will depend on many parameters including: the relative income and wealth of the debtor *vis-à-vis* the creditor, the ability of the debtor to increase its per capita real income, etc.

REFERENCES

Davidson, P. (1972) *Money and the Real World*, London, Macmillan.

Eichengreen, B., Tobin, J. and Wyplosz, C. (1995) Two Cases for Sand in the Wheels of International Finance, *Economic Journal* **105**, 162–72.

Garber, P. and Taylor, M.P. (1995) Sand in the Wheels of Foreign Exchange Markets: A Skeptical Note, *Economic Journal* **105**, 173–80.

Greenway, D. (1995) Policy Form: Sand in the Wheels of International Finance, Editorial Note, *Economic Journal* **105**, 160–1.

Hicks, J.R. (1967) A Suggestion for Simplifying the Theory of Money, in *Critical Essays in Monetary Theory*, Oxford , Clarendon Press.

Hicks, J.R. (1979) *Causality in Economics*, New York, Basic Books.

Kenen, P. (1995) Capital Controls, the EMS and the EMU, *Economic Journal* **105**, 181–92.

Keynes, J.M. (1930) *A Treatise on Money*, London, Macmillan.

Keynes, J.M. (1936) *The General Theory of Employment, Interest and Money*, London, Macmillan.

Keynes, J.M. (1980) *The Collected Writings of John Maynard Keynes*, D. Moggridge (ed.), London, Macmillan.

Vicarelli, F. (1984) *Keynes: The Instability of Capitalism*, Philadelphia, University of Pennsylvania Press.

Williamson, J. (1987) Exchange Rate Management: The Role of Target Zones, *American Economic Review Papers and Proceedings* **77**, 200–4.

Comment

Giancarlo Gandolfo

The starting point of this paper is the confutation of the statement according to which in completely free and efficient exchange markets all speculative activities are necessarily stabilizing. I agree with this starting point, since I have myself never believed in the theoretical validity of the statement being criticized, a statement that dates back at least to Milton Friedman's 1953 essay on the case for flexible exchange rates, where he tried to prove that profitable speculation is necessarily stabilizing.

All subsequent literature has never been able to give a satisfactory *general* proof of this statement, and I am stressing general because it is of course possible to show that it holds under some set of *ad hoc* assumptions, but not in general, as many counter-examples have shown (see, for example, Gandolfo, 1995, Ch. 17).

Professor Davidson gives us an additional element to confute the statement, which is that the mainstream opinion 'conflates the concept of speculation with the concept of arbitrage. Since the latter is always a stabilizing force, orthodoxy insists that the former is also always a stabilizing force'. I am again in agreement with this confutation.

However, I would not consider this as the main contribution of the paper. The reason is that, being myself an international economist, in the current literature I cannot find much advocacy for the statement under criticism. It may still be advocated by Milton Friedman and acolytes, but most international economists do not accept it, for even the most orthodox ones recognize that empirical evidence is definitely against the assumption of efficiency of foreign exchange markets (see, for example, Taylor, 1995), which means that a necessary condition (under the orthodox view) for the validity of the statement is rejected by reality.

Let me now come to what I consider the main contribution of the paper, namely a precise and well-designed proposal for the reform of the international monetary system.

Professor Davidson starts from the observation that the main cause of the current problems of the international monetary system is indeed the presence of destabilizing foreign exchange speculation, which in turn is free to operate thanks to the complete liberalization of financial capital flows. This is certainly true, and before coming to the presentation of his plan, Professor Davidson offers us a number of interesting considerations. Since I am here in the position of discussant, I will not list those with which I agree, but a couple with which I disagree.

The first is the statement that 'fixed exchange rate systems are associated with better global economic performance than flexible systems'. This may be true, but the facts given by Professor Davidson are not a proof, as they suffer from the 'post hoc ergo propter hoc' fallacy.

We cannot simply compare different periods, say period A under fixed and period B under flexible exchange rates, and say that fixed exchange rates are better than flexible rates because economic performance was better in period A than in period B. The same criticism holds if we let A and B stand for different countries (or groups of countries).

The correct methodological approach is to ask what would have been the performance in period (or country) B if exchange rates had been fixed rather than flexible, and what would have been the performance in period (or country) A if exchange rates had been flexible rather than fixed. Only if both comparisons turn out to be favourable to fixed rates can we reach the conclusion stated by Professor Davidson.

I know that this is a very difficult task, since economists cannot run experiments under controlled conditions as physicists and chemists can, but, after all, economic models, econometrics, and simulation experiments have been invented exactly to help us in making such hypothetical comparisons. And I do not know of any such experiment *conclusively* showing the claimed superiority of fixed over flexible exchange rates *in general*. The evidence is mixed, as there are both studies showing that for some countries and periods exchange rate volatility has exerted a negative effect upon export demand (for example Arize, 1995; Chowdhury, 1993) and studies showing the absence of such an effect (for example Menon, 1994; Flood and Rose, 1995).

The second concerns the parallel drawn between the Marshall Plan and point 3 of provision 6 of Professor Davidson's plan. According to this point, one of the ways for a surplus country to spend its accumulated credit balances is by providing unilateral transfers (foreign aid) to deficit countries. We should remember that, under the Marshall plan, the gift by the US to Europe was automatically beneficial to the US because this was the only country where at that time the recipients of the gift could buy the commodities they needed. Under the Davidson plan, the gift by a surplus country to a deficit country would *not* be automatically beneficial to the donor, because the recipient country can buy commodities anywhere.

All in all, I find Professor Davidson's plan for the reform of the international monetary system a welcome signal that the widespread concern about the current non-system is stimulating the members of the profession to offer policy makers food for thought in the form of precise plans.

However, I feel that it is very unlikely that a precise and detailed plan (Professor Davidson's or any other) can be adopted. After all, the plan that gave birth to the Bretton Woods era was adopted because at that time the situation was *extraordinary*: there had been a world war, the United States were the winners and had an overwhelming economic force.

Now, the theory of the obstacles to international policy coordination, on which I have no time to dwell here (see Gandolfo, 1995, Ch. 20), shows that under *ordinary* circumstances it is very difficult if not impossible to enter a cooperative agreement, a difficulty which is an increasing function of the detail (that is, of the loss of degrees of freedom of national autonomy) of the agreement itself. Needless to say that any reasonable person would prefer *ordinary* to *extraordinary* (in the sense used here) circumstances, hence we should be prepared to put up with a certain amount of uncoordination.

If we adopt this point of view, and I do adopt it, it is clear that the Tobin tax, though far from being the best possible solution (as Professor Davidson's rightly shows in his criticism of it), requires a much lower degree of coordination. Hence it lies in the realm of the possible rather than in the realm of wishful thinking. In my opinion, it belongs to the set of constrained optima, namely to the set of the best solutions under the constraint of the minimum amount of international coordination.

Further to this, there is a final point that I would like to make. This does not come from me as economist, but from me as science-fiction reader. I have been reading science-fiction almost since I learnt to read, which means for the last fifty years. In these fifty years I have seen many of the apparently wildest innovations presented in science-fiction novels become reality. Hence I have no hesitation in believing that in the not-too-distant future what I call *extraterrestrial* banking may become a reality. By extraterrestrial banking I simply mean the building and launching of a satellite sufficiently far in the space to be outside the jurisdiction of all governments of the planet Earth; this satellite can become the basis of what I dub *off-Earth* banking.

The Davidson proposal may be able to cope with off-shore banking, but not with off-Earth banking. Further, nothing could prevent the issuance of satellite money, let me call it the *SMU* (*Sidereal Money Unit*). And since we economists all know that money is not what authorities declare legal tender, but what is generally accepted by the public as money, I see no theoretical impediment to the *SMU* being generally used rather than Davidson's IMCU not only at the level of earthly central banks but also at the level of the general terrestrial public.

Let me also add that, if one takes too dirigistic an approach to the reform of the international monetary system (such as the one envisaged by Professor Davidson's plan may look to the owners of hot money), then – as the history of mankind shows – one simply stimulates the search for profitable alternatives. The satellite alternative is certainly technically feasible. It is probably not yet economically profitable, but it may become so after the implementation of Professor Davidson's plan.

To conclude: in principle I agree with the author that we would need to throw boulders rather than grains of sands or pebbles in the flow of international speculation. But if the throwing of boulders may cause a flood (as in my satellite science-fiction tale), then I remain satisfied with the pebbles, which means some form of the Tobin tax.

REFERENCES

Arize, A.C. (1995) Trade Flows and Real Exchange-Rate Volatility: An Application of Cointegration and Error-Correction Modelling, *North-American Journal of Economics and Finance* **6**, 37–51.

Chowdhury, A.R. (1993) Does Exchange Rate Volatility Depress Trade Flows? Evidence from Error-Correction Models, *Review of Economics and Statistics* **75**, 700–6.

Flood, R.P. and Rose A.K. (1995) Fixing Exchange Rates: A Virtual Quest for Fundamentals, *Journal of Monetary Economics* **36**, 9–37.
Friedman, M. (1953) The Case for Flexible Exchange Rates, in M. Friedman, *Essays in Positive Economics*, Chicago, University of Chicago Press.
Gandolfo, G. (1995) *International Economics II – International Monetary Economics and Open-Economy Macroeconomics*, Berlin, Springer-Verlag.
Menon, J. (1994) The Theory of Exchange Rates and Traded Goods Prices in the Short Run, *Economia Internazionale* **47**, 55–68.
Taylor, M.P. (1995) The Economics of Exchange Rates, *Journal of Economic Literature* **33**, 13–47.

4 Unemployment and Social Needs

Giorgio Lunghini

> The annual labour of every nation is the fund which originally supplies it with all the necessaries and conveniences of life which it annually consumes, and which consist always, either in the immediate produce of that labour, or in what is purchased with that produce from other nations.
>
> *Adam Smith*

THE ECONOMIC POSSIBILITIES FOR OUR GRANDCHILDREN

At the Madrid conference of 1930 (Keynes, 1930), J.M. Keynes maintained that both of the two opposed errors of pessimism would be proved wrong in our own time: the pessimism of the revolutionaries who think that things are so bad that nothing can save us but violent change, and the pessimism of the reactionaires who consider the balance of our economic and social life so precarious that we must risk no experiments. Keynes maintained that the disease of technological unemployment (unemployment due to the discovery of means of economizing on the use of labour outrunning the pace at which we can find *new* uses for labour) would be only a temporary phase of maladjustment, and that mankind would have solved its economic problem in a hundred years' time. In the light of that prediction, man ought to find himself faced with his real, his permanent problem, in just over thirty years from now: how to use his freedom from pressing economic cares, how to occupy his leisure time, which science and compound interest will have won for him, to live wisely and agreeably and well.

Lord Keynes was not a madman who heard voices. The heaven on earth that he envisaged can be realized, but not so soon and not so easily. In the two-thirds of a century which have passed since then, mankind has not progressed in the direction of freedom from want or freedom from the need to sell oneself for a livelihood. We have left the age of anxiety from which Keynes sought release, for an age of waste, not of freedom and moderation. Despite the subsequent developments in science and technology and the accumulation of capital, perhaps indeed because of them, the enormous anomaly of unemployment in a world full of needs is even more serious now than it was then. The appalling proliferation of commodities and the growth of unemployment are accompanied by old and new kinds of poverty, wars between the poor and a general barbarization of the material relationships of existence. Economic theory and the art of government are unable to explain, and uninterested in solving, our most pressing economic and political problem: too many commodities, too few jobs.

In the following paper, I shall maintain that the orthodox pharmacopoeia has no medication to cure or even alleviate this new variety of capital's chronic malaise, the contradiction between waste and penury. The establishment of greater harmony between the labour process and the needs of society must be sought elsewhere, outside purely mercantile logic.

THE PRODUCTION OF COMMODITIES AND UNEMPLOYMENT

Neo-Ricardian critique has definitively clarified the theoretical limits of the production function, in particular of the concept of 'capital' which it assumes. Despite this, we frequently continue reasoning as if the relationship between production and living human labour were governed by a simplified production function, in which the amount produced depended solely on the amount of labour involved. Hence, without questioning the soundness of this mechanism, it follows that the number of workers employed depends on the quantity of produce since, if the production function is monotonic, so too is its inverse function. The implications of this paralogism for economic policy is that all that is needed to increase employment is the neoclassical synthesis prescription of reducing real wages and relaunching the production of commodities.

In recent years a structural change has come about in the capitalist world of production and reproduction of commodities and society. Nowadays a trend is evident which can be roughly described as in Figure 4.1.

Figure 4.1 Production of commodities and workers employed in recent years

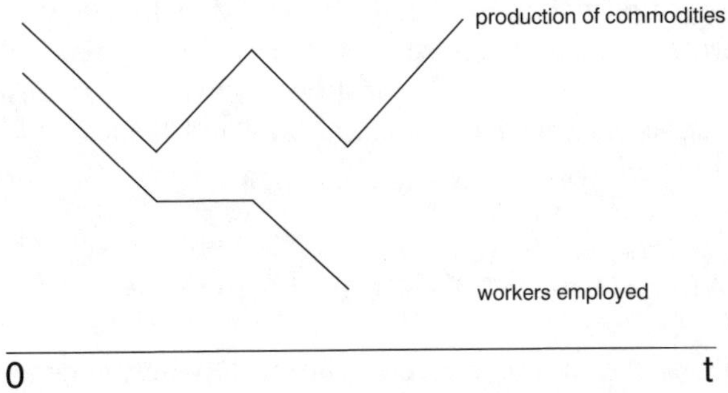

The stable and biunivocal coupling of the production of commodities and the employment of living human labour has changed. It is still true that if production declines, employment falls, but the opposite, if production recovers then employment also recovers, is no longer true. Unemployment becomes crystallized through technological and organizational restructuring and tends to become irreversible (*tends*: unless new stability factors or counter-causes intervene). As long as there is durable growth in the economy, the consequences of technological and organizational restructuring are not felt very much. When production falls each individual manufacturer cuts employment. When production recovers but with no further prosperous waves expected, all the individual manufacturers will find it economic to exploit the technical and organizational changes which allow them to save on human labour, so as to avoid employing new workers. The tendency of unemployment to be irreversible is the other side of the tendency of the rate of profit to fall. This is the structural aspect of the capitalist flexibility of employment. The labour force is a commodity, the demand for which is downwardly mobile only.

This 'stylized fact', which seemed highly daring when first put forward some years ago, is now a journalistic commonplace, borne out by statistics and confirmed by econometrics. A recent, most comprehensive, survey of the literature (Bean 1994) on the subject of unemployment (in Europe; the American situation is different, but equally threatening (Eatwell 1995)) shows that the traditional way of considering the problem, in terms of supply and demand of the labour force on the labour market, cannot explain the most serious feature of unemployment today, which is its persistence. I believe that this is a direct result of the orthodox, pre-Keynesian, and pre-Ricardian-Marxian way of formulating the problem, that is, in terms of partial equilibria. This stylized fact itself, which ought to constitute the main premise of any argument on unemployment, demands an answer to three questions: *What are its causes? How can the existing employment be maintained?* and *What should be done with the unemployed?*

WHAT ARE THE CAUSES OF UNEMPLOYMENT?

It can be said that the altered relationship between commodity production and employment has meant the end of the Taylor-Ford-Keynesian model and the establishment of new models of production, consumption and control of society, in a situation still dominated by the sole purpose of realizing profits. This model, which had distinguished the dynamics of postwar industrial economies up to the mid-1970s, was characterized by: (a) the mass production of standardized consumer durables; (b) a process of extensive capital accumulation; (c) social compromise on sharing productivity gains between capitalists and workers; and (d) policies directed at stabilizing aggregate demand and the social order.

Now that the consumer durables market has become progressively saturated, process innovation prevails over product innovation, and the time horizons of investment decisions are narrowed, while the geographical ones are widened. The introduction of new technologies into production processes is not translated into great investment projects capable of generating multiplier effects which at least would compensate for the saving in workers, but rather in an overall reduction in the technical coefficients. New investments are shorter-term than the traditional ones. In a situation of growing uncertainty this inhibits the employment of a regular force on long-term contracts and encourages 'flexible' arrangements in the factory, the labour market and society as a whole, economically convenient to capitalists.

Intensifying and lengthening production time and overtime in the factories and contracting out overhead costs to society are preferable to taking on more workers. Flexibility is fostered in the factories by means of new organizational models of relations among workers, and between workers and machines, which embody coercion as working rhythms imposed and controlled by the worker himself. In society, flexibility is introduced by means of an ideological use of the principle of efficiency and a political use of unemployment. Capital, on the other hand, frequently prefers speculative investments to those yielding a material surplus. In the Ricardian-Keynesian sense, rent prevents the accumulation of productive capital, and effectively it counts politically in as much as it prefers unemployment to cost inflation.

None, much less the whole set, of the circumstances from which the Fordian paradigm originated can be repeated spontaneously or be the purpose of credible economic policies. Today any compensation theory is untenable, and it is inconceivable that increased productivity, at effectively sustainable rates, should bring increased employment. The material basis for that paradigm is unrepeatable in the production sector. A policy of high wages in the distribution sector is also unrepeatable. The commodities market is unlimited and the demand for jobs is unlimited. Capital has no native land and seeks labour where it costs less, while the supply of labour remains basically restricted to domestic markets. Wages are only an accounting item in production costs.

If the dynamics of commodity production and the dynamics of employment are asymmetrical, then the policies designed to encourage capitalist accumulation can, at the most, maintain the existing employment level. In themselves they will not generate more jobs. A relatively high level of employment is no longer profitable. The terms of the relationship between capital and wage-labour, whether of conflict or compromise, have changed, as have the terms of the agreement between capital and the national political class with regard to the structure of the welfare state. To use an ambiguous expression from the 1930s, one could say that this is a form of 'mistaken rationalization', rationalization which, while lowering the production costs of a single business, raises the social costs of production 'thus enriching the individual and impoverishing society'.

The economic and social costs of long-term mass unemployment are greater than those of moderate inflation. However, narrowing the time horizons of capital, of politics and of the good family man himself, renders the long-term prospects immaterial. It is here that the economic question emerges as a social and political question. The industrial reserve army gradually takes on the function of a political reserve army, which is the most efficient form of coercion at this stage. Capital controls society on the labour market by means of the industrial reserve army and on the political market, by means of the political reserve army.

HOW CAN EXISTING EMPLOYMENT LEVELS BE MAINTAINED?

The second problem goes hand in hand with the problem of the industrial vitality (of agriculture in many countries) and of the related activities. Today a labour and employment policy must be principally a real industrial policy, and must pursue objectives aimed at stabilizing the economic cycle rather than intensifying recovery phases (this is implicit in the dynamics of the 'stylized fact'). A real industrial policy is the exact opposite of a policy of 'competitive' devaluation of the exchange rate, of wages and of the welfare state. True, in an economy open to exportation and importation, the problem of employment immediately becomes one of competitiveness on international markets. Increased competitiveness however cannot pass for an overall reduction in the cost of labour. If one considers that the world is a closed system, a universal reduction in the cost of labour would result in a general crisis of overproduction. On the other hand, the east Asian model of development does not seem to be universally applicable, mainly for cultural reasons.

Designing a model of civil, rather than savage, competitiveness means, at one and the same time, designing a model of development and a model of social order which are mutually coherent. Defining a development model means deciding what the wages of the workers involved directly or indirectly in the production should be, and also what the surplus, the extent and structure of consumption and the tax rate should be. Defining the social order means defining the expenditure on the care of people and of nature, particularly education and research. This means deciding on the amount of the social product which is destined for future generations, it means establishing to what extent the weak pay for their weakness and the strong enjoy the advantages of their superiority.

WHAT IS TO BE DONE WITH THE UNEMPLOYED?

The stylized fact mentioned at the beginning means that achieving a saleable surplus product is a necessary, but not a sufficient condition for reducing unemployment. Even in the presence of a fortuituously rapid growth, the third problem would remain unresolved. One could argue that a high surplus product would make unemployment tolerable, since one could transfer to the unemployed the purchasing power required to satisfy their demand for commodities. The argument is correct from the point of view of accounting, but it is short-sighted from the economic and political one. It overlooks the fact that the other side of mass unemployment is a mass of unsatisfied social needs, such needs as the market cannot and does not satisfy.

The solution most discussed in Europe today by those who do not believe in the official pharmacopoeia is an overall reduction in the working hours. This idea ('working fewer hours, everyone working') has two interpretations, which are frequently confused. Both stem from the observation that the labour socially required to produce a given quantity of goods has diminished and continues to diminish: proof of this is the growth of unemployment. There are two possible ways of dealing with this. One is to exploit the available technology to save labour instead of jobs, and reverse the present relationship between machine and living human labour. The other is to redistribute the working time so as to absorb the unemployed. These two possibilities would never coincide, not even when fully in force, that is, at the end of the not brief transition period which both would require, hence they must be kept distinct from each other.

With regard to the first approach (which is that of Paul Lafargue and Keynes) all that need be said here is that this is the road to be taken unhesitatingly by those who hold dear their own and others' liberty. However it is a long, arduous road for many reasons, some of which Keynes himself mentioned. There must be a high rate of capital accumulation, no civil conflict, wars or exceptional demographic increases. Relative needs, those needs which exist only in so far as their satisfaction makes us feel superior to our peers, should not boom disproportionately. One must be able to sing and want to join in the singing, to behave differently from the normal run of rich people today and be willing to share one's 'bread' and disdain love for money. In other words, one must presume that the 'economic problem' has already been solved.

The other approach to a shortened working week sees the decrease of the share of the wage-earners as an already achieved, if partial, liberation from labour and reducing the hours as one solution to unemployment itself. This is a goal which certainly ought to be pursued right now, although it has limitations and there are obstacles which must be taken into account if it is to be an efficacious solution and not conflict with the long-term one. A policy of reducing the working week (for the same wage) nowadays arouses obvious and probably insuperable opposition from capitalists, but particularly it assumes that commodities can satisfy all needs. An overall reduction in working hours should instead serve to reduce the labour involved in producing commodities, not to increase the number of workers thus engaged.

In the actual state of the world, labour redistribution is a goal to strive for constantly, but one which is extremely difficult to implement in any one country, if for no other reason than the constraints on competitiveness in the sector producing a trade surplus. Under current conditions, the reduction in the working week (and in wages) in the various countries risks being a form of respectable company compromise between capital and the labour employed, which however does not reduce unemployment and remains within the logic of commodity production. The idea which justifies policies to reduce the working week (for the same wage) is that of sharing productivity gains between the firms and workers, in terms of less time spent working rather than a wage increase for the latter. Therefore, it assumes high starting wages and a flourishing social and economic situation, tending towards full employment: the exact opposite of the current situation.

Reducing working hours requires a radical reorganization of the production process, so as to render it compatible with a more humane process of social change and, therefore, it assumes that there is social control over the technical change which today seems impracticable. In short: a general reduction in working hours presupposes full employment, it is not a way to attain it.

UNEMPLOYMENT AND SOCIAL NEEDS

In a capitalist society there is a dual contradiction:

Figure 4.2 The capitalist society dual contradiction

Social needs	Unemployed workers
Production of commodities	Wage-earning workers

Commodity production is equivalent to wage-labour and frequently our attention is drawn to this relationship only. The other side of unemployment consists of unsatisfied social needs which occur mainly in the social reproduction sphere. The relation between producing exchange-value and abstract labour has a dual negative aspect consisting of the relation between needs which capital does not satisfy and labour which capital does not employ. Market rationality, with its underlying contradiction between capital and wage-labour, is paralleled by the contradiction between penury and waste outside the market. This dual contradiction is intrinsic to the capitalist mode of production. But once the correspondence between the dynamics of commodity production and the dynamics of employment disappears, then this dual contradiction becomes economically and politically disastrous. Wasted labour and unsatisfied social needs grow together.

VALUE IN EXCHANGE AND VALUE IN USE

In so far as commodities tend to be solely exchange-values, one must move out of the commodity sector to produce use-values. What prevents this from being grasped is the naïve or culpable conviction that commodities can satisfy all needs, or that there is equivalence and commensurability between value in exchange and value in use, between the price of commodities and their capacity to satisfy the absolute needs of individuals and of society. Exchange values assume some value in use, since otherwise commodities would not be sold and profits could not be realized. In capitalist production, however, the production of use-values is incidental. (The so-called Baumol paradoxes – a Mozart quartet always takes roughly the same performance time – appear so because one forgets that it is production for use).

THE PRODUCTION OF MONEY BY MEANS OF MONEY

Capitalist production is not so much production of commodities by means of commodities as production of money by means of money. Were it possible, the *immediate* conversion of M into M′ would be preferred (as speculation does, which in fact is a zero-sum game). Commodities could satisfy all needs only if exchange-values always coincided with use-values. The problem would be purely redistributive, in the sense that all that would be necessary would be to give all individuals, whether employed or not, an adequate sum of money. The actual irrationality of the market, which registers and satisfies only needs endowed with purchasing power, principally relative needs, would disappear. Money, however, only enables us to buy commodities, and the commodities which capital decides to produce are only those that promise and permit a profit.

In the capitalist process, satisfying needs is only a stage in the process itself, not its end. A great liberal and upright market supporter, Luigi Einaudi, put it in a nutshell very authoritatively:

> It must be clearly understood that, in affirming that the market is the appropriate instrument for directing production in the sense of producing goods and services, precisely in the quantity and of the type which meet men's demand, is not affirming that the market likewise directs production to produce goods and services in the quantity and of the type which the same men might desire. The latter make the demand which they can using the means and money which they have available. If they had other and greater means, they would make a different demand: for the same goods in greater quantities or other goods of a different type. Markets satisfy demands, not needs.
>
> [Einaudi, 1994, p. 278]

TOO MANY COMMODITIES, TOO FEW JOBS

The level of capitalist production is not decided on the basis of the relationship between production and social needs, the needs of socially developed mankind, but rather on the basis of the profit rate. Commodity production stops, not when needs are satisfied, but when profitability dictates it. Even if commodity production recovered there would not be significant variations in employment unless in menial, occasional and low-income jobs. Policies directed at encouraging greater capital accumulation could generate a greater surplus product, but they would not resolve this contradiction.

The solution to this problem – too many commodities, too few jobs – must be sought elsewhere, outside the capitalist and market dimension of society. To borrow Claudio Napoleoni's illuminating assessment: the situation from which we must be delivered is the reification of the world, the absolutism of production, producibility as the ultimate criterion. Why concentrate attention on what workers can *have* or can *do*, and not also, and perhaps principally, on what they can *be*? However, it is not a question of exiting from capitalism to enter something else. It is a question of widening as far as possible the difference between society and capitalism, in other words, of enlarging the area in which man is not identified with subjectivity turned upside down.

ABSTRACT LABOUR AND CONCRETE LABOUR

The solution I propose is that socially useful jobs, involving concrete labour (as opposed to abstract labour employed in the production of commodities), must be promoted and organized. These socially useful jobs should be *immediately* directed at producing use-values, capable of satisfying the social needs which commodity production does not satisfy. According to J.M. Keynes, just as there are absolute needs and relative needs, there are technically individual services and technically social services. The state's most important action, through appropriate institutions yet to be created, should deal, not with those activities which private individuals already perform on the market, but with those functions beyond the range of individuals and of the market, with those decisions which otherwise would not be taken, what otherwise would never be accomplished. So doing, the function of the state becomes once more irreplaceable.

Today it is a question of devoting part of the surplus deriving from the production of commodities to a social surplus, to setting up, not unproductive labour (in the Smith-Marxian sense of the word) directed at satisfying relative needs, but to promoting jobs directly aimed at satisfying absolute social needs. This labour is to be employed, not in the commodity production sphere, but in that of social reproduction and environment maintenance. Broadly speaking this is mainly caring for people and nature. These are necessary jobs which the labour market and the commodities market do not register.

THE CHARACTERISTICS OF CONCRETE LABOUR

By definition and in contrast with abstract labour, concrete labour is labour intensive. This does not mean that it requires primitive technologies. On the contrary it may require refined and innovative techniques. It does not consist in menial works, indeed it requires ability, a professional approach, sensitivity to solving problems rather than an aptitude for repetitive tasks and responsibilities. While socially necessary abstract labour stems from the techniques adopted in commodity production and is exchanged on the labour market, concrete labour depends on inexhaustible social needs, and is exchanged, not on a market, but in society. Robots and workers are not necessarily destined to replace each other along a given isoquant.

Since it is directed at satisfying social needs, concrete labour, of necessity, has a marked regional aspect and requires and imposes democratic forms of monitoring, local control of demand and decentralized organization of the supply. Concrete labour is not exposed to international competition and must conform to criteria of efficacy rather than competitive efficiency. Without changing the money wages permitted by the capitalist economic situation and the relationship between capital and wage-labour, the use-value yielded by concrete labour would bring about an increase in real wages without affecting profits and without inflationary repercussions.

There ought to be no insurmountable obstacles such as those indicated by Kalecki: the aversion of 'industrial managers' to public intervention in industrial relations; the aversion to public spending on public investments or subsidies to consumption; the aversion to social or political changes resulting from full employment. Concrete labour should not be a burden, but an enrichment, for abstract labour, since producing use-values directly satisfies social needs and also indirectly improves the conditions and the productivity of the exchange values yielded by abstract labour.

TWO PROBLEMS

The two sectors envisaged here, the sector of abstract labour which produces commodities and therefore capitalist surplus and that of concrete labour directed at satisfying social needs, must be considered as two distinct, but not separate areas, as the two extremes of a *continuum* which winds through the 'private social' sector: cooperative firms, non-profit organizations, voluntary work, and so on. (With regard to this so-called third sector, it is often forgotten that the 'private social' – apart from voluntary work – only satisfies privately advantageous social needs, that is, those which can be satisfied.) The two sectors intersect and are interdependent in a non-hierarchical but complementary relationship. One could speak of a production of commodities and use-values by means of use-values and commodities (both basic products).

Although conceptually simple, realizing this design is not. At least two problems must be mentioned: how to finance concrete labour, and how to govern relations between the two sectors.

HOW TO FINANCE AND MANAGE CONCRETE LABOUR

The only solution to the first problem, at least in the early stages, is fiscal transfer. Intensifying the average tax burden by increasing the tax rates is inconceivable, both nationally and internationally, though a battle against evasion and avoidance is conceivable. A choice must be made between the three big groups of income: wages, profits and rent, which nowadays is principally financial rent. The choice can only fall on rent, which slows down the accumulation of capital, offsets any rise in employment, appropriates productivity gains and distorts consumption models. Although it is true that profit and rent are intertwined, profit can survive without rent, while the opposite is not true. This, in a certain sense, is a political problem of capital.

As for the second problem (managing the two sectors, their relationship and the shifting area where they overlap), it should be remembered that the two extreme forms of managing the economy are the Market, interpreted by an able auctioneer crying tempting prices, and a plan decreed by an omnipotent Dictator. A reasonable criterion for deciding which to choose or to exclude is to ask oneself what form of social reproduction is permitted or imposed by either form of economic and social administration. In reality the outcome is the same. Both cases, allowing the Market to rule, or delivering oneself up to the Dictator, are equivalent from the point of view of economic theory. Relationships between men are tyrannically reduced to relationships between things.

WELL-BEING AND SOBRIETY

As has been pointed out to me, creating a non-commodity sector to employ those not engaged in that of commodity production, for producing use-values instead, raises a thorny problem with regard to the redistribution of labour and commodities between the two sectors. The two possible mechanisms for commodity redistribution are imposition or market. Both are open to objections.

A supporter of the second would object to the first on the grounds that workers in the commodity sector would not easily give up a good part of their enjoyment of commodities, in exchange for the services provided by concrete labour. Those who trust the market as a mechanism for the rational allocation of resources and commodities would also object that it is incomprehensible why the very concrete services are not produced as commodities, that is, by the commodity sector itself. The first objection embodied in the words 'not easily' is political. Indeed it is not an easy political problem to design, against the spirit of the times, a model of economic development and social order which is both prosperous and sober.

THE 'SOVEREIGNTY' OF THE CONSUMER

The second objection is analytic and can be summarized in the axiom: *everything can be produced in the form of a commodity*. Consumers may be ignorant, and unaware of how they might benefit from the goods and services still unknown to them, or whose consumption has not yet been advertised, because the firm capable of producing them profitably does not yet exist. All that would be needed, then, is to make potential needs emerge as obvious needs and then ensure their satisfaction by converting those goods and services into marketable commodities. This is a real problem: how can unsatisfied needs be made to emerge, if knowledge of them does not already exist (which I do not believe), and, therefore, a corresponding demand. The problem is that of the effective sovereignty of the consumer.

One may doubt this sovereignty, since the consumer's choice is necessarily and always limited to the alternatives available in the market. It is possible that the vast majority of the choices recorded by the market are in reality second choices, if compared with the choices which consumers might make were the necessary alternatives available. Taking for granted that consumer preferences are given and static is politically shortsighted, while it is analytically infantile to overlook the fact that neither unemployment nor unsatisfied social needs would exist if it were economic for capital. It must be demonstrated and proved convincingly (and this is the job of politicians) that a model of economic development and social order, which is both prosperous and sober, can be advantageous to the majority of citizens.

MARKET FAILURE

The market may be a necessary, but it is certainly not the sole, condition for democracy. Mass unemployment and the mass of unsatisfied social needs are the two real failures of the market, bankruptcies to which the market itself cannot be receiver. Homeopathy is of doubtful efficacy.

The commodity sector of the economy today is essential for producing the surplus required by the capitalist mode of production. It is however incapable of resolving the contradiction between unsatisfied social needs and unemployment, nor is any dictator capable of doing so. Setting up concrete labour projects requires intermediary government levels between the Market and the Dictator and different forms of society. Keynes's *The End of Laissez-faire* (Keynes, 1926) gives us an idea:

> I believe that in many cases the ideal size for the unit of control and organization lies somewhere between the individual and the modern State. I suggest, therefore, that progress lies in the growth and the recognition of semi-autonomous bodies within the State-bodies whose criterion of action within their own field is solely the public good as they understand it, and from whose deliberations motives of private advantage are excluded, though some place it may still be necessary to leave, until the ambit of men's

altruism grows wider, to the separate advantage of particular groups, classes, or faculties – bodies which in the ordinary course of affairs are mainly autonomous within their prescribed limitations, but are subject in the last resort to the sovereignty of the democracy expressed through Parliament.

OUR PROSPECTS

The design outlined above has been thought out in terms of developed western countries, but it could perhaps stimulate a more general discussion. The main problem seems to be too many commodities and too few jobs, in addition to the explosive contrast between mass unemployment and a mass of unsatisfied social needs, which is evident all over the world, but obviously to different degrees and in different forms. The choice we are faced with, I believe, is dramatic. It is not between well-being and austerity, it is between possible forms of austerity: the poverty which awaits us if we let things take their course (a poverty predictably garbed in new forms of authoritarianism), or strict sobriety.

The apologia of the market conceals a plan to erase politics, and reduce it to administrating what already exists. Revealing this convincingly is the task of politics, of politics as a critique and as a plan: a critique of the existing state of affairs and of the ideological rationalization which makes the existing the 'sole thought', and a plan for a new model for development and new forms of government. A model of resource allocation ought to ensure an adequate and appropriate combination of commodity and social surplus, and a global system of cooperative government. In an age of worldwide markets, politics must also become worldwide.

It is vital for the fate of humanity that Western Europe, North America, Japan and the newly industrialized countries set themselves long-term horizons and direct their scientific and technological potential to reconciling economic efficiency, social justice, a sustainable environment, cultural diversity and political democracy. The premises and objectives of so-called 'plans for structural adjustment', which in fact are frequently directed at cutting wages and employment, must be baulked to resist the logic of competitiveness as the absolute, unconditional value. The task is not easy if one considers the ideas which inspire organizations such as the OECD, which has observed that in the majority of countries where unemployment is currently at the level of ten years ago or lower, the inequality of incomes has become more marked and in countries where social security and public transfer payments are directed at avoiding increased inequality, unemployment has not noticeably decreased. Hence the doubtful conclusion that the fight against unemployment forces us to accept, and even to accelerate the growth of inequalities.

Intelligence and courage are needed to deal with the problems which this short century delivers to us. Political economists too have a great deal to do if they want to help solve these problems. The task of politics is to regulate the relationship between the production process and the social reproduction process. At the root of our incapacity, as economists, to grasp the risks of the new forms of unemployment, and their consequences in terms of a tendentialy irreversible exclusion of ever greater masses of men and women from 'civil society' (which is the complex of material relations of existence), lies our inability to perceive the unbreakable bond between the process of production and the process of social reproduction. We do not need Marx to grasp this connection, Classical Political Economy is enough. Quesnay, Smith and Ricardo understood it well. The capitalist production process is circular, a process of reproduction. They were so aware of this that they considered the modes of social reproduction as determinants of wages, of prices and income distribution, therefore, of the very destiny of capitalism.

This idea has been abandoned by modern economics, which sees consumption, rather than the reproduction of the social process, as the purpose of the economic process. The production process is seen as a process of production of commodities whose value is established by the market, forgetting that the prior reproduction of people and nature is necessary in order to produce commodities, forgetting that social use-values are basic products. Reducing the production-reproduction process to the single stage of direct production has very serious repercussions when the labour socially necessary for direct production tends irreversibly to diminish and is not employed elsewhere, that is when labour is *wasted*. I believe that if we, as economists, want to go forward, it is time for us to look back.

NOTE

In this paper I continue the discussion of ideas first put forward in Lunghini (1995).

REFERENCES

Bean, C.H. (1994) European Unemployment: a Survey, *Journal of Economic Literature* **XXII**, 573–619.

Eatwell, J. (1995) Disguised Unemployment: the G-7 Experience, *UNCTAD Review*, New York and Geneva, United Nations.

Einaudi, L. (1994) Sull'economia di mercato, introduzione alla politica sociale', in R. Bocciarelli and P. Ciocca (eds), Rome-Bari, Laterza.

Keynes, J.M. (1926) *The End of Laissez-faire*, London, Hogarth Press (*The Collected Writings*, vol. **IX**, 272–94).

Keynes, J.M. (1930) The Economic Possibilities for our Grandchildren, *The Nation and Athenaeum* (*The Collected Writings*, vol. **IX**, 321–32).

Lunghini, G. (1995) *L'età dello spreco. Disoccupazione e bisogni sociali*, Torino, Bollati Boringhieri.

Comment

Claudio Gnesutta

The preparation of this comment on Professor Lunghini's paper, immediately posed two problems, one of a personal nature, the other of a general character. The former refers to the fact that, for some time now, I find myself in sympathy with what he has been writing on the subject, and with what he has presented in the paper. This will no doubt weaken the critical function I have been called upon to fulfil. The second difficulty stems from his appeal to economists to look for solutions to the structural problem of unemployment 'beyond the purely mercantile logic'. If we broach this area of speculation we must call into question many of the analytical instruments we have acquired in order to broaden and suitably redefine the subject under discussion.

In response to Professor Lunghini's appeal and with reference to the content of his paper, there is no doubt that the central question raised – here as well as in other essays – is that the present 'mode of development' of our economies is characterized by the 'atrocious anomaly of unemployment in a world full of needs'. I share this view and, to a large extent, the analysis of the causes which lie at the root of this contradiction and the ways to overcome it. Therefore, I limit myself here to making some remarks on one general question and to explore one analytical issue which I hold to be pivotal, despite its great complexity. This is the suggestion to interpret the production process as 'the production of commodities and use-values by means of use-values and of commodities', both being 'basic products'.

I said I largely agree with Professor Lunghini's thinking on the present 'mode of development', characterized by slow real growth and a growing disequilibrium in income distribution. I wish to point out that, compared with the recent past, we are experiencing a transformation in institutions and in economic policy, which backs up the structural, technological and social innovations. These changes are marked by the subordination of needs (of society) to efficiency (of the economy). It is widely acknowledged that at the root of this 'mode of development' lies a competitive tension; as a consequence, the price-elastic production is moving towards low-salary locations, while price-inelastic production is favouring high-salary ones. At an international level, the income differential between the two sectors is very wide and the globalization of the economy accentuates the pressures on differentials which already exist between countries. There follows a tendency for society to become polarized and, as a consequence, the weakest sectors of society experience a general lowering of expectations.

In the meantime, the new 'mode of consumption' is playing an increasingly decisive role in this polarization of society. Although few economists have written on this subject, it seems opportune to note that these new production relationships have become associated with specific sets of values and corresponding life styles and, therefore, with specific interpretations of existing social relations. The emphasis on this takes us back to a theme in the paper where the need 'to design, against the spirit of the times, a model of economic development and social order both rich and sober' is expressed. In my view, this should be deepened in order to have a better understanding of the contradictions which exist between the needs of economy and the needs of society, interpreted as an expression of the social processes accompanying the new production structure. Rather than point out the difficulties attached to the 'project' proposed in the paper, I wish to stress that this task would require a long and complicated cultural debate, which should be rooted in the economic and social structures.

The ongoing process can be interpreted as a sort of Schumpeterian process of 'creative destruction' in which not only the structure of productive capital is involved, but also the social nexus, and the democracy itself. Even if this were true only in part, we could not remain indifferent in the face of the widespread costs of destruction and the uncertain benefits of the 'creative' process; this is particularly so if we consider that 'spontaneous' tendencies do not seem capable of achieving the increased capacity for growth which could be expected from greater flexibility in social relations.

Summing up, my appreciation of Lunghini's paper rests on the following: the macroeconomic perspective adopted (centred on the functioning of the system), the political standpoint (not to passively accept spontaneous forces) and the urgent need for a profound cultural analysis (in order to redefine our own vision of ourselves in the world). This is all the more appropriate so if we consider that these aspects constitute a strong conceptual link with the sensibility and scientific commitment of Fausto Vicarelli.

Moving on to the analytical aspect, it seems to me that if the concept of 'the production of commodities and use-values by means of use-values and of commodities' is to remain a meaningful formula, it is necessary to submit it to careful analysis. However, I shall limit myself, for the time being, to the three points which seem to me the most problematical and the most pertinent to Lunghini's paper.

The first question concerns the identification of which use-values are to be included in the production process defined by Lunghini. A general definition of this category is not mentioned in his paper, but it is identified through a generic, although meaningful, reference to main activities 'of caring for people and nature'. In spite of such an 'elastic' concept, with wide margins of indeterminacy, we cannot say that it prevented the founding of any analytical structure based on it. It should also be pointed out that an alternative means of dealing with the problem does not exist, given the present state of economic thinking. (Analogous treatment of the problem is to be found in Delors's White Papers.) Yet, recourse to a list of activities rather than to one general criterion reflects, essentially, the procedure (a conventional one) which determines the most accepted concept of the domestic product currently in use.

Moreover, the category 'use-value' is far from alien to economic thinking, and to the field of national accounting in particular. This relates to the distinction, which took shape from the theory, between the product (domestic product) and welfare (based on the notion of 'net economic welfare' derived from the seminal work of Tobin-Nordhaus); in fact, it is well-known that the concept of domestic product fails to represent a satisfactory measure of economic well-being. The difficulties which are faced by accounting based on the concept of well-being are due not so much to the complex problems of valuation but to the fact that there must be a consensus (a convention, in fact) on the kind of activities generating use-values (of a positive or negative nature). The problem is not the recognition of the existence of concrete labour and of use-values – they obviously exist – but, rather, of rendering them socially visible. Their social recognition should also be possible on both the theoretical and the accounting level, and the accounting value should reflect the social value. It should be noted that the proposal of giving theoretical status to this aspect would, in fact, make the analytical structures of the economist dependent on an 'elusive' element, whose determination would derive from valuations (of a political and social nature) extraneous to the discipline of economics proper. If this were so, the relativism of many technical prescriptions would be exposed, in that they would be based on contexts which make use of different sets of use-values chosen as 'economically' relevant.

Second, in order to give an analytical form to the production process proposed by Lunghini, we must specify in a meaningful fashion the extent of both production processes, that is of commodities and of use-values; only in this way can the nature of the interaction between the two sectors be described. With regard to this, it is pertinent to remember Fausto Vicarelli, who expressed a similar position at a Trade Union meeting; Vicarelli pointed out that accumulation consisted not only in machinery and equipment, but also in schools, hospitals and sports fields. He described the two activities as being in competition in one respect (in that they both depend on the same resources for their production) but that they were also complementary (more use of social capital would improve the conditions of production and, therefore, the productivity of capital aimed at the production of commodities).

With the aim of formally reconstructing this process, it may well be appropriate to use a simple input-output model composed of three sectors (producers of commodities, producers of use-values, and final users), in which the two production sectors are stucturally integrated. From this representation we at once obtain the means by which the user sector (that is, the whole population) benefits from production; the resulting combination of commodities and use-values constitutes the 'mode of consumption' of that society. In addition to this, the accounting model reveals the nature of the interaction between the two production sectors; while the dependence of the sector of use-values on that of commodities is to be expected, the reverse dependency is by no means automatic. In order to make sense of the interpretative model, in fact, it is necessary to identify the origin and destination of the production of use-values. Clearly the failure to identify the respective transactions would hinder a valuation of the costs and benefits generated by the production process in its entirety. In their absence it would not be possible to estimate either the use-values engaged in the production process of commodities, or those values incorporated in the growth of human and social capital also used by the sector of commodities.

It must be said that a representation of this kind poses another problem which is no less complex: the valuation of use-values in terms comparable to those attributed to commodities by market prices. The need for an 'objective' index in order to give a quantitative dimension to use-values introduces, in fact, another 'subjective' element into the model (in the form of a political or social valuation). To conclude, the identification of an activity constituting a use-value, its quantification and valuation, are all essential elements to enable us to obtain a description of a society whose process of reproduction is made up of commodities and use-values which are closely linked in a relation of complementarity.

Finally, the determination of what consitutes use-values and of how much social value they incorporate would allow the quantification of the actual transfer of value between productive sectors. We should also note that, in the exchange between the two sectors, some transactions take the form of monetary exchanges while others are exchanges in kind. In so far as use-values cannot be calculated, the sum of monetary exchanges undervalues the reintegration of resources destroyed in the production of commodities. This gives a distorted measure of the potential growth of a country and provides, albeit with reference to a macroeconomic dimension, an analogy with the Pigouvian analysis of the gap between the individual and the collective valuation of economic results.

One obvious implication of the approach adopted here is that distributed monetary income is not a good index of the 'product' of the two sectors. The income of the commodities sector would be a gross value-added (because the value of use-values destroyed is not taken into consideration); yet, the savings would be undervalued (because it would not take into account the use-values directed at the accumulation of human and social capital). It follows that, as commodity production is overestimated, any necessary monetary re-allocation from this sector is considered unjustified, albeit wrongly, from the social point of view.

Not only, within the production sector of use-values, activities exist which do not involve any monetary transactions, either from the point of view of input or from the point of view of output (this is true, for example, for various forms of voluntary work). The failure to detect these situations also prevents us from reconstructing other forms of interdependence between the two sectors, as, for example, in the case of the readiness to do 'unpaid' work when people have more time available or are less concerned with the exigencies of survival, as a result of reduced work time or the existence of a 'citizen income'.

To sum up, on a par with the gross production of commodities, different social structures produce a different set of results in terms of welfare. Any choice as to which of these socio-economic models should be favoured involves going beyond the present concerns of the economist. But, if the choice leads to a process of redistribution (monetary or in kind) of resources which does not correspond to the perceived idea of welfare, it is highly probable that the 'economic' forces will reject the 'social' choice. It is also clear that the choice of a socio-economic model implies a specific combination of goods (commodities and use-values) for use in the collectivity which must be accepted as the present mode of consumption. From what has been said so far, I wish to underline the fact that a stable macroeconomic equilibrium can result only from an acquired social cohesion, which in turn accrues from a global 'mode of development'. It is to the transformation of both the 'mode of production' and the 'mode of consumption' that Lunghini's proposal for 'a welfare project in sobriety' is closely linked.

There is no doubt that Lunghini's argument meets with difficulties of an analytical nature (the identification of use-values, their social valuation, the support of institutions appointed to produce them, the extension of the redistributive process, and the structuring of the 'mode of consumption'), but I cannot, however, fail to remember the many times in which Fausto Vicarelli, warning that 'real problems are never simple', not only urged an adequate investigation of problems, but also reminded us that an important part of our activity is to 'appeal to reason', to find a consensus for proposals founded on a careful anlysis which did not lose sight of the objective of collective welfare. A lesson to be learned from Lunghini is that the way in which the employment problem is faced has profound implications for the 'form of democracy', understood as an instrument of choice and social control.

Undoubtedly this perspective brings another problem to the fore, that is the concrete existence of 'a body' able to promote and control a solution in accordance with needs which are in line with social expectations and future prospects. In his paper there is the tendency to place reliance on bodies other than the classical producer of use-values, that is the State. Yet even though the call for 'intermediary government levels between the Market and the Dictator and different forms of society' is a stimulating idea, we must not forget that, whatever institutions Lunghini is referring to, they would have to come to terms with the different 'preferences' and 'hegemony' which prevail today in the Market.

In fact his proposal would oblige us to undergo a cultural transformation, and assume a different vision of 'polis', one which could render the redefinition of life-style (in terms of sobriety) credible and the connected process of redistribution acceptable: 'It must be demonstrated and proved convincingly (and this is the job of politics) that a model of economic development and social order both rich and sober can be advantageous to the majority of citizens'. However, I am in no position to answer the question of how and where we can achieve within an appropriate time scale a cultural elaboration of such a proportion and depth that could prove to be sufficiently convincing. This is a question I will address not to Lunghini, but rather to all those who see in his proposal a possible and credible way of achieving the balanced development of our society.

Part III

Capital Accumulation: Real and Financial Aspects

5 Instability, Volatility and the Process of Capital Accumulation

Jan A. Kregel

INTRODUCTION

It is ironic that the breakdown of the golden-age of post-war capital accumulation in the 1970s should have signalled the crisis of Keynesian economics. Ironic, for as Fausto Vicarelli pointed out, Keynes's entire theoretical edifice was constructed in order to interpret the instability of capitalism, indeed 'the stimulus to his analysis was always some moment of capitalist crisis'. In contrast to those announcing the 'crisis of Keynesian economics' in the face of the increasing instability of the 1970s, Vicarelli argued forcefully 'that Keynes's thought has direct relevance to the present moment of capitalist crisis' (Vicarelli, 1984, p. 184). Yet, as a result of the crisis, the majority of economists have abandoned Keynes's theory in favour of what has come to be called the 'New Classical' economics, which seems to exclude instability by definition, or the inappropriately named 'New Keynesian' economics, which seems to rely on the failure of the perfectly competitive market to allocate information efficiently.

Vicarelli's carefully argued case that Keynes's economics was even more appropriate to periods of crises than to the Golden Age of post-war stability has been completely ignored by most professional economists. The present paper will try to recall and reinforce some of Vicarelli's arguments, drawing on his interpretation of Keynes to integrate it with some more modern theory.

THE EXPLANATION OF ECONOMIC INSTABILITY

Even before Keynes wrote there was broad agreement that economic instability was caused by 'imperfections' which were represented by mistaken forecasts of the future and associated disappointment in expectations (cf. Kregel, 1977), or from mistaken government policies (extending to the very existence of government) producing inappropriate expectations (which is what the Treasury View seems to have been), or most simply the absence of competitive conditions. By and large they tended to be maintained after Keynes, and were still prevalent at the time of the 'crisis in Keynesian economics'. All of these explanations implicitly accepted the self-adjusting operation of the market mechanism. This explains why the rational expectations hypothesis had such a powerful and immediate impact, for it simply brought expectations formation within the already accepted self-adjusting mechanism. If information was also a commodity (Stigler), then a perfectly competitive market should eliminate any information failures such as erroneous expectations, whether from the private sector or by government intervention. If the automatic equilibration of supply and demand by prices in competitive markets is accepted, and economic agents are assumed to have the cognitive ability of the average first-year economics student with a middling competent instructor, then sooner or later, but none the less eventually, there should no longer be mistaken forecasts of the influence of economic events on prices. And the impact of government policy decision should also be anticipated. Thus, at a stroke, the existing explanation of instability was eliminated. Exogenous supply side shocks become the only possible explanation. It is not surprising that the New Keynesians counter-attacked in the area of the economics of information and that their response was in terms of an 'impossibility theorem' concerning the existence of perfect competitive markets for economic information.

Yet, Vicarelli did not base his explanation of Keynes's instability on the failure of the operation of the market for information. Indeed, when Keynes realized that his *General Theory* was being interpreted in terms of the 'differences between effective demand and income'[1] he declared that the theory of 'effective demand is substantially the same if we assume that short-period expectations are always fulfilled' (XIV, p. 181).[2] Indeed, in the *General Theory* Keynes had already suggested that 'the existing market valuation, however arrived at, is uniquely *correct* in relation to our existing knowledge of the facts . . .' (1936, p. 152; see also, XIV, p. 114). And this is not an isolated passage. Throughout his writings Keynes appears to accept even the strong form of the informational efficiency of markets.

In Keynes's view, the source of instability was not to be found in informational market failure, any more than it was to be found in the existence of uncompetitive product markets or labour markets. Instead, Keynes's analysis of instability was based on his belief that there was a basic difference in the way the price mechanism operated with respect to consumption goods and to capital, or investment goods. This is evident from the fact that, in contrast to acceptance of the assumption that short-term expectations were always realized, he considered that it would be inappropriate to assume that long-term expectations, which determine 'what the entrepreneur can hope to earn in the shape of future returns if he purchases (or, perhaps, manufactures) "finished" output as an addition to his capital equipment' (p. 47), could be assumed to be realized. The reason for this difference is that 'it is the nature of long-term expectations that they cannot be checked at short intervals in the light of realized results' (p. 51).

Since the stability of the price mechanism is based on an error correction mechanism which causes mistaken expectations to be eliminated, if it is impossible to determine whether or not long-term expectations are correct, then it is also impossible for the error correction mechanism to automatically produce adjustments converging towards a uniquely correct valuation on the basis of existing information. In the long run, not only are we all dead, but no purposive action or reaction based on realization or disappointment of expectations can take place.[3] Thus, the 'nature' of the operation of the price mechanism as it applies to investment decisions must be different.

Keynes notes that the problem could be avoided by assuming 'a world in which economic goods were necessarily consumed within a short interval of their being produced' (XIV, p. 113). But this would imply a world without growth and capital accumulation. Another alternative would be to reduce long-term expectations and the corresponding results of the decisions based on them to a time dimension similar to that applied to short-term expectations, such as are implicit in the Swedish *ex-ante* and *ex-post* approach. But, Keynes also rejects this approach as impracticable. In any case, Keynes notes that the comparison of expectations with realizations is only of importance if this causes expectations to be changed. However, 'the original expectations . . . which led the firm to acquire the capital equipment' will no longer be relevant if conditions have changed after the investment decision has taken place, since 'current decisions will most appropriately be based on current expectations'. Thus, only if conditions are unchanged through time will comparison of expectations with realizations be relevant, but this would require that expectations are always fulfilled or that decisions based on erroneous expectations have no impact on current conditions. This solution, Keynes argued, was the equivalent of considering only the 'current yield of capital equipment, which would be correct only in the static state where there is no changing future to influence the present' and 'has the result of breaking the theoretical link between today and tomorrow' (p. 145). That all this was caused by the diverse nature of the accumulation because 'It is by reason of the existence of durable equipment that the economic future is linked to the present' (p. 146).

If it was impossible to determine whether the expectations concerning an investment were satisfied, then the self-adjusting competitive market mechanism could not be applied to the investment decision. Indeed, he argued that in the application of the competitive mechanism to investments 'facts and expectations were assumed to be given in a definite and calculable form. . . . The calculus of probability . . . was supposed to be capable of reducing uncertainty to the same calculable status as that of certainty itself' (XIV, pp. 112–13).

While the appropriate treatment of the impact of the future on current economic decisions was the subject of much debate at the time of the publication of the *General Theory*, by the end of the war economists' concerns had been diverted to the empirical estimation of Keynesian consumption functions, investment functions, income multipliers and the like. Again, ironically, these exercises employed econometric theory which was based of the same 'calculus of probability' that Keynes had rejected as the basis for decision-making (cf. Hamouda and Rowley, 1996).

KEYNES AND INSTABILITY

Keynes believed that the problems caused by the decision to invest could only be recognized in what he called a 'monetary production economy' and defined as an economy 'in which changing views about the future are capable of influencing the quantity of employment and not merely its direction'. (1936, p. vii). It is only by recognizing the importance of changing views on the operation of the price mechanism that the instability of the capitalist system could be explained.

Although the theory of effective demand in a monetary production economy had all but disappeared in the post-war golden-age of Keynesian economics, Fausto Vicarelli was among the small group of economists who continued to recognize their importance. Even before the advent of the rational expectations hypothesis, he had recognized that the instability that Keynes was discussing could not be explained by errors in expectation or imperfection in information. This is evident not only in his book, but also in his assessment of the contributions of the New Classical Economics which had been erected on the basis of rational expectations. In one of his last published articles (1985–86) Vicarelli does not direct his criticism of the approach to the assumptions made about expectations, instead he draws attention to the restoration of the idea that capitalist accumulation is based on 'natural laws', which would naturally establish the expansion of investment which would produce full employment. Once this automatic mechanism is accepted, Vicarelli argues, it really makes no difference how expectations are introduced for, following Hicks, the problem simply becomes specification of the means by which agent expectations come to reflect the objective facts of the economy. As Keynes had argued, it is as if the process of adjusting expectations to their correct values had no impact on the current conditions in the economy. If there are 'natural' or 'objective' laws producing current economic conditions, independently of agents' expectations, then there will be objective probability distributions which can be estimated with increasing certainty by standard statistical procedures. But the real point of difficulty concerned the existence of the natural law, the specification of the objective process generating the results which expectations would reflect, not with the process of predicting them.

In his book Vicarelli notes the importance for Keynes's ideas on instability of the debate between Hayek and Keynes over the existence of a neutral monetary policy. It is important because it is based on a similar point. The existence of a 'neutral' monetary policy requires the existence of an objective, or 'real', system based on an automatic adjustment mechanism which exhibited endogenous stability and which could be disturbed by 'monetary' factors. By demonstrating that there was no reason for an economy absent money to be stable, Sraffa showed a neutral monetary policy to be, not impossible, but irrelevant to the goal of economic stability.

Even if expectations are perfect, if there are no natural forces at work to produce equilibrium in the system, instability will exist; errors and imperfections and incomplete knowledge cannot then be the cause of instability. This is the monetary production economy in which monetary and real factors cannot be distinguished. Following Keynes's idea that a new kind of price mechanism dealing with investment goods is needed, Vicarelli suggests that the appropriate response to the New Classical economics based on the rational expectations hypothesis is 'A Keynesian microeconomic theory, based on the particular features of a monetary economy' (p. 312).

THE BEGINNINGS OF THE NEW MICROTHEORY

The beginning of Keynes's concern with the difference between the determination of the prices of current output and investment goods, and thus with how future conditions impinge on current supply and demand, is in the criticism he received from his younger colleagues for the inconsistency in the explanation of the determination of the prices of consumption goods and capital goods in the *Treatise on Money*. 'Richard Kahn, a pupil of Keynes's . . . noted an unjustified asymmetry between the price level theory for consumption goods . . . and that for capital goods . . . the price level for consumer goods was said to be determined by demand and supply, while the price level for investment goods was attributed to "external" causes . . .' (Vicarelli, 1984, p. 101). Despite the encouragement of the younger economists, schooled in Marshall's price theory, to make the price of investment and consumption goods symmetric, Keynes resisted. The basic reason, Vicarelli notes, was that 'Keynes had, however, long ceased to consider savings as automatic demand for investment. It was futile, therefore, to expect him to ferret out a symmetry between reciprocal excesses of demand and supply in the two sectors' (*ibid*., p. 102). That is, the demand for investment goods could not be discovered in looking at what was left from income after the demand for consumption goods had been satisfied (the definition of saving), without particular assumptions about the characteristics of the supply curve of investment goods. Vicarelli points out that Keynes chose to make neither adjustment.

Keynes instead sought to incorporate the importance of the future on the present, the diverse determination of the prices of investment goods, the impossibility of comparing expectations with realizations, by 'the introduction of the concepts of user costs and the marginal efficiency of capital' (*ibid*., p. 146) into the Marshallian theory of supply and demand. This reworking of supply and demand is Keynes's new 'microtheory' for a monetary production economy.

MARGINAL EFFICIENCY AND USER COSTS

The marginal efficiency of capital, as Keynes was quick to admit, was not a real innovation, for this approach is already to be found in the work of Veblen, Marshall, Myrdal, Schumpeter and many others. Leaving aside specifics, marginal efficiency is based on the idea that the calculation of the return on an investment project can be handled in the same way as the yield to maturity is calculated on a fixed coupon bond, or, as Keynes suggests, as the value of a finite series of periodic annuity payments. Just as the yield to maturity calculates an average rate of discount that equates the purchase price of a bond to the present value of its periodic coupons, the efficiency of capital calculates the average rate of discount that equates the purchase price of the investment to the present value of its expected future net receipts. Formally, this is correct, but as a measure to represent the impact of a series of future events on the present, it has substantial drawbacks.

This is because the calculation of the internal rate of return of any stream of net periodic payments relies on the assumption that the reinvestment rate of interest is known and constant, implying a flat yield curve or that the risk of the investment is constant over its life. It also fails to deal with the fact that bonds and investment projects differ in the certainty over the size of the future net receipts and the possibilities of changing the shape of the flows of these receipts through shut down or delay of the project. Finally, when there is variation in the size of the expected future receipts, or fluctuations in interest rates or slope in the yield curve, are allowed, there may be multiple internal rates of return, precluding any precise definition of the yields which must be compared across different investments.

The reswitching debate should have taught economists what finance theorists have always known when they discuss the drawbacks of the internal rate of return as a reliable tool in capital budgeting. Keynes must have been aware of these problems for he quickly shifts his discussion from the internal rate of return definition of marginal efficiency to comparison of the demand and supply prices of capital goods, better known today as 'net present value' analysis. This eliminates the ambiguities caused by multiple internal rates of return, but, the other difficulties surrounding the calculation of the present value of the future costs and receipts from a project remain. For example, the difference caused by the fact that bond coupons are perfectly known and the periodic net proceeds of an investment are not still remain, as do the difficulties concerning the appropriate discount rate. Formulating the appropriate course of future interest rates in the form of changes in the shape of the yield curve will be no easier than the estimates of the expected periodic net yields. Keynes recognizes this problem when he speaks of the 'complex of interest rates for various terms which will rule in the future' being reflected in the 'complex of rates which will rule today' (p. 143). Today we would simply talk of the spot yield curve. In addition, there is the question of the appropriate discount rate to be used.[4] Despite all these complications, of which Keynes seems to have been aware, his basic point is simply to emphasize 'The marginal efficiency of capital is of fundamental importance because it is mainly through this factor (much more than through the rate of interest) that the expectation of the future influences the present' (p. 145). Keynes also warns that it is only 'after giving full weight to the importance of the influence of short-period changes in the state of long-term expectation as distinct from changes in the rate of interest, [that] we are entitled to return to the latter as exercising, at any rate, in normal circumstances, a great, *though not a decisive*, influence on the rate of investment' (p. 164, italics added). It is perhaps unnecessary to highlight the difference between this position and the determination of investment in the standard Keynesian model by means of changes in the rate of interest relative to a fixed state of expectations.

The second aspect does, however, present a real innovation: the introduction of user costs into the calculation of supply prices. User costs are often presented as an elaborate calculation of depreciation, or as the difference between the current costs involved in the operation or use of assets relative to the maintenance costs of keeping them idle.[5] But, such an interpretation makes no recognition of the role of user costs in expressing the impact of the future on present returns through the appropriate adjustment to supply prices.[6]

The necessity of specifying the role of user costs in entrepreneurial decision making is expressed in this passage from an early draft of the *General Theory*:

> The employment of the factors of production to increase output involves the entrepreneur in the disbursement, not of product, but of money. The choice before him in deciding whether or not to offer employment is a choice between using money in this way or in some other way or not using it at all . . . The only question . . . is to choose . . . that way which will yield the largest profit in terms of money. It must be remembered that future prices, in so far as they are anticipated, are already reflected in current prices, after allowing for the various considerations of carrying costs and of opportunities of production in the meantime which relate the spot and forward prices of a given commodity. Thus we must suppose that the spot and forward price structure has already brought into equilibrium the relative advantages, as estimated by the holder, of holding money and other existing forms of wealth. Thus if the advantage in terms of money of using money to start up a productive process increases, this will stimulate entrepreneurs to offer more employment . . . For the entrepreneur is guided, not by the amount of product he will gain, but by the alternative opportunities for using money having regard to the spot and forward price structure taken as a whole.
>
> (Keynes, 1936, XIII, pp. 82–3)

It is necessary to calculate the appropriate supply price incurred in production of output and the present value of the net sum received per unit of output (the demand price or forward price), in order to identify the 'actual nature of the business decision' as the comparison of the spot prices, current supply prices and forward prices. If the return available from engaging in current production to be sold at the expected future price is greater than the return available from buying existing output at the prevailing spot price and holding it for sale at the expected future price (or simply selling for future delivery at the forward price) then employing labour will provide a return greater than any 'alternative opportunities for using money' (or the costs of borrowing the money expended) and decisions will be taken to create output and provide employment. This comparison of the alternative rates of return provided by holding capital idle, using existing capital equipment to produce output, or ordering new capital equipment, was thus the key to determining the offers of employment.

The calculation of 'whether it is expected to pay a firm in possession of capital equipment to spend money on incurring variable costs' to produce either consumption or investment goods will then require a precise calculation of the amount of money spent on 'the employment of a given volume of labour by an entrepreneur'. This will be given by 'the amounts which he pays out to the factors of production for their current services' and 'the amounts he pays out to other entrepreneurs for what he has to purchase from them' plus 'the *sacrifice* which he incurs by employing the equipment instead of leaving it idle, which we shall call the user cost of the employment in question' (1936, p. 23, italics supplied). User cost plays a central role in determining supply price, but not so much in terms of maintenance costs, as the 'sacrifice' related to the decision to produce or not produce.

The calculation of the future return expected (whether it is expected to 'pay') by a firm from operating its existing equipment to produce output by employing labour will be based on the difference between the expected sales value of the output and the sum of costs paid to factors, including the user costs of non-labour inputs: 'in a given situation of technique, resources and factor cost per unit of employment, the amount of employment, both in each individual firm and industry and in the aggregate, depends on the amount of proceeds which the entrepreneurs expect to receive from the corresponding output'.

The origin of the concept of user cost is the analysis of short-period price adjustment in volume two of the *Treatise on Money*.[7] The problem that Keynes was trying to resolve was how the price adjustment mechanism would operate to restore equilibrium in conditions of excess supply. If future prices were expected to fall, then it would be rational to sell excess stocks as soon as possible, aggravating conditions of excess supply. The only way to stop a fall in price would be for prices to have declined to a point at which expectations were reversed. If prices were expected to rise, then it became rational to hold supplies off the market in the hope of selling them at higher prices in the future. However, holding supplies for future sale involved costs, of financing, storage, insurance, and so on. The expected rise in price would have to be sufficient to cover these costs before it would become rational to hold back supplies. This would cause supply to contract and start the process of price recovery. If the expected price rise more than covered the costs of storage, then a decision to sell at the current price would mean the 'sacrifice' of the higher net profit from holding to sell at the higher expected future price. This sacrifice of potential gain,

Keynes argued, should be included among the prime costs of supplying commodities today. In this way, expectations of future conditions had a direct impact on current supply prices and decisions to sell or hold a commodity should be made by comparing current selling prices with costs including the prospective future gain.[8] Thus the prime costs of using the commodity today would be the sum of the factor cost, which in this case is its current market value, plus the benefit which will be sacrificed by its current use, or its user cost. In this case prime costs are greater than the current market value, so it is more profitable to hold the commodity for future sale or use in production. User cost is then the present value of the increased return that could have been earned if the use of the commodity had been postponed to a future date. In this way the future exerts an influence on the present supply via the inclusion of user cost. Alternatively, if spot prices are expected to be lower in future, user costs would be negative and would act to reduce supply prices relative to current spot prices. It is thus profitable to 'use' current stocks by selling at current prices, leading to conditions of excess supply and downward pressure on prices. Thus, the response to the question that Keynes had posed in the *Treatise,* whether there was any automatic tendency for prices to move so as to restore equilibrium prices, was that it would depend on expectations of future prices and the costs of carry, primarily, the rate of interest. There was an appropriate combination of expectations and interest rates which would produce adjustment, but there were more combinations which would produce market breakdown and collapse.

Thus, the present value of expected future returns produced the influence of the future on the present demand prices of capital goods, while user costs produced the influence of the future on present supply prices.[9] This is the new microtheory of supply and demand that Keynes proposed as a substitute for the traditional theory which was only concerned with current conditions and the calculation of current yields.

However, one additional step was required, before the choice facing the entrepreneur in using his wealth could be fully specified. The rate of interest enters into the calculation of demand prices through the specification of the rate of discount and it enters supply prices through the impact of the cost of carry on user costs. Recall Keynes admonition to give 'full weight to the importance of the influence of short-period changes in the state of long-term expectations as distinct from changes in the rate of interest.'

It was for this reason that the *General Theory* differed from the *Treatise on Money* by the introduction of a distinction between the determinants of the marginal efficiency of capital and the rate of interest (compare 1936, p. 173). With the newly defined marginal efficiency to determine the rate of return on capital goods, liquidity preference, built on the concept of 'bearishness' from the *Treatise,* was to determine the rate of interest. Liquidity preference and the concept of the 'liquidity premium' have also caused difficulty in interpretation, but it seems clear that they are a straightforward extension of the idea of user costs to determine whether it is profitable to hold money for future use, rather than using it today to purchase investment or consumption goods. If money is 'used' today to buy investment goods, or consumption goods, or to buy financial assets (which includes bank lending to either households or entrepreneurs) to gain a return this means that the money will no longer be available to be 'used' at a future date when the prices of the assets or goods will be different. The 'user cost' of spending money today to acquire an asset or good will then be the present value of the potential future gain or loss that has been foregone or avoided by parting with money today. This future gain or loss will depend on the expected forward prices of investment goods, consumption goods and financial assets.

With respect to other financial assets, the user cost of money is the foregone gain (or loss) that could have been earned (or avoided) by waiting to purchase financial assets at lower (higher) prices and higher (lower) yields. The use of money is defined as becoming 'illiquid'. The premium which is required to convince holders of money to become illiquid is thus the equivalent of the 'user cost' of money. Liquidity preference will determine this liquidity premium and is thus linked directly to the expectation of the future movement of prices. The rate of interest can then also be represented as the relation between the spot price and the expected future prices of money. But, no one should be surprised by this, for Keynes insisted that his definition of the rate of interest, in difference from the 'real' rate determined by the forces of productivity and thrift in traditional theory, was 'nothing more than the percentage excess of a sum of money contracted for forward delivery, *e.g.* a year hence, over what we may call the "spot" or cash price of the sum thus contracted for forward delivery' (1936, p. 222). The complete specification of the new microtheory for the monetary production economy in which the future has an influence on the present thus requires the application of user costs to money as well as capital goods. It was thus possible to answer the question of whether it would 'pay' to employ labour and produce output by comparing the returns from holding money as given by the user cost of money, of holding capital goods (or any other durable) idle in terms of the return as given by user costs, and the return from using the capital goods with labour to produce consumption or investment goods as given by the marginal efficiency of capital. Only if the return on the latter could be held above the two former types of investment, would capital accumulation take place and employment be provided. This would require the appropriate manipulation of user costs, that is, expected future prices, and interest rates (which were also determined by expected future price movements). The explanation that Keynes offered of underemployment equilibrium turns on the different behaviour of supply and demand prices as supplies change, financial assets prices behaving in a different way than the prices of produced goods.

FROM INSTABILITY TO VOLATILITY AND BACK

The instability of the system then was the result of the fact that it was impossible to compare expectations with results, that there was no 'objective' referent upon which expectations might be based. The representation by means of user costs of this position provides us with an alternative way of seeing this point. Recall that one of the criticisms of the net present value calculation taken over from bond valuation was that it did not take into account the possibility of a variable holding period, for example, a decision to postpone an investment, or shut down a plant during its expected operating period. It thus ignores the value of 'imbedded' options in investment projects.[10]

Note that the decision not to 'use' a commodity or capital equipment in production is the equivalent retaining the privilege of doing so in future. Thus, the value of the decision to hold includes the equivalent of the value of a call option written at a strike price equal to the current spot price. The value of the position is thus its current spot market value plus the value of the option. This is precisely equivalent to the argument that prime costs should include user costs. At the same time, the user cost of money is equivalent to a call option on a deposit at the current interest rate. Alternatively, holding money uninvested in a portfolio allows you to forgo the sale of an investment asset to realize an unanticipated need for liquid funds. This is equivalent to the value of a put on the investment position written at the expected future appreciation of the asset.

Alternatively, anyone wanting to sell without losing the possibility of future profit could do so by purchasing a call option with a strike equal to the current spot price. Thus, if the price rises he can always reverse his prior sale at no net gain or loss by exercising the option and then sell at the now higher market price. On the other hand, if price is expected to fall, a covered call option could be written at the current spot price. If the price falls the premium is retained. If the options were traded in the market, the price of the option will be set by the balance of those who expect prices to rise and those who expect prices to fall, just as user costs are determined by the expectation of price rises and price falls. For the covered call, writers will be supplying the options for the buyers at a premium which is fixed by the balance between them. However, option pricing theory allows the value of options to be fixed without the existence of actual markets to set prices with reference to market conditions. This provides a response to the criticism of those who argue that the appropriate futures markets will not exist, or that the specification of expectations is purely subjective and thus irrational. Thus, instead of saying that supply prices have to be adjusted for user costs, we could say that supply prices which are corrected for the impact of the future on the present include the appropriately calculated values of the imbedded options.

This provides us with an understanding of why Keynes might have considered expectations relatively unimportant with respect to the short-period decision to produce. Consider the relation between spot and forward prices. If a commodity is purchased today to be held for sale in the future, interest costs will be incurred to finance the spot purchase. If expected future prices exceed current spot prices by more than this amount there is a profit to be made by buying spot and holding for forward sale. This would represent the user cost of the position.[11] If contracts can be drawn for forward delivery then there is a profitable arbitrage trade of buying spot and selling forward if forward prices exceed spot prices by more than the interest costs less the convenience yield. This will eventually bring the spot and forward prices into a relationship in which the market expectation of the forward price is given by the current spot price and the carry costs given by the rate of interest and convenience yield.

The calculation of present values requires the specification of future prices, discounted at the rate of interest. If future prices are given by spot prices plus the inclusive carry costs, then dividing them by the rate of interest will give spot prices. There is no need to formulate expectations about future prices – knowledge of current interest rates and current spot prices is sufficient to place a value on the commodity in any future period.[12] The present value of the expected future returns can be determined directly from spot prices without reference to expectations of future conditions, and from the appropriate interest rates. All reference to the relationship between expectations and realizations can then be eliminated.

In fact, once the idea of user costs as an option is recognized it is possible to go one step further and calculate the value of the ownership of productive capacity as equivalent to owning the plant and equipment, valued at the existing spot or scrap price, plus an option on the returns that could be generated from hiring labour to produce and sell the output from operating the plant. The exercise price of this option would be the payment of the prime costs of production, primarily wages and inputs.[13] Thus, the value of capital equipment could be determined directly from current spot prices and the value of the option to use the plant to produce future incomes.

Again, the absence of markets is no particular problem, as the formula for option values only requires information on the maintenance costs of the plant, its current operating costs, current output prices and any costs related to starting if the plant is not currently operating. All of this is currently available information and in no way requires specification of expectations or relies on comparing expectations with realized results.

But, there is one crucial additional piece of information which is required in order to calculate the option values. This is the volatility of output prices. The standard deviation of product prices is the only value which is not expressed in current market prices. It is the only 'unknown' which we still have to solve. But, this is precisely what is not, and cannot, be known. This is Keynes's point with reference to traditional theory. Only if the future replicates the past, only if we can use the calculus of probability and assume that realizations come from a stochastic process with zero mean and normally distributed errors, can we assume that past volatility is a good guide to future volatility. This, indeed, is the world of rational expectations. If we are not, and the future has an impact on the present, then Keynes's theory is fundamentally different from the traditional theory. If, as Davidson (1982–83) has argued, the world is not ergodic, or as Minsky has argued, if conditions of stability lead to endogenous changes in risk assessments, then volatility cannot be predicted from the past and there is no basis upon which we may produce an estimate of what it will be in the future. But, if volatility cannot be predicted correctly, then options prices cannot be calculated correctly. We are thrown back to the problem of how changes in the state of expectations are produced. It is the determination of price volatility which determines whether or not the economy is stable or unstable. Volatility will then determine stability and with it the process of capital accumulation. This is just another way of putting Keynes's basic point, that it is not realization of expectations, but whether or not their formation has an impact on the evolution of economic affairs which is of importance.

This is the explanation which Fausto Vicarelli gave. It was based on the impact on expenditures which results from the failure of households to calculate correctly the user cost of money generating an income multiplier process which changes conditions and thus causes a shift in expectations. Or by a failure on the part of bankers to calculate the user cost of money correctly yielding an expansion of loans and the money supply producing an auto-regressive impact on those decisions.

Obviously, Keynes's own explanation of expectations formation is based on his *Treatise on Probability*. It is important to note that Keynes distinguishes between the probability of the occurrences of possible states of the world and the probability of propositions concerning explanations of those states. The former relates to the objective occurrences of a natural process, while the latter relates to hypotheses upon which to base action. The former will produce stability, the latter instability because the former allows the prediction of future volatility from past volatility, the latter does not.

NOTES

1. 'Income, i.e. realized results as distinct from effective demand' (XIV, p. 180).
2. Keynes notes that 'a producer estimates what he will get for a product when it is finished when he decides to begin producing it to-day with the existing plant' on the basis of his short-term expectations (1936, p. 148; see also pp. 46–7).
3. As a rough analogy, it is impossible to determine if a long-distance train will arrive on time by comparing its average speed at any point during the journey with that required by the timetable, for it is always possible for it to make up or lose time until the scheduled arrival time is past. Indeed, it may require variable speeds in order to obtain open track.
4. Where Keynes also notes that this risk adjustment will tend to be variable, falling as the economy expands and thus reinforcing a boom and rising in a decline, reinforcing the duration of a slump.
5. Davidson (1987) is the major exception, but he notes that the concept has been primarily employed in the analysis of depletable natural resources.
6. Here, it is important to note that while Keynes's theory was grounded in effective demand, he himself identifies his major departures from traditional theory in the analysis of supply. Recall the argument that labour had no way of choosing its desired position on the labour offer curve. User costs made a similar point concerning the supply curve of output. This point is important, not only because one of the supposed failings of Keynes's theory which led to the crisis in Keynesian economics of the 1970s was the absence of the analysis of supply factors, but also, as Vicarelli points out, because the basic point of disagreement with the new Classical economics based on the rational expectations hypothesis concerns the specification of the supply curve (Vicarelli, 1985, p. 305) and the natural rate of interest. Thus, the specification of the theory of effective demand also implies a basic difference in the specification of the supply side.
7. This analysis is converted into spot-future price form in Kregel (1993).
8. To those unaccustomed to thinking in terms of spot and forward prices the idea may be seen by considering a commodity such as wheat. Today, at time t, the value of the commodity is given by its current market (spot) price S_t. To determine whether the commodity should be sold or held for future sale will be determined by the spot price, S^*, expected to prevail at some future date, $t + T$, T days distant. Alternatively, if there is a market where the commodity may be contracted for future delivery, the forward price quoted today at time t, for delivery in T days, will be $F_{t,T}$. In general the difference $F_{t,T} - S_t$ must be sufficient to cover the cost of holding the commodity for T days. This 'carry' cost may be defined as cS_t. If the difference $F_{t,T} - S_t$ were more than this a profit could be made by simultaneously buying the commodity spot and selling it forward, holding it for the T days to be delivered at $t + T$. The carry cost will include the costs of financing,

maintenance, storage, insurance, etc. In a balanced market, $F_{t,T} - (1 + c)S_t = 0$ and the present value of the commodity will then be given by $(F_{t,T})/(1 + c) = S_t$. The expected spot price should also equal the forward price, so $S^*_{t,T}=F_{t,T}$. However, if there is imbalance in the market and there are expectations of say a rise in price which is greater than c per period, then $S^*_{t,T} > F_{t,T}$ and the difference represents the profit sacrificed by current use, u. Then c must be adjusted for u to yield (c – u) as the carry cost for holding. This is also often called the 'convenience yield' of a stock of a commodity.

A decision to 'use' the commodity today, either by selling it or as an input in production means foregoing the gain in value which will occur between t and t + T, which is given by the present value of $F_{t,T}-S^*_t$, or uS_t. This is the 'user cost' associated with the commodity.

9. Note that user costs enter the calculation of both investment and consumer goods supply prices for the decision facing the producer of investment goods is the same as that facing the producer of consumption goods, to evaluate appropriate the prime costs of production including those from using non-labour inputs and capital equipment to produce today rather than in the future.
10. This analysis builds on an interpretation of Chapter 17 that I shared with Fausto Vicarelli. Its most recent version is Kregel (1996).
11. Recall that this cost is the equivalent, with opposite sign, of what is called the 'convenience yield' of holding stocks of a commodity. When we are dealing with capital equipment, excess capacity may indeed have a 'convenience yield' similar to stocks of primary inputs which should also be included in the 'user costs' of using current equipment at 'full capacity'.
12. If there is a convenience yield, then the appropriate discount rate would be the marginal user cost.
13. Cf. the analysis suggested in Brennan and Schwartz (1985).

REFERENCES

Brennan, M. and Schwartz, E. (1985) A New Approach to Evaluating Natural Resource Investments, *Midland Corporate Finance Journal* **3**, 37–47.

Davidson, P., 1982–83, Rational Expectations: A Fallacious Foundation for Studying Crucial Decision-Making Processes, *Journal of Post Keynesian Economics* **5**, 182–98.

Davidson, P. (1987) User Cost, in *The Palgrave Dictionary of Economics*, London, Macmillan.

Hamouda, O. and Rowley, R. (1996) Ignorance and the Absence of Probabilities, in C. Schmidt (ed.), *Uncertainty in Economic Thought*, Cheltenham, E. Elgar.

Keynes, J.M. (1930) *A Treatise on Money*, London, Macmillan.

Keynes, J.M. (1936) *The General Theory of Employment, Interest and Money*, London, Macmillan.

Keynes, J.M. (1973a) *The Collected Writings of John Maynard Keynes, Vol. XIII, The General Theory and After, Part I, Preparation*, London, Macmillan.

Keynes, J.M. (1973b) *The Collected Writings of John Maynard Keynes, Vol. XIV, The General Theory and After, Part II, Defence and Development*, London, Macmillan.

Kregel, J.A. (1977) On the Existence of Expectation in English Neoclassical Economics, *Journal of Economic Literature* **15**, 495–500.

Kregel, J.A. (1993) Keynesian Stabilisation Policy and Post-War Economic Performance, in E.Szirmai, B. van Ark and D. Pilat (eds), *Explaining Economic Growth*, Amsterdam, Elsevier, 429–45.

Kregel, J.A. (1996) The Theory of Value, Expectations and Chapter 17 of *The General Theory*, in G. Harcourt and P. Riach (eds), *The Second Edition of Keynes' General Theory*, London: Routledge, 251–72.

Minsky, H.P. (1986) *Stabilizing and Unstable Economy*, New Haven, Yale University Press.

Vicarelli, F. (1984) *Keynes: The Instability of Capitalism*, Philadelphia, University of Pennsylvania Press.

Vicarelli, F. (1985) From Equilibrium to Probability: a Reinterpretation of the Method of the *General Theory*, in F. Vicarelli (ed.), *Keynes's Relevance Today*, London, Mcmillan.

Vicarelli, F. (1985–86) Natural Laws and Economic Policy: Some Considerations on the Theoretical Foundations of the New Classical Macroeconomics, *Journal of Post Keynesian Economics* **VIII**, 298–314.

Comment

Augusto Graziani

I shall comment on four specific points touched upon in Jan Kregel's paper. They concern short-term expectations, the typical instability of a monetary economy, the distinction between micro- and macroanalysis, and the so-called crisis of Keynesian economics.

SHORT TERM EXPECTATIONS

Kregel remarks that in the *General Theory*, short-term expectations are always realized. This is of course totally correct. It may be worth adding that the complete realization of short term expectations is in some sense a condition for the very validity of the theory of effective demand.

Keynes makes the point that 'The amount of labour which the entrepreneurs decide to employ depends on the sum (D) of *two* quantities, namely D_1, the amount which the community is expected to spend on consumption, and D_2, the amount which it is expected to devote to new investment' (*General Theory*, p. 29). He also says that 'the behaviour of each individual firm in deciding its daily output will be determined by its short-term expectations – expectations as to the cost of output of various possible scales and expectations as to the sale-proceeds of this output' (*General Theory*, p. 47).

If we want output and employment to be determined by aggregate demand as determined by the actual behaviour of consumers and investors, we must also admit that producers are able to foresee correctly the level of 'the two quantities', or that they are able instantly to correct supply so as to keep it constantly in line with demand.

THE INSTABILITY OF A MONETARY ECONOMY

The definition of instability suggested by Kregel deserves some further comments.

Kregel considers as inherently unstable an economy in which future events influence current decisions. He also adds that instability is typical of a monetary production economy. Now the two definitions need not overlap in that in a monetary production economy present-day decisions are certainly under the influence of expected future events but it is not immediately clear why this should be so only in monetary economies.

In a monetary economy, by definition, money expenditure is required for any transaction, and therefore also for financing investment. Money holders compare the possible advantage of keeping money idle with the return expected from investment. If the first exceeds the second, liquidity yields more than any capital good and no investment will be undertaken.

In order to analyse this point, Kregel goes through an elaborate reasoning. He shows that, if correctly understood, the element of total cost named by Keynes 'user cost' is not only the excess of the actual cost of running a plant over the cost of keeping it idle, but more generally the opportunity cost of making use of a good now instead of using it in the future. As Kregel shows, a similar decision can be assimilated to the decision of an operator in the stock exchange.

So far, it seems that fluctuations in investment provoking instability in the entire economy are typical of a monetary economy. Kregel dwells at lenght on this point and develops a detailed reasoning in which he starts from the dual theory of prices developed by Keynes in the *Treatise*, and ends up by showing how, according to the state of long-term expectations, it can be more profitable for an investor to keep money idle instead of engaging in any productive activity. Kregel states however that the same reasoning commonly applied to money balances can be applied to real goods as well, in that the state of long-term expectations can induce an agent to keep a plant idle instead of operating it, just as it can induce to keep money idle. There are various possible outcomes resulting from the state of long-term expectations: (a) an agent can decide to keep money idle and to postpone investment; (b) the same agent can decide to keep his plant idle instead of using it for producing finished goods; and, finally (c) an agent can decide to keep his finished goods in stock instead of selling them on the market. The generalization introduced by Kregel in the definition of user cost allows him to outline a general theory of idle resources – idle resources being either money, or idle productive capacity, or stocks of finished goods. Even in a barter economy, it seems that the future can influence current decisions, just as it can in a monetary economy. The difference lies in the fact that in a barter economy no money is present; as a consequence, if the demand for investment goods declines, the demand for some other good must increase and no aggregate demand failure takes place.

In spite of the threefold dimension of idleness sketched by Kregel, it seems that, in a Keynesian framework of aggregate demand, the really relevant variable is investment and that the really relevant idleness remains the one connected with money balances.

It would seem, therefore, that, of the two definitions of instability put forward by Kregel, one based on the influences exerted by future expected events, the other on the monetary nature of the economy, the second should prevail.

MICRO AND MACRO ANALYSIS IN KEYNESIAN ECONOMICS

Kregel implicitly touches on the question concerning the relationships between macro and micro analysis in the Keynesian model. His point is that the Keynesian model is based on specific micro-foundations which are typical of a monetary production economy. In a similar economy, the behaviour of those who own productive capacity and must decide whether to use it or keep it idle, as well as the behaviour of those who own liquidity and must decide whether or not to invest it in new productive capacity is dominated by long-term expectations.

While it is unobjectionable that similar micro-foundations are different from the well-known traditional neoclassical micro theory, the question can be raised whether Keynesian macrotheory, or any other macrotheory, should really be grounded on microfoundations based on individual behaviour. While it is totally legitimate to start by analysing individual behaviour and derive a macro-theory by way of aggregation, it seems equally legitimate to proceed the other way round, namely by defining at the outset the structure of an economy according to its macroeconomic features and by deriving from this preliminary definition the individual behaviour that is consistent with the reproduction of the same structure.

In more than one way it might seem that the second procedure is the one Keynes had in mind. The way in which Keynes treats investment decisions, as clearly outlined by Kregel, is most significant in this respect. Keynes insists on the fact that the dominant variable in the decision to invest is not interest but the marginal efficiency of capital, and he adds that the presence of some seemingly irrational element cannot be ruled out (the famous appeal to the animal spirits of entrepreneurs). This as well as other elements present in the *General Theory* suggest that Keynes had in mind a monetary production economy in its macro-structure and that the pattern of individual behaviour he was trying to define was one not necessarily rational in itself but necessarily consistent with the perpetuation of the macro-structure he had initially defined.

THE DECLINE OF KEYNESIAN ECONOMICS

A final comment concerns an initial remark made by Kregel. Ironically, he says, Keynesian theory, a theory designed to demonstrate the instability of capitalism, was abandoned just when the golden-age of capital accumulation broke down – namely just when Keynesian theory was most urgently needed to explain the instability of market economies. Perhaps the succession of events appears more logical if the direction of change is reversed. The dominance of free-market ideology produced two main consequences. On the one side, Keynesian theory was replaced by a rehabilitation of neoclassical formulations, on the other side stabilization policies were abandoned. Both produced the break-down of what had been a long period of stability and growth. If, as Kregel might imply, Keynesian theory was abandoned 'as a result of the crisis', we might be induced to adhere to the widespread idea that Keynesian theory is no longer valid and Keynesian policies are no longer applicable. I do not think that this is the message Kregel meant to convey. Anyhow, it may be worthwhile emphasizing that this conclusion is far from having been demonstrated.

Comment

Guido M. Rey

In order to discuss Kregel's paper, I shall turn back to the method that Fausto Vicarelli and I used to adopt *while working together* – he would formulate the theoretical outlines and my task was to analyze the economic policy aspects and empirical components of the theoretical model. They were very pleasant moments that I recall with nostalgia and great sadness.

Kregel has the merit of having correctly set out Vicarelli's thinking in interpreting Keynes, as regards both the question of the instability of capitalism and his rejection of the idea of a capitalism based on natural laws that agents are able to identify, even where these laws are associated with probabilistic laws and can thus be formulated in conditions of certainty equivalence. Fausto was, therefore, convinced that there was an important and active role for economic policy and that one of its tasks was to reduce instability in order to foster real capital accumulation, since full-employment equilibrium could not be considered a stable equilibrium. His approach was based on a thorough understanding of Hicks's theory of capital and of the role of interest rate, which made it possible to introduce expectations concerning the dynamics of markets and to reason as if the future, which is generally expected by operators in an economy having a finite time horizon divided into periods defined in relation to the duration of capital, were known. Furthermore, he clearly appreciated the conceptual difference between the expected rate of return on investments and the interest rate on securities having the same time horizon, and in this respect he was highly critical of the Keynesian synthesis put forward by neoclassical economists. Lastly, Vicarelli also recognized that the role of the price of investment goods has to be considered in a different way to that of the price of consumer goods in the equilibrium of markets, both static and dynamic.

Vicarelli saw innovations as playing a fundamental role, as in the real world techniques could not be considered as given; indeed, technical progress was the disruptive force that made it impossible to reason in static terms or even in conditions of certainty equivalence. This brings me to the first consideration arising from my analysis of Kregel's work: the hypothesis of given techniques he adopts in developing his dynamic microeconomics. It is just a consideration, of which Kregel is perfectly aware, and therefore rather than as a criticism it is intended as a stimulus to deepen the study of this aspect of the model.

A model based on information and the role of information naturally cannot ignore this variable since the rate of innovation in the ICT sector, for example, is measurable in months and not in the years typical of consumer goods. Moreover, investment in research is so important that investing in government securities or similarly 'safe' assets does not really provide viable alternatives, since the risk attaching to the first type of investment cannot be compared with that associated with the second type and can only be borne by large investors and suppliers of finance.

The second aspect of the model that attracted my attention concerns the way in which Kregel treats expectations in the case of consumer goods, from the standpoint of both producers and consumers. His theory retraces many of the arguments embodied in the analysis of the instability of markets based on inventory cycle, and in fact inventories are the most obvious expression of uncertainty and mistaken decisions. If I expect rising prices, I will reduce today's supply to the market and build up inventories; this will cause prices to rise, up to the point and until the time at which expectations reverse and I increase the supply to the market, with adverse effects on employment. Such textbook models are well known and have served to explain the economic cycle on the basis of the analysis of inventories and expectations concerning actual demand. This would be in relation to the time needed to carry out new investments in order to equilibrate demand and supply at time t + n.

Their weakness, and unfortunately Kregel's model suffers from this inconsistency, is that the microeconomics of individual decisions is not always consistent with the aggregation at a macroeconomic level. For the economy to be governable, there must always be a counterparty, and this counterparty must have expectations that are inconsistent with those of the whole market. In order to address this issue, it is necessary to introduce a central operator with responsibility for equilibrating the market directly or indirectly. The operator's macroeconomic objectives must give priority to the stability of markets. In other words, a role is assigned to economic policy once more.

Another interesting aspect of Kregel's model is the introduction of 'user costs' as an option implicit in the supply price. The model, though, has the drawback of introducing a choice that does not seem to be within reach in reality, that of a producer who decides not to produce, not because he would make a loss but because he does not intend to forego a larger future gain and, therefore, prefers to remain liquid.

Even disregarding these monetary and institutional aspects, Kregel's model again fails to take the technological obsolescence of plants into account, so that this hypothesis is valid from the theoretical standpoint and for limited quantities, since re-entering the market generally entails high costs. The hypothesis thus applies to small investments by small businesses, perhaps to what in Italy we call the underground or irregular economy, but certainly not to the large firms typical of modern capitalism.

It is worth noting that the information structure of the model is better suited to describe small and medium-sized firms, which have a limited quantity of information and therefore must rely on the ability of the market to convey the information necessary for the market to operate efficiently. But this is the description of a perfectly competitive equilibrium that is far from the reality of the oligopolistic markets that characterize today's economy.

However, I believe that the above consideration enhances the importance of the thesis of Kregel's paper – the instability of capitalism – that his contribution develops by incorporating in his model the volatility of prices associated with the expected variability, or better the probability distribution, of expected prices.

By this means Kregel states that the presumed stability of the full-employment equilibrium cannot be demonstrated in a dynamic context. This is so even where there are arbitrage mechanisms that result in market prices incorporating the options associated with the decision to produce or purchase investment goods in order to reduce the disequilibrium between supply and demand in the different periods into which the time horizon of producers and consumers is divided.

Kregel's contribution is extremely important because he refocuses attention on the question of the instability of capitalism, basing his conclusions on dynamic aspects that had been forgotten by those who considered information to be a good available to all and failed to consider information asymmetry, by trusting in market arbitrage to incorporate this factor.

The question of the volatility of prices introduces a price distribution that is consistent with an imperfect-information model and hence to some extent inconsistent with Kregel's own, whereas he considers that the user cost of capital, or better the cost of foregoing liquidity, can be incorporated into production decisions; a hypothesis that is valid for the purpose of incorporating uncertainty, but not for forecasting the path of market prices (that is of prices in future markets if we also divide goods according to their availability at different times).

There is also a 'time' problem in the probability distribution of prices. If this distribution varies with their path, uncertainty becomes endogenous, so that it is no longer possible to relate expected prices to the present ones only, because these are not independent of the prices that will prevail in the future. The problem takes on special importance in connection with expectations concerning the future demand for goods that incorporate technical progress in both products and production processes, since the investment goods involved in the latter make far-reaching changes in the frontiers of efficiency and hence in expected prices.

6 The Relevance of Keynes's Thought on Financial Markets

Giangiacomo Nardozzi

INTRODUCTION

The relevance of Keynes (*Attualità di Keynes*) is the title of a book that Fausto Vicarelli edited in 1983, containing papers dedicated by leading Italian and non-Italian scholars to Federico Caffè at a conference held in Rome. Fausto arrived at Keynes by a complex path starting out from quite different interests. He was moved by a powerful ethical tension to envision and to try to unravel the essential problems of economics – those having importance for the present state of our society and, above all, for its future.

To speak of the relevance of Keynes's thought on financial markets affords me the opportunity to resume a dialogue, interrupted ten years ago, with one who was both friend and mentor. A dialogue founded on spontaneous conversations that started out from facts, were constantly underpinned by the doctrine and debates on the interpretations of economic thought, and generated hints to follow up or, in some cases, research projects.

It is in this spirit that I wish to set forth some simple ideas that I shall sum up in five points in support of the relevance of Keynes and in a short concluding illustration of how I have sought, and continue to seek, to translate this relevance into the practice of my work in research and newspaper comments on the behaviour of financial markets. To retrace the path from this work to a theoretical systematization that will develop Keynes's thought is a hard task, surely beyond my powers. But already the attempt to understand how markets actually work in Keynesian uncertainty enables us to perceive – 'on the spot', so to speak – the limits of the dominant theory that, as Hyman Minsky wrote, 'may satisfy the politicians need for a villain or a scape goat, but . . . offers no useful guide to a solution of the problem' (Minsky 1986).

FIVE POINTS IN SUPPORT OF THE RELEVANCE OF KEYNES

The first point is that today, as never before, we live in a monetary economy in the Keynesian sense. In an economy where money is a device for accumulation of wealth that serves to protect us from the uncertainty largely generated by the monetary nature itself of the capitalistic organization of production as described by Keynes in his draft of the General Theory of 1933 (Keynes, 1933). As in Keynes's time so today, the importance of the concept of a monetary economy lies in its contrast with a cooperative or, for Marx, mercantile economy, where the influence of money can be regarded 'as something so to speak separate from the general theory of supply and demand' (Keynes, 1936, Preface). But it also lies, and to a greater extent than in Keynes's time, in the fact that uncertainty takes on more weight the morc wealth is accumulated in assets immediately convertible into money, like financial assets. As Minsky states, Keynes's theory offers the best description of the 'Wall Street Economy' in which our wealth increasingly relies on the financial markets. In financial markets the Keynesian 'urge to action' finds its fullest realization, and hence the ways in which that action tries to overcome the uncertainty that might obstruct it take on extraordinary importance.

The second point is that we are currently faced with a problem of particular significance in Keynes's theory. Unfortunately, this problem is generally addressed with instruments that, even if updated, still remain pre-Keynesian. The problem I have in mind is how to govern the financial markets that cause interest rates to undergo movements that are ample and unexpected but characterized by a downward rigidity around values that, in real terms, are very high with reference both to the history and growth of the economies. This problem, which is central to the General Theory, is now a very serious one, and is recognized as such at the summit meetings of the countries that govern the world economy.

Over the last fifteen years the long-term nominal rates of the leading countries as a whole have fluctuated widely in a decreasing trend as compared to the peaks at the beginning of the 1980s, which were only seldom recorded since the beginning of the nineteenth century. The real rate has also been falling, but has levelled out at a stable trend around a value still high in the history of capitalism – namely, double the mean rate of growth.

This phenomenon defies explanations based on the neoclassical fundamentals of thrift and productivity and their variants, on which the international institutions have concentrated, especially the OECD (Dean *et al.*, 1990; European Commission, 1994; OECD, 1994).

The rate of saving of the G-7 countries fell during the 1970s, but in a proportion only slightly greater than the simultaneous reduction in the rate of capital accumulation (Ciocca and Nardozzi, 1996; Group of Ten, 1995). The diminution in the propensity to save can largely be accounted for by the increase in public deficits. But the empirical evidence of an effect of increasing public deficits on interest rates remains inconclusive (Group of Ten, 1995). On the other hand there is evidence of a positive correlation, for the countries as a whole but not individually, between real rate and public debt/GDP ratio (Phelps 1994; Helbling and Westcott, 1995; Izzo 1996). But this econometric evidence is not supported by the theoretical arguments regarding the links between public debt and interest rate. In particular, the evidence fails to confirm the idea of a correlation between growing public debts and greater risk of easy monetary policy and hence of inflation, since the increase in the ratios of debt to GDP occurred between the 1970s and 1980s while inflation was notably diminishing. On the other hand, a reduction rather than an increase is recorded in the capital productivity of industry which should reflect the scarcity of private capital crowded out by the public debt, as well as the expected rate of return that regulates the position of the neoclassical schedule of investments (Ciocca and Nardozzi, 1996). Also the variant of the theory, that locates the cause of high real rates in the strong demand for capital by the more recently industrialized Asian countries and the economies in transition, is found to be unsatisfactory by the very upholders of the thesis of capital scarcity (Group of Ten, 1995). The same can be said of the opinion which holds that the increase in rates can be retraced to the removal of administrative controls in some countries (*ibid.*).

The third point is that in public opinion and among the operators there is now a very widespread demand to understand the behaviour of the financial markets. It appears increasingly difficult to fathom the why and wherefore of the price fluctuations of financial assets. This not only because they run counter to the trend of what the pre-Keynesian economics of the textbooks dubs 'fundamentals' (thrift, productivity, inflation) but also because often the markets appear inconsistent, giving opposite meaning to the same information on the variations of the same variables; or obstinately concentrating exclusive attention on certain variables in one period, then immediately afterwards on other variables (as emerges from research on the behaviour of the New York Stock Exchange in Nardozzi (1995)). This demand for comprehension of the behaviour that dominant economic theory seems unable to satisfy may suggest a reappraisal of Keynes, seen as a theoretician of the irrationality of the markets, of the uncertainty that allows them to function only on the basis of whims, the instinct of animal spirits, imitation. And this may be a reason for the tiny group of scholars opposing the dominant theory to take heart. But to go any further will not involve focusing on the precarious elements in the psychology of the financial markets that set 'speculation' against 'enterprise', on 'When the capital development of a country becomes a by-product of the activities of a casino, the job is likely to be ill-done' of Chapter 12 of the *General Theory*. Such orientation threatens to spill too hastily over into other disciplines (like the psychology of behavioural finance which, unmindful of Keynes, seeks to bridge the gaps in the present economic theory (the *Economist*, 1994)); it deserts our own discipline before that discipline has expressed what it has to say on a purely economic matter like the determination of prices of financial assets. And it risks leaving a person who asks us for enlightenment on the behaviour of financial markets with the flat alternative between believing an ever present informational efficiency moving prices according continually changing expectations on the fundamentals, or believing them to be subject to elements of irrationality, to be examined in detail elsewhere, that preclude the aforesaid efficiency.

The fourth point in the relevance of Keynes lies not in the fact that the frequently disorienting behaviour of the markets stems from irrationality; but, rather, the opposite – namely, that the markets are swayed by international investors of huge dimensions who employ large resources in order to satisfy a highly rational need to understand the overall economic picture that will provide them with some certainty upon which to operate, as Keynes said, without losing their sleep. A conviction, that is, enabling them to act on the basis of the objective datum constituted by the Keynesian probability not subject to human whim but rationally deduced from the circumstances. Here is the most interesting ground that economists should continue to till. Because, among other things, it involves the closest, most fruitful contact between our profession and those who govern, control or, in the case of the investors, make the financial markets. Valid above all in this area is the lay attitude (of which Fausto Vicarelli, though a deeply religious man, was master) that in academic controversies between schools of thought succeeds in seizing the point that almost always characterizes them – namely, the fixing on questions relating to ambits, to problems of different kinds that, as such, may assume more or less importance according to specific situations. Anyone professionally concerned with financial markets will ultimately be scarcely interested as to whether or not their behaviour is rational in accord with economic models of prices of financial assets. What professionals really want is the understanding of the reasons of the market that may refer to all kind of considerations and to different models according to the circumstances.

If this is the demand coming from financial professionals to economists, then we find a fifth point in support of Keynes. That is the philosophy of practice, of what can reasonably be believed in order to act in given circumstances, rather than what is true or false on the basis of a given economic theory, which is important for understanding the behaviour of financial markets. This is precisely the message coming from Keynes's method (Carabelli, 1988). The guide to action consists of what can reasonably be expected. This reasonableness implies the formation of judgements that are probable because reasonable (rational beliefs) which can be relied on (because what Keynes calls the weight of the argument is good), where the probability, not understood as calculation of frequency of events, depends on the amount of relevant knowledge favourable or unfavourable to a proposition. The relevant knowledge is made up of information, or reasons, varying according to circumstances. The choice, the selection of such knowledge from the huge mass of available information, is performed by means of a judgement on the circumstances of an essentially intuitive nature that circumscribes the information to be considered. This idea of the probable as that which is reasonable and remains so even if the predictions produced by it turn out to be unconfirmed by what actually happens, is the key suggested by Keynes for an analysis of the financial markets that proves useful both for investors and central bankers.

The pursuit of reasonable judgements in order to be able to act is the task constantly performed by financial markets – a complicated task, with two orders of difficulty. The first is that the relevant knowledge available may be insufficient to form rational beliefs in which even a certain amount of confidence can be placed (the weight of the argument is too low). The second is that probabilities can hardly be measured quantitatively. They may be put in order of more or less probable, but they may equally turn out to be not comparable owing to the diversity of the reasons underlying the relevant knowledge of them (Carabelli, 1994). These reasons may be mutually conflicting: for instance electoral reasons may conflict with an increase of central bank's interest rates in order to forestall inflationary expectations or the fitness of containing a speculative bubble may suggest a rise in rates not motivated by the trend of inflation. Only when these difficulties do not allow reliance on rational judgment is recourse had to whims, to instinct, to imitation, or the decision is postponed (preference for liquidity).

PUTTING THE RELEVANCE OF KEYNES INTO PRACTICE

These five points, in my view, call for an analysis of the behaviour of financial markets starting out from their need to reach rational beliefs in Keynes's sense. This type of analysis entails 'field' research attempting to identify how, in the shifting contingencies of history, the market seeks to attain the formulation of judgements – just as the scholar should do, according to Keynes's philosophy. Where by 'market' I mean the operators who obtain and process the information in order to shape rational beliefs that spread by imitation, thus giving rise to a convention.

Ciocca and I embarked on this research to understand the phenomenon of the high cost of money that has by now been a characteristic of the leading economies for fifteen years (Ciocca and Nardozzi, 1996). We sought to identify the facts considered, and the schemes of interpretation adopted, by the markets in periods crucial for the evolution of interest rates. Straining Keynes's thought, we called these by the name of 'conventions': meaning that they are produced not by twists and turns in the mass psychology of a large number of ignorant individuals, but by the rationality of informed individuals pursuing reasonable judgements grounded on all the elements that are considered decisive for action (here following the interpretation of Joan Robinson as recalled in Nardozzi (1996)). And we showed how these conventions worked to produce exceptionally high real interest rates between the end of the

1970s and the mid-1990s. In this work, dedicated to Fausto Vicarelli, we tried to apply Keynes's approach to account for a stylized fact, the high cost of money, that emerges from consideration of a long period. But the same approach can be followed in analysing the behaviour of the financial markets so as to get a basic knowledge, so to speak, that will enable us to find our way around among the sudden and often unexpected shifts in securities prices and, also, better to understand the possibilities of governing them. Here the reference is not to the episodes of daily or very short-term volatility in which trading is performed, but, rather, to the price fluctuations that are important both for the strategies of investors and for the central banks and governments.

This analysis of the reasons of the financial markets starts out from consideration of the behaviour of securities prices in the light of the interpretations supplied by the markets themselves with the opinions of operators (reading the *Times* . . .), analysts, institutions whose daily bread is the situation of the markets. These interpretations constitute the material from which inductively to extract the information, the facts, that combine to make up the relevant knowledge and the confidence accorded to the rational beliefs formed from it.

The evidence supplied by this material is very plentiful and may provide a variety of indications. I shall here confine myself to noting some more general ones that currently seem to bear on the problem of governing the financial markets.

The knowledge relevant for the markets seldom consists of stylized facts concerning the trend of the aggregate (G-7 or G-10) made up of the leading economies; and hence the fundamentals (saving, investment) that, according to pre-Keynesian theory, should regulate the common trends of interest rates.

Normally, as we know from the practice of macroeconomic counselling, the knowledge relevant for the markets starts from what is happening at the centre, from facts regarding the economy and the economic policy in the United States, Japan and Germany. The prime difficulties in arriving at an opinion usually concern the United States. The problem stems from the particular flexibility of American capitalism, in as much as it is able to stand a wide variability in rates of inflation, unemployment, interest and exchange. This flexibility is especially reflected in monetary policy which unfolds in a context that takes account of several elements, hence of a variety of reasons (in the Keynesian sense), that may come into conflict with one another. In its code and its practice, the US central bank enjoys much more freedom of action than its German counterpart in the trade-off between growth and inflation. It is also particularly attentive to the stability of the financial system since it has to face the world's most sophisticated, most innovative, most restless financial markets; it is sensitive to the electoral cycle leading to renewal of the administration, and cannot ignore the effects of its policy on the trade war with Japan and the coverage of the huge current account deficit. All of which compels the financial markets to choose from among conflicting reasons, and induces shifts in the relevant knowledge and wavering between different rational beliefs. This is much less the case with the other two economies of the centre, the Japanese and the German, which are highly structured, the former around a model containing strong elements of planning and the latter around one in which the independence of the central bank and the maintenance of monetary stability serve as a continual point of reference. As regards Japan, the main reason for uncertainty in the financial markets lies in the relations with the United States. In view of the impact that movements in the US and Japanese financial markets have on the rest of the world, this reason is of fundamental importance in establishing a hierarchy in which first place is taken by the relations between the United States and Japan, with Germany in a subordinate position. By now, this hierarchy, which counts as 'fundamental' for professional investors, has come to be used by the markets to resolve the uncertainty stemming from the cyclical lags between the US and European economies and that stemming from the contrasts between German and US monetary policy. Proof of this are the problems of decoupling between the German, and hence European, rates and the US ones.

Rational beliefs on the predictable behaviour of the centre provide an important guide for choosing the relevant knowledge to make judgements on other countries. Significant here is the impact of such behaviour on the specific situations of the individual country that, as we know, provokes wider fluctuations in the interest and exchange rates for the countries at greater risk. The interest of the international investors in these countries, and hence the size of the fluctuations in their interest and exchange rates, depend on the earning opportunities that, in the judgement of the investors, occur on the markets of the centre. When on these markets there seems to be nothing further to earn, one moves to the markets at greater risk. This attitude has recently been theorized by the house of J.P. Morgan (The *Economist*, 1996; Morgan 1996) which has devised an index of the appetite for risk that depends on the conditions obtaining in the markets of the leading economies. When in these markets the interest rate is low and there is little volatility, the appetite for risk grows and there is an upward movement of the exchange rates and of the prices of securities of the countries at greater risk. According to this study, which might almost have been suggested by Keynes, the appetite for risk belongs in what are called 'regimes' of few months duration, the succession of which generates the long-term path of exchange rates. The advice to the investor, at whom this study is aimed by one of the leading operators on the markets, is to try to understand the regime in which the market operates in order to obtain an outperformance.

According to this view, accentuated movements in interest and exchange rates can be accounted for by the uncertainty that may arise regarding the monetary policy of the United States, by the uncertainty stemming from problems of coordination among the three leading countries, by the alignment of the German rates to the US ones, by the situation of the financial markets of the centre that may urge reallocation of portfolios towards the peripheral countries, by the return towards the centre, called 'flight to quality', as soon as either the opportunities have been fully exploited or problems arise in these countries, even as an effect of their initial attraction for investors (Mexico). The reasonable judgements that determine these movements are shaped by different kinds of information and reasons that vary in time, where news or expectations regarding the fundamentals, especially inflation, often are only their starting point (I refer to the judgements that take root generating the price fluctuations that influence the strategies of the investors and the central banks, rather than the day-to-day movements of prices that often react to proxy news of inflation). These judgements, which involve all sorts of considerations, are however able to modify the fundamentals through the effect of the interest rates on the trend of the economies and on public deficits. Soros's statement to the effect that 'We create the fundamentals' may take on a dual significance: that it is the investors who decide what is important in shaping their judgements; and that it is these judgements that affect what economic theory dubs the 'fundamentals' (and also the behaviour of the central banks).

From these very summary hints at the evidence coming from the practice of macroeconomic counselling to operators on the financial markets and from the press, it can be seen that the relevance of Keynes lies also in the fact that the investors responsible for the fluctuations of prices of financial assets are themselves far more Keynesian than the majority of the economists who interpret these prices. Keynesian not only in the sense that their activity is guided by what can be reasonably expected on the basis of rational beliefs which they continually pursue by evaluating the mass of circumstances; but also in the sense of starting out from the complexity of governing the economy in order to shape these judgements. If that is true, then it is an illusion to suppose that the problem of governing the financial markets can be solved by applying the simple recipe that emerges from the periodic meetings between the economic ministers and the governors of the central banks of the leading countries: namely, to confront the markets with significant steady progress in containing public deficits and reducing inflation – that is, in the pre-Keynesian fundamentals – and vigilance over the phenomena of volatility in order to control it. Such a recipe is of scant importance for markets governed by investors who actually operate according to Keynesian rationality-reasonableness in conditions of uncertainty. For the distinction between price movements justified and not justified by these fundamentals does not tally with the process of formation of rational beliefs in which the relevant knowledge is not exhausted by the trend of public finance and inflation; to be sure, these latter may be part of it, but they may be lesser reasons or contrast with other reasons drawn from the knowledge.

Reasons other than the trend of the fundamentals of public finance and inflation will continue to sway the behaviour of the financial markets even in a future that envisages the alignment of the leading countries with further reduced public deficits and an almost zero risk of inflation, together with a broad-based single European currency. At which point, to be sure, the markets will no longer have to take account of the risk of inflation, and the movements of interest rates now generated by investors shifting among the EU countries will calm down as these countries adopt the single currency. But the new context will itself give birth to other reasons. The attention of the financial markets, currently attracted inter alia by analysis of the opportunities offered by the individual countries of the EU, will focus on the relations between the United States, Japan and the Euro countries as a whole. The size of the market of this bloc will call into question the hierarchy that currently acts as a guide to reduce the uncertainty stemming from the comparison between the three capitalisms, US, Japanese and German. European economic policy will become rigid, both at fiscal and at monetary level. And at that point – since it can no longer be brushed aside with the recipe of the fundamentals and no longer confused by the divergences or convergences of the European economies – we shall find ourselves face to face with the problem of government of the economy that was most dear to Keynes: how to devise a policy to contrast the instability of capitalism stemming from uncertainty. The reasons of the healthy finance and monetary stability may be outweighed by the uncertainty posed by the confrontation between the Euro bloc, the United States and Japan; or by the effects of too rigid fiscal and monetary policies on the growth of the European economies and on unemployment, which could undermine social cohesion.

What elements have we for believing – as governments would like us to believe – that the financial markets will settle back on the fundamentals of pre-Keynesian theory and, with the 'fundamentals' for reasonable action continually created by them, will cease to generate instability and to keep the real cost of money high?

NOTE

I acknowledge the help of Anna Carabelli and Pierluigi Ciocca for their comments on a previous draft of this paper.

REFERENCES

Carabelli, A. (1988) *On Keynes's Method*, London, Macmillan.

Carabelli, A. (1994) Keynes on Mensuration and Comparison, in K.I. Vaughn (ed.), *Perspectives on the History of Economic Thought*, Aldershot, Edward Elgar.

Ciocca, P. and Nardozzi, G. (1996) *The High Price of Money*, Oxford, Clarendon Press.

Dean, A. *et al.* (1990) *Saving Trends and Behaviour in OECD Countries*, Paris, OECD Economic Studies.

The *Economist* (1994) *Mind over Matter*, 23 April.

The *Economist* (1996) *Time to Whet Investors' Appetites*, 24 February.

European Commission (1994) *Recent Developments in Long Term Interest Rates and Their Implications*, II/618, Brussels.

Group of Ten (1995) Saving Investment and Real Interest Rates, A Study for the Ministers and Governors prepared by the Deputies, *typescript*.

Helbling, T. and Wescott, R. (1995) *The Global Interest Rate*, Staff Studies for the World Economic Outlook, Washington DC, IMF.

Izzo, L. (1996) The High Level of the Expected World Return on Financial Assets during the 1980s and the 1990s: a Tale of Tequila Effects, *typescript*.

Keynes, J.M. (1933) The Distinction Between a Cooperative Economy and an Entrepreneur Economy, in *The Collected Writings of John Maynard Keynes vol. XXIX*, London, Macmillan.

Keynes, J.M. (1936) *The General Theory of Employment, Interest and Money*, London, Macmillan.

Minsky, H. (1986) *Stabilizing an Unstable Economy*, New Haven and London, Yale University Press.

Morgan, J.P. (1996) Investors' Changing Appetite for Risk: A New Approach to Short-run Developments on the Foreign Exchanges, *Foreign Exchange Research*, 10 July.

Nardozzi, G. (1995) Il mercato interpreta la propria volatilità: evidenze dalla borsa di New York (1976-92) utili per un miglior dialogo tra economisti e operatori, in G. Nardozzi (ed.), *Rapporto IRS sul mercato azionario*, Milano, Edizioni Il Sole-24 Ore.

Nardozzi, G. (1996) Joan Robinson and the Rate of Interest These Days, in M.C. Marcuzzo, L.L. Pasinetti and A. Roncaglia (eds), *The Economics of Joan Robinson*, London and New York, Routledge.

OECD (1994) *Economic Outlook*, Paris, OECD.

Phelps, E. (1994) *Structural Slumps*, Cambridge, MA, Harvard University Press.

Vicarelli, F. (ed.) (1983) *Attualità di Keynes*, Rome-Bari, Laterza.

Comment*

Marcello de Cecco

According to economic textbooks, a high real interest rate should bring a rise in the savings rate and cause private investors to increase their private commitment to fixed-rate securities. The opposite was true last year. The seasonally adjusted savings rate in 1995 ranged between 12 per cent (first quarter) and 12.5 per cent (fourth quarter); the Bundesbank's reading for the first quarter of 1996 was an unchanged 12.6 per cent. During this period, however, the real interest rate rose above 5 per cent, thus marking a multiyear high. Looking back on the past two decades, we note that a high real interest rate does not automatically boost savings. What encourages people to increase their savings is a high nominal rate, or a minimum rate level. The current minimum rate is 7 per cent; in the previous interest-rate cycle (1978 to 1985) it was slightly higher (about 8 per cent). Nominal rates at or above this level attract private investors to fixed-interest securities. If the nominal rate for 10-year bonds is below this level, purchases by private individuals – traditionally the principal investor group in the bond market – tend to be measurably restrained . . . It is a well known phenomenon . . . that the savings rate falls when the nominal rate declines. In the mid-1970s and early 1980s, for instance, when fixed-interest securities produced double digit yields, savings rates – 16.2 per cent in 1975 and 14.8 per cent in 1981 – were at the upper end of the multiyear range. In the years of the lower rates, by contrast, when the coupon rate for public bonds temporarily showed a 'five' before the decimal point, the savings rate was at a modest 12 to 13 per cent.

The above passage is music to the ears of the Keynesian true believer. It confirms, with figures from the real world experience of a contemporary developed country, Germany, what Keynes stated as his theory of the rate of interest in 1936. The passage is all the more remarkable because it is extracted from *Money and Capital Markets,* a Newsletter issued by the Bayerische Landesbank. The anonymous drafter of the Newsletter demonstrates total ignorance of Keynesian theory, as he states that neoclassical theory is economic theory. He is certainly not engaging in a tongue in cheek experiment. He is perfectly honest, and his results become, because of his earnestness, all the more credible. In the passage, we find not only Keynes's nominal interest rate theory, but also his theory of the critical rate of interest. A little later, the unknown German economist adds that, having in mind a critical rate of interest, German investors have shunned bonds in 1996 because they 'tend to park funds from maturing investments as well as new savings in . . . low-yielding but highly liquid investments. Savings deposits, for example, were up about DM 45 billion at mid-year on year end 1995, while bond purchases by non-banks in the first six months of the year showed a decline of more than DM 50 billion.

'It is difficult to say when private individuals will return to the bond market,' the unknown German economist continues. 'In the light of past experience, however, it would seem safe to predict that buying interest will remain tepid as a "six" appears before the decimal point'. To make it absolutely sure that he has rediscovered liquidity preference theory, our German economist concludes his analysis by stating that 'If interest rates stay at a low level, the gap between short-term and long-term rates will increase the risk for "parkers"'.

These are thus good times for Keynesian economics, as it tends to be independently rediscovered by non-Keynesian economists, who totally ignore that what they just found out was completely mapped and charted exactly 60 years ago.

Our unknown German economist, who is probably quite young, can be pardoned for ignoring Keynes's contribution to interest rate theory and his theory of liquidity preference. In German universities, because of unfortunate historical experiences, Keynesian theory is tainted with dirigism and that smacks of nazi and communist totalitarianism. It has, therefore, with notable exceptions, been for all practical purposes expunged from economics syllabuses for the greatest part of the post-war period.

Keynes and his monetary theories ought to be known, however, to such learned leading-edge economists as Messrs. Sala y Martin and Mulligan. They teach, respectively, at the University of Chicago and at Columbia University. In a very interesting paper, which appeared in the CEPR Discussion paper series in March 1996, they study the 'application of financial technologies' by members of the American public, and from what they find they derive implications for money demand and monetary policy.

In the 'non technical summary' of their paper they resume their findings as follows: 'The paper argues that 59% of all US households do not hold any interest-bearing assets, and 53% of those who hold cheque accounts do not hold any interest-bearing assets'. How to explain this remarkable fact? The key point – according to our authors – is that, in order to use (interest-bearing) assets, households must 'adopt the technology' and this adoption is costly. The financial technology is costly in the sense that people must be financially skilled to programme their choice spreading their savings between interest-bearing and non-interest bearing assets. Education they find to be a good proxy of financial skill. Moreover, there is a certain intercept in the quantity of assets held from which the holding of interest bearing assets starts. This intercept they call the extensive margin. Its relative height is determined by nominal interest rates. Therefore, rational people will forgo the potential yield from interest-bearing assets and stay with zero-yielding assets if they are not skilled enough to make the investments and if they do not have enough total assets. There is therefore a certain entry-level which depends on total financial wealth, on education, and on the nominal interest rate.

Here we have a rediscovery of Hawtrey plus Keynes. It is a pity that neither the first nor the second are mentioned in the text or the extensive bibliography appended at the end of the paper.

Liquidity preference is therefore alive and well, even if it is called by other names, in Chicago and at Columbia University. What better proof can we provide of the relevance of Keynes's monetary thought? As to the formal ignorance of his writings demonstrated by our two examples, we can conclude by remembering what the great Italian jurist Piero Calamandrei used to say in his lectures: 'How lucky it was that the Library of Alexandria was burned so many centuries ago! Had it remained in existence, how many original works would have not seen the light in our era!'

NOTE

Editor's Note
*This comment, although unrelated to the paper being discussed, is published all the same owing to its intrinsic interest.

Part IV

Social Choices, Economic Policy and Moral Values

7 Setting and Monitoring Poverty Standards: Drawing on the Parallel with Macroeconomics

Anthony B. Atkinson

This paper has its origin in my concern to integrate consideration of economic and social policy. Economic and social issues are too often discussed in isolation, whereas they are deeply interconnected. We cannot separate economic and social policy. As I argue in the paper, macro-economic policy interacts with anti-poverty policy.

I hope that this choice of subject is an appropriate one for this paper in memory of Fausto Vicarelli. While I try to present an objective analysis, I conclude with a definite policy recommendation. The paper combines the detachment of the academic economist with social commitment to the combating of poverty. What I am arguing in this paper is the importance of an official poverty line. Reducing poverty should become an explicit object of policy. There should be a poverty target, which governments accept as a commitment and there should be an official *Poverty Report* assessing how far the target has been reached.

This draws on the parallel with macroeconomics in a way that I shall describe in a moment, but first I should explain that I am concentrating here on poverty in 'rich countries', like Italy and – my particular focus – the United Kingdom. In so doing, I am not suggesting that poverty in Africa, for example, is less important. I should make clear at the outset that I regard poverty on a world scale as a problem of even more pressing significance. It is indeed my own personal judgement that world poverty has a *priority*. At the same time, I do not accept that this leaves no room for consideration of poverty in the countries of the European Union. This is a proper subject of our concern.

DRAWING A PARALLEL WITH MACRO-ECONOMIC PERFORMANCE TARGETS

In October 1992, after the pound left the Exchange Rate Mechanism, the UK government launched a new macroeconomic strategy, at the heart of which was a formal target for the rate of inflation. Although low inflation had been long an avowed objective, there had not previously been an explicit quantitative performance standard. The government now announced its intention to keep inflation within a range of 1 to 4 per cent. These were fine words, and the problem was to make them credible. Credibility was sought by increasing the role of the Bank of England, including the innovation of introducing a quarterly *Inflation Report* (for example, Bank of England, 1993), providing statistical evidence about inflation and its prospects, together with a commentary. Quite a number of countries have adopted inflation targets. As the IMF Survey recently observed: 'they provide a transparent guide to the conduct of monetary policy, whose commitment and credibility can be assessed' (11 November 1996).

The argument I am making here is that those concerned with the abolition of poverty can draw on the parallel with macroeconomics. It is not an exact parallel, but there are at least two reasons why it is relevant. The first is that macroeconomics has been remarkably successful in its public relations. A large proportion of political attention, and media time, is devoted to macroeconomic issues. As a result of the Keynesian revolution, aggregate economic performance has come to have first call on our attention, with issues of distribution appearing irregularly and less urgently in political debate.

The second important reason is that choices made in the macroeconomic sphere have profound implications for the achievement of social objectives. Nowhere is this more apparent than in the case of the Maastricht criteria. Achievement of the convergence criteria may require a level of employment which seriously damages the earnings prospects of the poor; adjustments in public spending may directly reduce the incomes of the poor. This has been recognized by those European Union governments which have argued for employment targets to be placed alongside those for government borrowing and debt.

Here I am taking the logic still further and arguing for a poverty target. In a European context, it would mean adding such a target to the convergence criteria. In the case of the UK, this would mean adopting for the first time an official poverty line.

DECOUPLING POVERTY STANDARDS AND BENEFIT SCALES IN THE UK

The fact that Britain does not have an official poverty line may appear remarkable in view of the predominance of poverty among the concerns that led to Britain having a social security system with largely flat-rate benefit scales: that is, benefits which are £X per week rather than a percentage of previous salary. It is however the ambiguous relation between the two – poverty standards and benefit scales – which may account for the failure to adopt a transparent national target. The ambiguity was evident in Beveridge Plan of 1942 which was the blueprint for the present social security system in the United Kingdom. Beveridge stated that: 'social insurance should aim guaranteeing the minimum income needed for subsistence' (1942, p. 14), and presented his proposed benefit scales as achieving that objective. But subsistence was not the only consideration influencing the determination of benefit scales. He was also constrained by what could be afforded and the need to keep tax rate down (Veit Wilson, 1989).

The ambiguity persisted when social investigators in the post-war period looked for a standard to judge the effectiveness of the welfare state. In their book published in 1965 which drew public attention to the persistence of poverty in post war Britain, called *The Poor and the Poorest*, Brian Abel-Smith and Peter Townsend (1965) took the National Assistance benefit scale as their starting point when measuring poverty, and later authors, including myself (Atkinson, 1969), followed their lead. The shortcomings of using benefit scales to measure poverty are however evident. As Abel-Smith and Townsend were well aware, any improvement in the assistance scale leads, on this basis, to an *increase* in measured poverty.

OFFICIAL POVERTY LINES IN THE EU AND THE USA

The problem is that there is no official poverty line in Britain. The government has been hostile to this idea. Indeed, one of the objectives of the Conservative party when in government in the UK was to attack the notion of poverty which had been adopted by the European Union. Whereas the British government has no official poverty line, the European Commission has established such a criterion, stating that: 'the poor shall be taken to mean persons, families and groups of persons whose resources are so limited as to exclude them from the minimum acceptable way of life in the Member States in which they live' (Commission of the European Communities, 1989, p. 9).

This is the definition contained in a decision of the Council of Ministers when approving the first Community Action Programme to Combat Poverty. In its evaluation of the Programme, the Commission took as the concrete implementation of this definition a poverty standard of 50 per cent of the average disposable income per equivalent adult in the country in question.

There can, therefore, be said to be an official European Union poverty line. And there are countries which have official lines, of which perhaps the best known is that in the United States. In 1964, when the War on Poverty was declared by President Johnson, the Council of the Economic Advisers defined the poverty line as a $3,000 a year for family and $1,500 for a single person. This was based on research by Mollie Orshansky, who subsequently produced a refined, more differentiated, poverty line adopted by the Office of Economic Opportunity (Orshansky, 1965). In 1969, the Bureau of the Budget issued a statistical policy directive which gave a modified version of the line official status throughout the Federal Government.

Although the US poverty line plays a role in the allocation of federal funds and in the determination of some individual benefits, there is an important separation between the poverty line and the determination of benefits: they are essentially decoupled. There is no guarantee that the cash transfer programmes will bring people up to the official poverty level. In January 1992, under the Aid to Families with Dependent Children programme, the maximum benefit, in the median state – since it varies by state – for a single parent family of three was only 72 per cent of the poverty threshold (Committee on Ways and Means, 1992).

The official poverty line is the basis for the US Bureau of the Census Current Population Report, *Poverty in the United States*. Recent reports (for example, US Bureau of Census, 1993) show that about 15 per cent of the US population, or some 35 million people, were living in families with incomes below the poverty level.

Figure 7.1 Comparative poverty rate: 1980–94

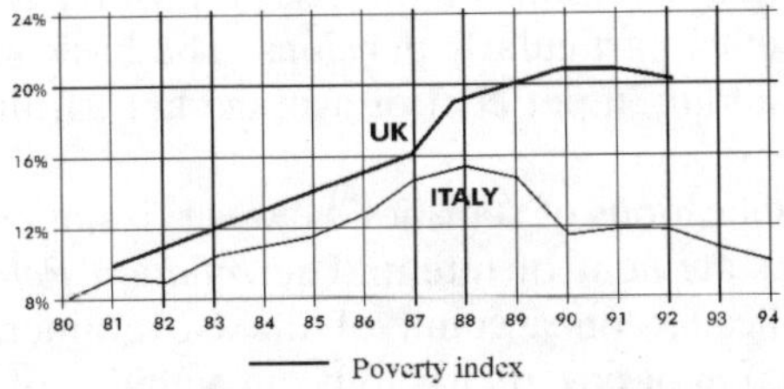

Fifteen million people live in families with incomes below *half* the official poverty line.

Such an official poverty report is published in Italy too. The Commissione di indagine sulla povertà e sull'emarginazione has produced a very valuable series of reports, including that on *La povertà in Italia 1980–1994*. This shows that the poverty rate in 1994 was around 10 per cent and that there had been a modest rise and then fall over the period from 1980, see Figure 7.1. The poverty rate reached a peak of 14.8 per cent in 1988.

AN OFFICIAL POVERTY LINE FOR BRITAIN?

The question we are asking in Britain is whether we should adopt an official poverty line decoupled from benefits scales. Should we interpret the poverty standard as performance target, like the 2.5 per cent for the rate of inflation? The parallel with inflation targets suggests, moreover, that the credibility of the government's commitment to this target could be significantly enhanced if we follow the Bank of England's innovation of the *Inflation Report*, and introduce a regular *Poverty Report* on the extent and the nature of poverty.

The nucleus of such a report already exists in the form of the valuable publication *Households Below Average Income* developed over the past 10 years by Department of Social Security (for example, 1995). If the official poverty line were to take the form of a percentage of mean income, as with the European Union poverty standard, then we already have much of the necessary material. This report shows, I should add, that the proportion below the poverty line was about the same as in Italy in 1981 – around 9 per cent – but increased very sharply to 20 per cent in 1992–93. Even if the levels of these figures are not comparable, the differences in the trends are striking and can be related to the policies pursued. In the UK one major reason for the rise in poverty is the cutback in the state benefits, particularly pensions. The basic state pension has fallen from about 30 per cent of average net earnings to about 20 per cent.

The simple publications of statistics, however, is not enough. What is required is a statement of intent. The *Inflation Report* acquires its special significance on account of the Government's inflation target. The reduction of poverty has to be an ambition of the Government, just like the reduction of inflation. The figures in the *Poverty Report* have to be seen as indicating how far we are from achieving a national goal.

RELATION OF POVERTY LINE TO SOCIAL SECURITY BENEFITS SCALES

Essential to the proposal is that the official poverty scale should be set independently of social security benefit scales. It is important to keep these separate. The poverty target is an *objective*, social security benefits are an *instrument*. The national performance standard, and the political commitment, would be set in terms of *outcomes* rather than social transfer policy instruments. The government would be committed, not to rising child benefit by £X, or pensions by £Y, but to reducing poverty. The outcome will of course depend on the choice of benefit levels, but it will also depend on other policies. As already noted, macroeconomic policy can potentially play an important role.

Separation of objectives and instruments means that we have to recognize that our aspirations run ahead of the current constraints. In terms of Tinbergen's theory of economic policy, the abolition of poverty is a *flexible* rather than *fixed* target (Tinbergen, 1952, 1954). Whereas the latter specifies policy objectives in absolute terms (the balance of payments must be in equilibrium or the borrowing requirement not exceed X per cent of national income), a flexible target is one that indicates the direction in which we are aiming but where it is recognized that there may be limits to the extent that it can be attained and to the speed of progress towards the goal.

In Europe we have seen the dangers of fixed targets, in the Maastricht criteria. I would like to see the fixed fiscal targets replaced by more flexible criteria. By the same token it does not seem reasonable to see the elimination of poverty as a fixed target. (We may here want to draw a distinction between poverty and destitution. There should be two levels of target.) Rather, it is a flexible target, the attainment of which is limited on account of the constraints faced by the government. Beveridge may have claimed in his 1942 Plan that the level of the subsistence standard determined the level of social insurance benefits, but in reality the choice of targets was influenced by what was feasible. Behind his proposals lay a balancing of the benefit levels with considerations of cost and incentive constraints. No one can reasonably expect poverty to be ended overnight.

THE CASE AGAINST A NATIONAL POVERTY OBJECTIVE

The adoption of such a performance standard may seem entirely natural. As Dr Johnson said: 'a decent provision for the poor is the true test of civilisation'. A national poverty indicator would provide a focus for such a concern, and the *Poverty Report* would inform public debate. The press and media would find such a poverty standard simple to describe, and there would be clear topical interest in the performance according to this target. In the United States, newspapers know when the annual poverty count is to be released and line up academic commentators. The regular performance test would contribute to keeping the issue on the public agenda.

What then are the arguments against? The first set of arguments are that we could not agree on the definition of a poverty line and contents of the *Poverty Report*. Academics disagree about fundamental conceptual issues; pressure groups disagree about their implementation. The second objection is that we can define an official line but its adoption would not contribute to the reduction of poverty. It would be mere rhetoric and make no difference. The third objection is that it *would* make a difference but in the wrong direction. It would be counterproductive.

Finally, there are those who can see no reason why a government should agree to a performance target. Why, for example, should politicians agree to a poverty target forming part of the European project? These then are four objections that I want to consider in the remainder of this paper.

COULD WE AGREE ON A POVERTY TARGET?

For some people, inflation is not regarded as a problem: they do not see why its reduction should be a national goal. Others feel that hyper-inflation is a problem, but that is not relevant to Britain. Latin American countries are the ones who need to worry about inflation. The same is true of poverty. Some people do not regard it as a problem. Others say that there is no poverty in Britain, feeling that this is only be found in 'underdeveloped' countries.

There is bound to be disagreement about national goals. Even among those who support the reduction of poverty, there is, as noted above, much disagreement about its definition. The academic literature is replete with discussion of the difficulties in defining a poverty line. From this literature may be seen the problems with the European Union 50 per cent poverty line. For some, the definition will already have closed too many options. It may not be adequate to measure poverty in terms of income, rather than expenditure, or the consumption of specific commodities, such a food or shelter. Income may be an intermediate variable, rather than an end in itself, allowing people to achieve a certain level of capabilities. For others, it will have left open too many questions. In work with Karin Gardiner, Valerie Lechene an Holly Sutherland (1993), I have shown how a '50 per cent of average income' criterion can be interpreted in very different ways, leading to quite different comparative rankings of different countries.

All of these pose formidable problems, and it is far from clear that we could agree on a national target. At the same time, there are four considerations which make the task of agreement easier.

First, there is an important difference between agreeing on a criterion according to which benefits are to be paid and agreeing on a definition for purely statistical purposes. We do not have to worry about the feasibility of the administrative apparatus for determining benefit eligibility. If it is an aggregate poverty statistic that is the end of product, then a certain amount of approximation may be acceptable. The simplicity of a '50 per cent of average income' criterion is positively an advantage in terms of transparency when it comes to public debate. There does not have to be the fineness of classification necessary to ensure horizontal equity in the payment of benefits. Members of Parliament will not find their constituents complaining because they have been left out of the poverty total!

Second, it may be possible to identify common ground even where there is not complete agreement. People may prefer an imperfect measure to one that matches their ideal in all respects. They may agree that the poverty line for a single person should be at least £X a week, even if they do not agree how much higher it should be. We may therefore set an official standard which the majority regard as too low, but which very few regard as too high. In his assessment of the US poverty line, Joseph Kershaw said that 'it worked' because: 'Although the definition undoubtedly classifies some people as nonpoor, it classifies very few nonpoor as poor' (1970, p. 13). Third, *one of the objects of the Poverty Report* is to divert attention from a single number. The *Report* should present a range of information, as well as informed commentary. The range will no doubt include different poverty cut-offs: the US Bureau of Census shows people living at 50, 75, 125, 150 and 175 per cent of the official poverty line. There will be different poverty indicators (for example with different equivalence scales, or different methods of up-rating over time), just as the Bank of England publishes different inflation rates (RPIX, RPIY, and so on) in its *Inflation Report*.

Finally, one hopes that the *Poverty Report* will contribute to the development of the poverty standard in a dynamic way. A good example is the research undertaken on family budgets, building up from individual budget items the costs of a 'modest but adequate' and a 'low cost' standard (see, for example, Bradshaw *et al.*, 1992). These budgets perform the valuable function of helping translate percentage of average income, or cash amounts, into actual living standards.

WOULD IT MAKE ANY DIFFERENCES?

One dismissive response to the proposal that the UK should have an official poverty line is that the Americans have had one for thirty years and it has made no difference. Indeed, the US record on anti-poverty policy is worse than that of European countries.

This dismissive view is not shared by all American observers. Among the few who have commented on this issue, the general opinion seems to be that it *does* make a difference. According to J. Tobin, writing in 1970:

> the Federal war on poverty, whatever else it has accomplished, has established an official measure of the prevalence of poverty in the United States. Administrations will be judged by their success or failure in reducing the official measured prevalence of poverty. So long as any families are found below the official poverty line, no politician will be able to . . . ignore the repeated solemn acknowledgements of society's obligations to its poorer members.
> (Tobin, 1970, p. 83)

This assessment was quoted approvingly some two decades later by Robert Haveman (1987) in his evaluation of the impact of social science research.

Nevertheless, it is an objection which one has to take seriously. The experience of the US may not carry over to Europe. How would the establishment of a national poverty target and publication of the *Poverty Report* affect government policy towards the poor? Economists often pride themselves on not being interested in rhetoric and may well feel that it is the substantive policy on which we should concentrate. It is not relevant what people *say* they do; all that matters is what they actually *do*. On the other hand, many non-economists believe that stated objectives are relevant, and that it may be useful to distinguish between these and the preferences which appear to underlie observed policy choices. Moreover, people may be led to change their priorities.

In order to explore this, we need to consider the motives which influence political choices by the different actors – or the theory of political behaviour/public choice. The answer clearly depends on the model of behaviour supposed to apply to the government. Many such models have been proposed and there is little consensus as to the most appropriate. Moreover, the most appropriate model is likely to vary over space and time. None the less, there is likely to be an element of 'principal/agent' in any explanation. The electorate, as 'principal', has to make choices between different manifestos in the knowledge that its 'agent', the government, will make the operative decision in the light of the information available at a subsequent date. Political parties are offering a 'contract'.

Viewed in principal/agent terms, there is evidently a difference between a contract written in terms of objectives and one written in form of policies. Which is preferable in terms of the final outcome is open to debate. Where there is a close link between policy and outcome, then a commitment to specific policy measures may be more effective. Suppose that voters choose between political parties each with a set of policy commitments/expectations, but after the election these commitments prove to be inconsistent with the constraints, such as those on public spending. When these conflicting commitments come to be reconciled, a specific promise to raise pensions by £Y is likely to strengthen the bargaining power of the Secretary of State for Social Security more than a generalized commitment to a national poverty performance standard. The latter can, after all, be addressed by other policy measures which do not involve public spending. But the latter argument is also the strength of the poverty performance standard. It provides grounds for raising the issue of combating poverty in all spheres of government policy. Cabinet papers from all ministers would have to include a statement as to how their proposal contribute to the reduction of poverty.

WOULD A NATIONAL POVERTY OBJECTIVE BE COUNTER-PRODUCTIVE?

Would the existence of the poverty target however have adverse effects? In planned economies, it was alleged that targets distorted government decisions in favour of the chosen objective and against other worthy goals (as epitomized by the tired joke of the Soviet factory which met its output target in weight by producing a single nail). The risk that the government would minimize the poverty statistics to the disregard of all other functions of social transfer is a major ground for concern, since the objectives of such transfers are much broader than the alleviation of poverty. They are intended to smooth income across the lifetime, to redistribute towards those with dependants, to provide for adversities such as sickness and disability which involve a loss of income but not necessarily poverty, and to provide a general sense of security. Although it would be small protection, I would like to see the terms of reference of the *Poverty Report* include a requirement to comment where an improvement in the poverty figures had been achieved at the expense of other social goals.

A narrower version of the same objection is that, if the government is to be judged on its poverty performance, then it may concentrate on those policies which lead to improvement in the particular chosen indicator (for example helping those who are just below the poverty line but not those more in need). It seems to me however that this is less potentially serious. The risk can be moderated by careful choice of the measure and by use of multiple indicators. The purpose of having a *Poverty Report*, rather than simply publication of the statistics, is that the commentary would draw attention to the limitations of the indicators and the emergence of the new forms of deprivation.

The introduction of the *Poverty Report* could, alternatively, have a negative impact by crowding out substantive measures to help the poor. Whether this would happen depends on the constraints on government action. If the binding constraint is public expenditure, then it seems unlikely that this is a serious obstacle. The main issue is that of 'political capital', and this mergers with the question whether or not the proposal would be accepted by any politician.

WHY SHOULD ANY POLITICIAN ACCEPT SUCH A TARGET?

Why should any politician accept such a poverty commitment? The answer I believe lies in the same reason for John Major's adopting the inflation target – the search of credibility. Let us take the case of the European Union. The European project is currently facing difficulty on account of the Maastricht criteria. Many confirmed Europeans are having doubts on account of the adverse effects of fiscal contraction on social problems. The fiscal criteria are adversely affecting employment and incomes of the poor. Adoption of a definite, if flexible, target for the reduction of poverty may reassure those who are concerned about the social dimension.

Of course, there may be a direct conflict with the fiscal criteria. At the same time, it may allow changes to be made in the structure of public spending. People may accept fiscal austerity if they are reassured that the weakest will be protected. It may be possible to scale back public spending in general if there is a guarantee that cuts will not fall on those below the poverty line. Moreover, as I have emphasized, anti-poverty policy is not just a matter of public spending. Employment policy, training programmes, and health policies may contribute as much or more to the reduction of poverty.

CONCLUSION

This paper has had an academic purpose, which is to examine a question which seems surprisingly little discussed – what would be the role of the institution of an official poverty line and the publication of an official *Poverty Report*. It has also had a missionary purpose, which is to argue the case for adopting this approach. I accept that there are legitimate grounds for concern, particularly that it would focus attention on the anti-poverty function of social transfers to the exclusion of other functions, but on balance I feel that there is a good case for the UK to introduce an official poverty line which is decoupled from benefit scales, to which there is a national commitment, and for there to be an official *Poverty Report* documenting and interpreting performance in the light of this performance standard.

The same applies at the European level, where a poverty criterion should be considered along side the fiscal criteria of the Maastricht Treaty. At the 1995 Copenhagen Summit on Social Development, the British Government, and other European governments, committed themselves to plan to: 'establish . . . strategies and affordable time-bound goals and targets for the substantial reduction of overall poverty and the eradication of absolute poverty.'

I have proposed one way of making a reality of that commitment.

NOTE

The present paper draws heavily on Atkinson (1996).

REFERENCES

Abel-Smith, B. and Townsend, P. (1965) *The Poor and the Poorest*, London, Bell.

Atkinson, A.B. (1969) *Poverty in Britain and the Reform of Social Security*, Cambridge, Cambridge University Press.

Atkinson, A.B. (1996) Promise and Performance: Why We Need an Official Poverty Report, in P. Barker (ed.), *Living as Equals*, Oxford, Oxford University Press.

Atkinson, A.B., Gardiner, K., Lechene, V. and Sutherland, H. (1993) *Comparing Poverty in France and the United Kingdom*, Welfare State Programme Discussion Paper 84, LSE.

Bank of England (1993) *Inflation Report*, Bank of England Quarterly Bulletin, February.

Beveridge, Lord (1942) *Social Insurance and Allied Services*, Cmd 6404, London, HMSO.

Bradshaw, J., Hicks, L. and Parker, H. (1992) *Summary Budget Standards for Six Households*, Family Budget Unit WP 12, University of York.

Commission of the European Communities (1989) *Interim Report on a Specific Community Action Programme to Combat Poverty*, Bruxelles, European Commission.

Commissione di indagine sulla povertà e sull'emarginazione (1996) *La Povertà in Italia 1980–1994*, Rome, Presidenza del Consiglio dei Ministri.

Committee on Ways and Means (1992) *US House of Representatives Green Book*, Washington, DC, US Government Printing Office.

Department of Social Security (1995) *Households Below Average Income 1979–1992/93*, London, Department of Social Security.

Haveman, R.H. (1987) *Poverty Policy and Poverty Research*, Madison, University of Wisconsin Press.

Kershaw, J.A. (1970) *Government Against Poverty*, Washington, DC, Brookings Institution.

Orshansky, M. (1965) Counting the Poor: Another Look at the Poverty Profile, *Social Security Bulletin*, **28**, 3–29.

Timbergen, J. (1952) *On the Theory of Economic Policy*, Amsterdam, North Holland.

Tinbergen, J. (1954) *Centralisation and Decentralisation in Economic Policy*, Amsterdam, North Holland.

Tobin, J. (1970) Raising the Incomes of the Poor, in K. Gordon (ed.), *Agenda for the Nation*,Washington, DC, Brookings Institution.

US Bureau of the Census (1993) *Poverty in US*: 1992, Washington, DC, US Government Printing Office.

Veit Wilson, J. (1989) *Memorandum. House of Commons Social Services Committee, Minimum Income*, London, HMSO.

Comment

Luigi Frey

There is room for agreement with A.B. Atkinson who states that the fight against poverty must be seen as closely related to macroeconomic policies. I agree with the two reasons he puts forward, namely the political *visibility* of macroeconomic strategies and the extent to which such strategies can *exert their effect* on social problems (especially when we consider the consequences of poverty and, more generally, of social exclusion brought about by unemployment). However, in my view it is important to add yet another reason.

Problems of poverty, and of human development generally, must in fact be viewed in relation to the medium and long-term *growth* of economic systems; indeed, the latest UNDP report on *Human Development* (UNDP, 1996) emphasizes the part played by this relationship for countries in different areas of the world. Such growth must be structurally balanced and seek to pursue the overall aims of human development. Macroeconomic strategies for growth, quite apart from those concerned with currency and price stability, become particularly important in the way they affect poverty trends in the various economic and social systems. This means that growth policies, with special regard to structural policies for investments (material and human), so dear to Fausto Vicarelli, acquire decisive importance for the fight against poverty in the wider field of human development.

However if the problems of poverty are to be considered in this perspective, a new definition of poverty has to be found and *synthetic indicators* have to be identified in order to clarify, in quantitative terms, the objectives to be pursued (as is done for the rate of inflation, to which Professor Atkinson devotes special attention).

Recent improvements in research work and in the attempts to measure indicators of human development have led to the conviction that income – even in its distributive aspect that helps to identify the means or medians from which concepts of the poverty line originate – is too limited a reference. In the first place indicators for education and health should also be included: the latter being of particular importance in economic and social systems where elderly people are present in increasing numbers. Further studies and discussions within the European Union (see European Commission, 1993) have taken the concept of social exclusion far beyond its connection with poverty lines, so that other components of *malaise* are included as well and here the question of satisfying needs for housing and personal safety (with regard to European countries) is also raised. It is no accident that emphasis is laid on aspects of *extreme poverty* (such as the homeless).

Furthermore these studies on the meaning of social exclusion press for reference to positive, rather than negative, concepts/indicators of social development, just as did the discussion on the results of the UN Copenhagen Summit (see Copenhagen Declaration, 1995).

It is also the case that it would be worthwhile establishing an *official poverty line* which could then become a simple point of reference like the rate of inflation. The fight against poverty could be based on this standard and appropriate macroeconomic strategies could be applied together with measures to stabilize currencies and prices. It must, however, be said that while this is not so simple as would appear at first sight (as R. Livraghi's researches on income distribution are showing: see Livraghi, 1996), the choice of a simple reference, compared with a more complex though more exhaustive course of procedure, does not make it any more likely that such a reference would be acceptable to those responsible for working out economic and social policies.

Reference to an example relating to problems of employment may be useful. It goes without saying that this is a matter of great concern in all European countries since unemployment is tending to increase; it is also widely recognized that the question of poverty, or of economic and social *malaise* generally, is related to unemployment. At the beginning of the 1990s an attempt was made to identify a very simple indicator (in the negative sense the rate of unemployment, in the positive the rate of employment) to place alongside monetary and financial indicators which, once accepted at national level, could be adopted as 'criteria of economic convergence' at the European level. Through a committee of experts formed at the DGV of the European Commission, I personally pressed for acceptance of the 'rate of employment', but the idea was rejected, partly because it was not considered acceptable to risk 'polluting' macroeconomic policies to the point of delaying or even adversely affecting the pursue of monetary and financial stability, and partly because paradoxically, the proposal itself implied the need for more articulated and complex indicators (for example, the rate of unemployment + the rate of unemployment among young people + the rate of long-term unemployment).

Might it not be advisable, in this context, for experts in social sciences to try to work out indicators that, while synthetically expressed, may also take proper account of the complexity of the problem to be tackled in the medium and long term by adopting strategies of economic and social policy with special attention being given to macroeconomic policies? In view of the limits of international 'convergence' now accepted by the bodies dealing with these policies at a national level, would it not seem advisable for experts to work out indicators that cannot only be used in national policies but can also be integrated and compared at international levels? The research made by the Luxembourg Income Study (LIS) into the comparability of information on income distribution among various countries comes to the conclusion that much can and must be done especially if we are to arrive at *official* indicators that can be translated into objectives of economic and social policy.

These remarks have not been made idly and it is hoped that they will be taken into account when drawing up and publishing official reports on problems of poverty, or rather, of social development for all. Agreement may be expressed with Professor Atkinson on the advisability of drawing up an official report at a national level that clearly sets forth the state and evolution of the problems of poverty, explicitly and precisely linking them to the economic and social policies adopted and/or proposed (particularly with regard to macroeconomic policies). The problems that have emerged from official reports on poverty in Italy (promoted by the Prime Minister's office: through the Committee on Poverty), and still more what appears from extensive experience gained by reports on problems of exclusion and social development in Scandinavian countries (see the contributions in the book edited by Frey, 1994), suggest the need for analyses and proposals that definitely go beyond a simple reference to the poverty line and the position of those concerned in relation to it.

Experience gained in Scandinavian countries further suggests how a fairly satisfactory basis can be created for comparing and integrating information on exclusion, or rather on social development, at an international level. Though somewhat hesitantly, the European

Commission is slowly moving along the same lines, in collaboration with Eurostat and urged forward by CEIES (a consultative committee on which users of statistical information are well represented; see material edited by Frey, 1994) and by a group of experts known as the 'Siena Group', so named because it was formed following a seminar in honour of Richard Stone held at Siena in 1993.

To what extent can Professor Atkinson's idea of an official British report on the problems of poverty be seen in the same light? It must be recalled, among other things, that in the United Kingdom the ONS produces a great deal of information on social problems (published annually in *Social Trends*) and that there is a large and growing collection of information and analyses by experts and research centres on social problems in which Professor Atkinson takes a leading part.

Would Professor Atkinson, who runs an important research centre (*Sticerd* at the London School of Economics) dealing with problems of social development and social policies, be willing to extend his role of drawing up and publishing official reports on poverty in the United Kingdom (thereby furthering the active participation by Britain in the slow process going on in Europe) and press for a clear statement on the aims of social development as part of balanced growth strategies in the European Union over the medium and long term, along the lines partly set forth in what is known as the Delors report?

Professor Atkinson has shown recognition of the work done by Professor Caffè and by our colleague Fausto Vicarelli. In view of the ideas expressed and the unceasing dedication of both Caffè and Vicarelli to the cause of a balanced social development, I feel sure that they would have wished to collaborate in any initiatives promoted by Professor Atkinson in this direction.

Anyone wishing to take an active part along the lines traced out by our so highly valued colleagues and friends will surely be ready, as far as may be possible, to participate in research and other activities (at national and European levels) that may be undertaken (jointly or singly).

REFERENCES

Commissione d'indagine sulla povertà e sull'emarginazione (1996) *La povertà in Italia 1980–1994*, Rome, Presidenza del Consiglio dei Ministri.

Copenhagen Declaration (1995) *Copenhagen Declaration and Programme of Action*, Copenhagen, World Summit for Social Development.

European Commission (1993) *European Social Policy, Options for the Union*, Department of Employment, Industrial Relations and Social Affairs, Green Book, Luxembourg, EC Publications Department.

Frey, L. (1994) (ed.) Lavoro e Benesserc. La costruzione di indicatori sociali, *Quaderni di Economia del Lavoro* **49–50**, Milan, Angeli.

Livraghi, R. (1996) I recenti perfezionamenti delle informazioni sulla distribuzione dei redditi e una migliore conoscenza della problematica del lavoro in Europa e in Italia, in L. Frey, (ed.) Le statistiche sul lavoro in Europa, *Quaderni di Economia del Lavoro* **56**, Milan, Angeli, 51–83.

Office of National Statistics (ONS), *Social Trends*, London, HMSO, (published annually).

UNDP (1996) *Human Development 1996*, New York, Oxford University Press.

8 Social Paradoxes of Growth and Civil Economy

Stefano Zamagni

INTRODUCTION

'The problem with reliance on the market as a moral code is that it fails to give moral credit to those whose sacrifices enable others to consider themselves freely choosing agents. By concentrating on the good news that we can improve our position, rather than the not-so-good, but socially necessary, news that we might consider the welfare of others as our direct concern, the market leaves us with no way to appreciate disinterest'.[1] While in agreement with the descriptive content of this statement, I would not endorse its conclusion. Indeed, my argument is that a too narrow interpretation of the notion of market economy has brought us to believe that 'the market leaves us with no way to appreciate disinterest'. I believe it is time to re-examine that very foundation of economic theory according to which rational economic man is conceived as a calculating self-interested maximizer. I argue for a more realistic and solid view that takes into account the possibility of visualizing a market society as composed of both a private economy and a civil economy.

As it will be shown in the following pages, civil economy is constituted by a kind of contract but not by a trade contract. Civil economy is based on the consent of its citizens that equals the consent of a contract of private law but it is a contract only by analogy. I will show that it is a contract only by analogy, not by identity with trade contracts. My hypothesis is that underlying the root of the development process there is the phenomenon of institutional reciprocity, that is the creation of social structures capable of engendering a flow of voluntary exchanges on the basis of mutual expectations of retribution. This is the basic idea underneath the notion of a civil economy strategy to overcome the many social paradoxes of growth.

CIVIL SOCIETY AND ECONOMIC DISCOURSE: A HISTORICAL PERSPECTIVE

Has the economic discourse something relevant to say on civil society issues? In this section I will try to find an answer to this question and I will do so on the basis of a historical perspective. An important line of research was opened up in Italy in recent years by scholars like R. Scazzieri, P. Porta, C. Poni, O. Nuccio[2] and others, enabling us to recognize the connection between civil society and the economic system, more specifically highlighting the multifaceted, profound significance of the relationship between the concepts of competition and civil society. This relationship 'does not represent a mere juxtaposition but a two-way implication' (p. 15) in that 'civil society and competition go together' (p. 52). While I am referring to Porta and Scazzieri (1996) for a more thorough analysis of the subject especially concerning the appropriate evaluation of the influence of the French tradition of 'Jacobin engineering', it is worthwhile to consider the historical path of what can be called the tradition of thinking in the field of civil economics. This tradition goes back to fifteenth-century 'Civil humanists', a tradition developing with ups and downs to the economic thinking of Italian enlightenment – the school of Lombard economists (C. Beccaria, P. Verri, G.D. Romagnosi) and above all that of Neapolitan scholars (P.D. Doria, F. Galiani, A. Genovesi) – and the more sophisticated theoretical conceptualizations of the Scottish enlightenment (A. Ferguson, D. Hume, A. Smith).

Among Italian renaissance authors, the following are noteworthy: Matteo Palmieri, whose *Della vita civile* (Of civil life), written in the middle of the 1430s, is of paramount importance; Leonardo Bruni, Chancellor of the Florentine Republic; Antonino da Firenze, Florence's Bishop; Bernardino da Siena to whom we owe the first organic contribution centred on the functioning of a civil economy. In his 1427 *Prediche*[3] Bernardino da Siena elaborates an argument that in present time language can be cast as follows.

There are two sets of moral rules: rules that can be conceptually expressed in the form of reputational human capital (they imply the subject's awareness that by infringing the norm he or she is going to incur substantial personal costs, as his or her reputation will undergo a severe loss because of this immoral behaviour) and rules whose enforcement depends upon constraints of a more internal nature, that is the agent's moral disposition. These moral rules, while highly beneficial to society, may bring no direct profit to those abiding by them. Such are all rules aimed at minimizing or neutralizing various opportunistic behaviours, from *free-riding* to *shirking*, which are the source of a society's decadence. This dichotomy generates a formidable question: to produce and enforce the first group of moral rules all one needs is a consistent body of laws combined with a well-oiled justice machinery as well as with external incentives in the form of reputational capital – in substance, a solid *private* economy – while to provide society with the other set of moral infrastructure one has to intervene upon the internal motivational structure of individuals, namely, upon their deep-rooted acceptance of shared values, which is tantamount to saying that a sound *civil* economy is required. In conclusion, in the long-term perspective, a market economy is sustainable providing both legs – the private one and the civil one – are able to function.

Concerning the contribution of the Italian enlightenment thinkers, I would like to point out that beyond undeniable differences among authors, what they all have in common is the stress on relationality as the essential feature of a person, a true anthropological assumption, from which the conclusion derives that the really scarce resource in economics is to be found in interpersonal relations. As M. Palmieri states in his *Della vita civile* (Of civil life): 'of all beings, man is the most useful to man. Thus he cannot hope to obtain from a different source the goods he can get from his fellow creatures'. This was also Giambattista Vico's position when, formulating his first law of society's evolution, he wrote that decadence sets in when individuals fail to find within themselves reasons to tie their own life to the life of others, not when material resources are becoming scarce. Along a similar line, Romagnosi writes in 1827: 'Political economy in general should embody the order of civilized societies . . . The unrestricted individual greed for wealth is attuned without subsiding by the continuing action of a well-built civil society, so that we have at the same time individual greed and intemperance but also participation and social equity'.[4] Along the same lines and, for some aspects, even more forcibly, scholars of the Neapolitan School express themselves, particularly Antonio Genovesi (*Lezioni di economia civile* – Lectures on civil economics, 1765) to whom we owe one of the first explanations of the reasons why man's economic behaviour is governed jointly by his soul's disposition and by material incentives so that a genuinely civilized society should not create an institutional setting that practically favours behaviours based on the latter, at the expense of those founded on the former. In other words, precisely because the gratification of ideal motives is as legitimate as that of natural impulses, a society claiming to be civil should not *a priori* discourage the growth of the former to the exclusive benefit of the latter.

Finally, a few words on Scottish enlightenment scholars, whose thematical horizon presents quite a few affinities with that of their coeval Neapolitan thinkers. In order to grasp the significance of their contribution to our present discussion, it is necessary to dwell on the influence exerted by the two main theories of political philosophy – contractualism and evolutionism – upon the attempts to justify the existence of coercive institutions, *in primis* the State. I am thinking here of the convergence as well as of the insurgency theories.

Hobbes is the most famous champion of convergence theories within the social contract tradition. The contractualistic model is based upon the distinction between the state of nature and civil society, the latter being in fact identified with the State. According to Hobbes, the process by which civil society is formed is identical to that through which the State is formed. In fact, state of nature is not yet civil society, but the 'war of everyone against everyone else'. The social pact or contract, on the other hand, putting an end to the state of nature and creating civil society, coincides with the creation of the Leviathan to whom all individual rights to self-governance are conveyed. Since the contract takes place between self-interested individuals and not between a sovereign and his subjects, it is conceptually impossible for the sovereign ruler – whether a monarch, an oligarchy or a democracy – to violate the pact. One can infer that no subject may ever feel released from obedience to the State whose specific purpose is the deliverance of people from the threat of war. This is how Hobbes's famous statement 'the purpose of obedience is protection' should be understood. Within the contractualist perspective the political result is right because it is rationally acceptable by anyone, not because it satisfies some independent criterion stating that something is right.

The notion of state of nature and the need for the contract to justify a given social-institutional setting were soon criticized by Hume, who fathered the theory of insurgency. Hume rejects the relationship established by Hobbes between individual motives and the features of the institutional setting. In the vision of Scottish moralists, the civil society's order appears not as the product of a 'project' but as the spontaneous consequence of behavioural norms that individuals learn to develop gradually in the course of centuries. The evolutionary approach of the Scottish school, more specifically of A. Smith's, suggests that the interaction of free agents may originate an order at the same time natural – because of its spontaneous occurrence – and artificial in that it is founded on the acceptance of social conventions. Therefore, if according to Hobbes the omnipotent State is the creator of civil society, Smith maintains that the latter comes conceptually before the State. So much so that in the absence of a well articulated civil society the prerequisite for the growth of the economic system, that is, the division of labour, is not existing.

In fact, the specialization resulting from such division, while positively affecting the system's productivity – as admirably depicted in Chapter I of *The Wealth of Nations* – tends to have a very negative impact on the 'poor', that is labourers performing the lowest jobs in the productive process. Chapter V of *The Wealth* offers a penetrating analysis in which the negative consequences are ascribed to the loss of 'versatility' (nowadays it might be called alienation), caused by the process of division of labour. It is, therefore, necessary for the 'government' to intervene in the realm of economic activities to prevent negative effects from exceeding the positive ones because such a condition would hamper the primary invisibile hand mechanism, namely market competition. For the market institution to be a lasting one in time, civil society must foster citizen's 'inclination' and 'disposition' to exchange, which in turn imply interaction between the market's invisible hand and the government's visible one. For if it is true that self-interest may suffice to ensure a frictionless coordination of economic decisions – albeit, as Smith puts it, 'not under the most pleasant circumstances'[5] – the society within which such coordination is due to take place is bound in the long run to break up unless the norms of justice are at least to some extent complied with, for justice 'is the main pillar upon which the whole edifice of human coexistence rests' (ibid.)

To sum up, in the evolutionist perspective, market and State stand out as the epitome of a covenant – due to repetitive transactions among subjects – whose nature was to make these basic institutions pass the acceptance test thanks to the stability they managed to achieve: they benefit everybody even though nobody was engaged in convergence procedures. One should note however that all this implies the existence of a civil society capable of keeping under control, by appropriately balancing them, such moral sentiments as self-interest and 'benevolence'. In his *Theory of Moral Sentiments* – that Smith himself considered to be more relevant and basic than the better known *Wealth of Nations* – the author writes: 'however selfish one may consider man to be, some principles are obviously embodied in his nature that make him share other people's good luck, and make other people's happiness necessary to him even though all he gets from it is the pleasant contemplation of it'. The clue is the term 'necessary'. Smith here seems to suggest that the attention to others is an essential and unavoidable feature of human nature and as such it is of vital importance to understand social choices, especially economic choices. Furthermore, the famous Smithian statement that 'it is not from the butcher's, brewer's or baker's benevolence that we can expect our lunch, but from their pursuit of self-interest', implies, for it to be relevant and convincing, that economic relations take place within a reciprocity network – this being the proper meaning of Smithian's *sympathy*.

The above overview is simply meant to highlight the fact that at least up to the first half of the nineteenth century the prevailing economic thought in England and in Italy sees interpersonal relations as a value *per se*, and the market as the institution capable of reconciling the fulfilment of individual self-interest and the pursuit of common good. From that time on, due to circumstances whose analysis is not within the scope of the present work, and for whose occurrence the influence of Bentham's utilitarianism is as decisive as French enlightenment,[6] the hyper-minimalist anthropology of *homo economicus* asserts itself in the economic science, and with it the methodology of social atomism. The concept of market thus established sees the market as an allocation mechanism that can be studied *in vacuo* disregarding the kind of society surrounding it. This explains why the market became, especially at the level of popular culture, the typical place in which moral sentiments like altruism, reciprocity, relationality and so forth have no space to express themselves freely. The grotesque vision of human nature as handed down to us by the traditions of utilitarian jacobinism eventually generated a twofold myth: that the private market domain coincides with the horizon of egoism, and that the State's sphere corresponds to that of collective interests (or solidarity). Hence the well known State/market dualism and above all the identification of the State *in toto* with the public sphere.[7]

Now, in quite a few circles the belief has recently arisen that the simultaneous and hypertrophic growth of the State and of the private market is at the basis of the many problems afflicting our societies in this time of transition from Fordism to post-Fordism. If this is so – as I believe it is – the answer cannot be a radicalization of the State versus market alternative, but a revival of all those forms of economic organization that shape a modern civil economy.

HOW TO BUILD A CIVIL ECONOMY

What should we do to reinstate, as rapidly as possible, civil society, restoring the role that in long-gone times it successfully performed? I am going to dwell on what I consider to be the foundations of an economic constitution of civil society. I start from one of the most serious paradoxes that seem to characterize the present phase of development: in spite of the apparent atomization of post-fordist economies, this age needs more, not less, collective decision processes; more, and not less, cooperative effort. Indeed, as the new political economy has convincingly demonstrated, at the origin of each 'market failure' we find the market inability to produce cooperative results, whose attainment is the effect of the presence within the economic system of significant trust networks. As Arrow says in a well-known essay a few years ago: 'one can plausibly maintain that most of the world's backwardness can be explained by the lack of mutual trust'.[8] The assumption underlying this proposition is simply that development demands high levels of cooperation and this in turn implies deep trust ties among economic agents.

At the empirical level, too, the connection between trust and development opportunities in a country or geographical area is ascertained. One may mention here Robert Putnam's accurate research, updating results obtained by Harvard politologists, and also the distinction outlined by F. Fukuyama in his 1995 essay *Trust*, between high-trust and low-trust societies.

Which are the necessary conditions for a society to improve trust structures? As by now ascertained, civil society is the ideal/typical place to foster dispositions to trust; not so the private market which is instead a trust-consumer. The question is, therefore: how can one deal with the problem of extending trust to larger economic structures, having started from short-range relations (within families, small groups in M. Olson's sense, and so on)? In other terms, how can we overcome the difficulties inherent in the connection between interpersonal trust and institutional trust, and those caused by trust variability and its institutional control? The strategy suggested by Roniger[9] seems to be convincing. As a first step one should 'concentrate trust around specific experiences and social actors' (p. 25). This is the so-called *focusing* process whose aim is to allow the two fundamental elements of trust – mutual acknowledgement of identities and engagement not to cheat nor betray – to develop as free gifts when the process starts. (This explains why the private market cannot be the *primum movens* in generating trust.) Take a cooperative or a non-profit organization: members comply with established norms and enhance the overall status of the institution as a trust-producer, or, better said, as a source of expectations of trust. The very existence of similar enterprises gives evidence of the presence in the territory of a stock of active trust.

Over time, focalization should lead to *generalized* trust 'based on more impersonal images of credibility' (*ibid.*) and marks the transition from interpersonal to institutional trust. Should this not be the case, the risk would be represented by small groups' parochialism and the predominance of corporate interests, with the easily predictable, inevitable consequences of a destabilized social order. Only when trust is generalized can it be looked upon as a public good generating positive externalities.

What should it be done to promote trust generalization? Several different actions can be taken, all of which appear to be connected, one way or another, with the achievement of a more equitable society. For instance, one cannot hope to generalize trust if social inequality tends to increase or become endemic. (Hence the need to move from an oligarchic on to a polyarchic society in which the decisional centres of economic and financial power are multiple and ubiquitous.) If the aim to be pursued is equity viewed as the equality of citizens' fundamental capabilities, the unequal distribution of income or wealth is not the only problem: the unequal production of income and the unequal accumulation of wealth also raise a problem. Trust generalization likewise implies on the one hand higher technical competence levels upon which trust certification is based – this being the key-role of the professions and of light bureaucracy – and on the other hand, that ethics codes adopted by corporations should reach that critical threshold beyond which the market can act as a reputation control device. And so on, to sum up, the winning strategy to generalize trust is to favour the creation of a new economic space, that of the civil economy.

In order to highlight the essential element of the civil economy one needs to start from a general statement. According to the usual, still prevailing conceptualization of economic activity, the functions the economic system is called upon to perform (from resource allocation to the distribution of goods and services produced) are accomplished within two traditional sectors: State and private market. As we know, operation in these two areas differs in two aspects: one is information, that is, messages about individual choices; the other aspect concerns the decisional rule by which results are obtained, given the information set available. Now, if we can identify the public economy with the set of activities organized and legitimized by coercive powers, and the private economy with the set of profit-oriented activities organized according to the principle of exchange of equivalents, the civil economy is represented by all those activities in which neither coercion nor profit are the *primum movens* or the ultimate target. In other words, while in public and private spheres the principle of legitimization of economic decisions is represented, in the one case by the right of citizenship, in the other case by purchasing-power, in the civil economy it is represented by the *reciprocity principle*.

In a recent study,[10] Kolm formalizes the reciprocity relation as a series of bi-directional transfers, independent of one other yet interconnected. Independence implies that each transfer is in itself voluntary, which means free; in other words, no transfer is a prerequisite for the occurrence of the other as there is no external obligation whatsoever in the mind of the transferring subject. This characteristic differentiates reciprocity from the familiar market exchange which too is a set of voluntary bi-directional transfers whose voluntariness is global in that it applies to the whole set of transfers, not to each single transfer in isolation. Put differently, the transfers implied by the exchange of equivalents are each the prerequisite of the other, so much so that the law can at any time intervene to enforce compliance with contract obligations. This is not the case with reciprocity, even though market exchange and reciprocity, both implying voluntariness, oppose command relations. At the same time, however, there is more freedom in reciprocity than in the exchange of equivalents as here transfer in one direction is made compulsory by transfer in the opposite direction. This is precisely why, with reference to the category of freedom, one can claim that market exchange places itself in an intermediate position between coercion and reciprocity. Reciprocity's other characteristic – bidirectional transfers – is what distinguishes this relation from pure altruism expressing itself in isolated one-directional transfers. In both cases however transfers are independently voluntary, hence one can infer that reciprocity takes up the intermediate position between market exchange and pure altruism.

Therefore, the reciprocity relation demands some kind of balance between what one gives and what one expects to obtain, a balance that is not expressed in a definite exchange relationship (or relative price), since it can vary according to the extent to which moral sentiments like sympathy and benevolence are practised by the subjects involved. Unlike market exchange and coercion, and like mere altruism, reciprocity in the end cannot be explained in terms of *self-interest* alone: motives and relations are basic elements of the concept of reciprocity. This is why economic literature locked on to the rational choice scheme[11] cannot account for reciprocity, nor can reciprocity be understood as a special case of a repeated game. One should recognize, however, that reciprocity owns a strategic dimension of its own, as it happens in any interaction among subjects: 'should the recipient of my transfer not reciprocate, at a later moment I will somehow put an end to our relationship'.

Where is the difference with reference to the exchange of equivalents? Such difference is twofold. In market exchanges the determination of the exchange ratio (the so-called equilibrium price) logically precedes the transfer of the object exchanged – only after buyer and seller have agreed on the house price is the property right of the house transferred. In the reciprocity relation instead the transfer precedes, both logically and temporally, the reciprocated object. Under reciprocity, the person who starts it has but one firm point: an expectation of reciprocation. Furthermore, as Bruno Manghi adroitly remarks,[12] 'The "altruistic" form of the relationship is at one time result and regulator of a continuous coordination of different meanings among interdependent agents. They are not "altruist" and "beneficiary" respectively before they meet, but that is what they become by interacting in the course of social processes' (p. 449). And further on, 'The sacrifice implied by altruistic acting is not a mere transfer of resources from one agent onto another, because what is at stake is not just to have, so-to-say, but also to be – to be with' (p. 450).

In the economist's language this means that reciprocity ties may modify the outcome of the economic game, whether by tending to stabilize cooperative behaviours by agents interacting within contexts of the prisoner's dilemma kind, or because the reciprocity practice tends to modify endogenously the preferences themselves, that is to say the form of individuals' objective-functions.[13] (To quote but one example: if I need help under circumstances enabling me to reciprocate only at a later time, while I cannot credibly commit myself, a rational agent in the sense of the *rational choice* paradigm, although he or she is in a position to help me will not do so if, knowing that I too am a self-interested individual, he or she expects that I will not have an interest in reciprocating his or her favour. Things will differ if my potential help-giver knows I practice reciprocity.)

The stress here should be on the fact that in quite a few cases the conscious pursuit of one's self-interest is incompatible with its attainment. It follows that in several instances an 'irrational' response in terms of reciprocity principle leads to better results than the answer conforming to the canons of the exchange of equivalents. One should notice that this paradox is exactly the opposite of the one set forth in the Smithian invisible hand. This too is a telling sign of the epochal transition from fordist to post-fordist society.

I now turn to the question: to what extent is reciprocity practised and how significant is it? Unlike what one might assume, even a casual examination suggests that it is a very widespread phenomenon especially in advanced societies. Not only it is practised within families, in small informal groups, by associations of various kinds, but the transactions network based on the practice of reciprocity as ruling principle is present in all those enterprises that fill the variegated non-profit world, from cooperatives in which reciprocity takes the form of mutuality, to voluntary organizations where reciprocity verges on altruism, on the free gift.

This remark provides the opportunity to single out a far-reaching principle concerning the evolution of any society. Social evolution is always favourably influenced by the presence of diverse rules presiding over the activity of various economic spheres. In fact the famous principle of comparative advantage applies not only at the level of goods and services but also for economic institutions. The market is much more than a mechanism driven by demand and supply forces alone. As a social institution it embodies specific founding rules, which in their turn are the product of cultural matrices, conventions, firmly established practices. On the other hand, citizens' and community's welfare is not just a given aspect that can be but negligibly influenced by human action, it is instead the consequence of the way adopted by human beings living in a society to shape community life.

This is why it does not make sense, nor does it help, to raise the question as to the choice between the reciprocity principle and the equivalent-exchange principle. It does not make sense because we do not possess any indisputable criterion to base our choice on. To avoid any misunderstanding, Pareto efficiency cannot provide such a criterion because it does not apply by definition to an economic set-up resting upon the reciprocity principle. On the other hand, it does not help in any way, indeed it causes damage because an advanced economy requires the implementation of both principles. It is unrealistic to think that all kinds of transactions can be based upon the 'culture of contract', namely, the exchange of equivalents. If this vision were to become the ruling one, individual responsability would coincide with the terms contained in the contract with grotesque consequences that can be easily imagined. If the culture of contract fails to integrate with the reciprocity culture, the potential of the system as a whole is going to be damaged. Hence the urgent need to help the civil economy sphere to take off.

To conclude, the most detrimental effect of the self-interest doctrine and of the culture of contract based on it is to lead us to believe that behaviours inspired by aims other than self-interest are conducive to economic disaster. By encouraging us to expect the worst of others such doctrine eventually brings our worst side to the surface. Moreover, it will eventually greatly hamper the utilization for practical purposes of dispositions such as trust, reciprocity and altruism, since it views them as merely intrinsic qualities of human nature, unrelated to the civilization process society is undergoing.[14] Nowadays we are aware that all this lacks any firm theoretical foundation.

WHAT CAN REASONABLY BE EXPECTED OF A VITAL CIVIL ECONOMY?

What would be the practical outcome of the implementation of what might be called the civil model of social order as sketched? This is not the appropriate place to dwell on the mechanisms of that vision of social order, even though the task must not be neglected.[15] I deem it more urgent to attempt an answer to the following question: which difficulties of our societies should a vigorous sphere of civil economy be expected to overcome? The answer is concealed in the following proposition: the social sustainability of the development process is nowadays jeopardized by the increasing frequency of three specific growth paradoxes: increased inequalities, at community as well as at personal level which go hand in hand with the rise of wealth and average income; jobless growth; putting into practice the liberal principle of the consumer's sovereignty. While these paradoxes are characterized by specific differences, they have two common features: none of them has directly anything to do with situations of material shortage. What they indicate instead are conditions of social shortage and we all know that such shortages are dealt with only by institutional changes (new poverties are certainly not caused by shortage of resources). The second feature is that all three paradoxes seriously endanger the very reasons of liberty understood in a positive sense. How can civil economy represent an accessible and successful path toward solving those paradoxes? I will start by the first one.

In a famous 1976 study, *The Social Limits to Growth*, Fred Hirsch introduces the concepts of positional goods and positional competition. In short, all goods whose demand cannot be met by economic growth – for the obvious reason that the very increase in wealth generates an increased positional demand – are called positional. Let's consider education. Up to a certain level, education is essentially a public good, one whose consumption cannot be ruled out and one that generates positive externalities. Beyond and above this level, however, education tends to become a positional good: even though it is in demand for its intrinsic properties, its consumption produces a decreasing utility as generalized consumption rises.

As Pagano indicates, positional goods possess two undesirable peculiarities. The first one is inequality: one can make use of a positional good only if it is unequally distributed among a large number of subjects (consider, for example, the case of goods such as power or status symbols). As to the other characteristic, the global rate of growth for positional goods is necessarily zero since it is impossible for everybody to raise the consumption of such goods.[16] Thus we realize why the new form of positional competition is dangerous. As Tocqueville foreshadowed with great insight, positional competition 'arises from equality as a prerequisite and aims at overcoming it: equality in principle sets in motion the quest for *de facto* inequality'. The worrying side of positional competition is that it symbolizes an actual case of destructive competition: instead of improving, it worsens both individual and social well-being by producing waste from affluence, so typical nowadays, and disrupting the social texture. An alarming case is the recent phenomenon of *gated communities* in the USA. As many as over four million Americans live in these artificial communities not so much for fear of crime – as one might be inclined to believe – but for meeting a peculiar positional demand: the desire to reconstruct a community and a sense of belonging.

What would be a credible answer to positional competition? Not the one offered by those who believe it should be found within private economy (let alone, within public economy) by accelerating the replacement process in consumption as suggested, for example, by Gershuny.[17] The most effective and cheapest antidote against positional competition is an intervention on the supply of *relational goods*. One might define a relational good as one that produces utility to the consumer only if shared with other subjects. Unlike private goods that can be enjoyed alone, and unlike public goods that can be enjoyed jointly by more subjects, a relational good – for example, the services to a person – has a twofold connotation. With respect to the production side, it demands the participation of all members in the organization, but the terms of 'sharing' are not negotiable. This implies that the incentive to participate in the production of the relational good cannot be external to the relationship among these members themselves: the other's identity does matter. With respect to the consumption side, the fruition of a relational good cannot be pursued overlooking the condition of need and the preferences of other subjects because the 'relationship with the other one' is a constituent of the consumption act.[18]

It follows that in the supply of relational goods, communication becomes the key-term. The more relational goods are the product of what is shared, and the more they result from a commonly shared background intention, the better they perform. As T. Nagel writes in a stimulating monograph about the meaning of altruism: 'Altruism depends on a recognition of the reality of the other persons, and on the equivalent capacity to regard oneself as merely one individual among many. Altruism is not to be confused with generalized affection for the human race. It is not a feeling' (1970, p. 3). And few pages later, he adds: 'The general thesis to be defended concerning altruism is that one has a direct reason to promote the interests of others – a reason which does not depend on intermediate factors such as one's own interests or one's antecedent sentiments of sympathy and benevolence' (ibid., p. 18).

We can now understand why relational goods are the very opposite of positional goods and in particular why the undertakings and the organizations of civil economy are a preferential place, the ideal 'factory' to produce relational goods. Indeed, if the private sphere of the market tends to exclude all subjects lacking purchasing power, the civil sphere tends to include everyone provided they are capable of reciprocity. Therefore, if the *primum movens* of growth in the post-fordist age is social capital, and if this in turn is but the sum total of relational goods, one infers that the expansion of a civil economy is the most effective strategy against the diffusion of the disruptive positional competition. Hirsch's favourite strategy is instead to get away from the market-oriented production logic, moving beyond the market. This happens because Hirsch – influenced by Marxian thought – sees the market as an institution including only the private sphere; the market, therefore, appears to him to be the locus of pure egoism. One should instead view the market as the result of a combination of private economy and civil economy.

Let us now consider the other paradox: jobless growth. As from the 1970s, our post-industrial societies are confronted simultaneously with a two-side affluence and a two-side shortage. On the one hand we have a relative overproduction of goods (goods and services that travel across the private market) combined with the second kind of plenty: unemployed work-power. On the other hand we face a situation of unsatisfied individual and collective needs for two reasons: groups of individuals cannot afford to meet such needs by addressing the private market (first shortage), and the currently operating welfare systems are no longer able to offer appropriate services to non-solvent subjects (medical care at home, baby-sitting, training to complete school education, and so on), nor can they provide for collective needs related to the environment, urban renovation, public spaces and so on. Hence the paradoxical contradiction of our age: unused labour and neglected needs.

Past experience shows that technical innovation waves more than compensated for the loss of jobs thanks to the parallel creation of new activities, industrial segments, services. From David Ricardo onward, economists and policy makers are divided into 'techno-pessimists' and 'techno-optimists', champions of the belief that technological progress destroys more jobs than it creates, and advocates of the contrary. Like so many other controversies, this one too was left unresolved, the crux being: how long is the 'compensation' time? The point is that the compensation process is neither immediate, nor adjustable to labour requirements in geographical or specialization terms. While it is comparatively easy to conform to minor incremental technical changes, a technological revolution like the one we are going through brings along an extraordinary amount of structural adjustment. To sum up, if its occurrence in the history of capitalist economies is not new, the unemployment problem nowadays presents aspects that cannot be ascribed to past cases.

Therefore, it is urgent to resort to new policies capable of combining the properties of today's technological trajectory (whose outstanding feature is that of *continuous* investment in human capital) with a wider sphere of personal freedom (compensation effects cannot be allowed to go their way, merely supporting their function by adjustments of the labour markets).[19] Fifty years ago J.M. Keynes considered mass unemployment in a wealthy society a shameful absurdity – one that it would be perfectly possible to eliminate. Our economies are nowadays three times as rich as they were in Keynes' time and he would be justified to consider todays' unemployment three times as absurd and dangerous, for in a society that is three times as rich, the inequality and exclusion it produces are at least three times as disruptive. Now, without detracting in any way from the relevance of several proposals that are being offered – all based upon a reformulation of the well known incentive models – I think one should acknowledge that these suggestions are not decisive, since today's unemployment is much more a question of social organization than a question of malfunctioning of the labour market, as indeed it was the case in Fordist economies.

My thesis is that action should be taken on timing-pattern rules (for labour, training, free-time and so forth). Timing rules are not given *una tantum* but they change according to the needs that become manifest during the various stages of society's evolution. New technologies free social time from the production process to an extent that was unthinkable previously. Current institutional labour-market frameworks and, more generally, our society's institutional structure turn this freed social time into unemployment. Following Gershuny's analysis and its inspiring concept of 'social innovation',[20] the issue is, in brief, the following. Since new technologies raise the system's average productivity – estimated to be a yearly 3 per cent – if a society wants unemployment figures to remain unaffected, it will have to step up its effective demand (consumption plus investment) at the same rate as labour productivity. As the investment increase is closely related to the consumption growth, the adjustment load will in fact be all upon consumptions. However, consumption of goods and especially of services, takes time. Therefore, *if* productivity rises, *if* one wishes to keep employment unchanged, *if* work-hours are to remain constant, consumption has to step up. This means that more and more strenuous consumption is needed just to permit an unhampered progress to the economy.

In a celebrated 1970 piece of work, Linder demonstrated that increased consumption would lead to a paradoxical outcome: the attempt to use up ever growing quantities of goods within one time unit lowers people's utility instead of enhancing it – that same utility that a rational agent should try to maximize. Luckily, however, the alternative I have just suggested is not the only one available. Another way would be an increase in the productivity of non-waged works thus obtaining results similar to those of a reduced schedule for the creation of new jobs; this way also permits the pursuit of other aims, such as the 'release' of an as yet just potential demand for services, but above all it makes feasible *intertemporal* labour flexibility.

This is where civil economy steps in with its strategic role: it allows that the transition from an organizational pattern based upon the eight-hour per day – five-day week for four consecutive weeks each month, to a model in which the same work-hours are distributed differently, will occur at basically zero social costs. The problem is not so much the weekly or monthly reduction of work-hours, but a much more structural one, that is, to control the temporal sequence of paid work so as to enable the worker to adjust the work-schedule to meet his or her requirements at different phases of his or her active life. Private companies, instead, should be enabled to abate the costs of a reorganization of the production process caused by new employment schemes. Summing up, the problem to be solved relates to the timing of work, training, leisure (strictly speaking), and the scheduling of workhours divided into labour paid according to market prices and hours not so compensated, but offered in one of the many aspects of civil economy, but by no means unpaid.

The idea that employment questions should be approached from the life-cycle viewpoint is based on the possibility of organizing the choice among work hours, training hours, family life, and leisure having in mind the entire life-span of individuals. A reorganization of the time patterns signals profound changes in life-style and a remarkable cultural advancement. In the Fordist epoch we got used to considering the concept of freedom of choice in terms of choice among the various market goods. In a post-Fordist age, an increase in individual liberty requires the concept of freedom of choice to be gradually extended to the choice of life-outlooks. This is the specific task of a civil economy because neither State nor private market would, if left to themselves, be able to guarantee that the costs of transition to the new structure are socially sustainable.

Finally, I come to the third social paradox of growth. One of the manifold aspects of the transition from Fordism to post-Fordism is a sort of reconciliation between labour and consumption, two fundamental segments of individual life that industrial society had forcibly kept apart. The reasons why this happened are well known: opulent consumption was to compensate for the loss of significance in individual work, hence the successful consumerist model. No less important are the theoretical reasons thereof: consumption of goods and leisure are the goal of economic activity just as natural resources and labour are the means resorted to for achieving those goals. A distinction of this kind generates disregard for a momentous fact: people are not only interested in the quantity of work they perform or in the amount of free time they give up, but also in the job quality. In fact, equal amounts of labour supplied in different jobs correspond to equal amounts of leisure time, but the well-being conditions of workers are bound to differ. The point is that agents' preferences should be acknowledged not only for consumption goods but also for specific jobs that for this very reason should not be considered as a mere mean.[21] This is tantamount to saying that one doesn't work for money alone, but also for the significance perceived in one's own productive activity; likewise consumption is not just based upon utility, but strives also to obtain advantages at a productive level.

With some generalization one might say that industrial society did not offer any alternative to acting as producers during work hours, and as consumers during leisure time. Post-Fordist society generates a third category: the producer-consumers, self-producing part of the goods they themselves consume.

This trend is expressed by a variety of related signals: when we collect cash-dispenser money we act as part-time bank clerks; shopping in a self-service supermarket makes us part-time shopkeepers; when we help ourselves at a refreshments kiosk we are part-time waiters, and so on. Under such circumstances, made possible by technology and therefore destined to be more and more frequent, productive systems shift labour costs on to the citizen/consumer, or, more generally, externalize part of production costs. Now post-industrial society tends to favour self-production both because leisure time versus paid labour cannot be filled up just with pastimes, and because people want to get involved, be busy, make use of and exchange the skills they are endowed with and that new technologies can turn into diverse activity promoters.

This is why it is impossible nowadays to determine *a priori* which activities are means and which are ends. The time is luckily on the wane when it was the institutional set-up that decided in which 'places' human activities were to be considered as targets and in which instead as means. Persistent compliance with such a scheme would not only lack any rational justification, it would also be conducive to evil consequences: if the only exogenously set targets are mere consumption goods and leisure, national income may continue to rise, yet the 'well-being' of people and their liberty can be heavily affected by the consequences of this condition. By the same token, increase in per capita income no longer warrants, at the present evolutional stage, a higher quality of life, for one fundamental reason: while the quality of life is gauged in terms of liberty range, viewed as possible self-assertion, increased income merely indicates that subjects can afford higher expenditure. Thus it may happen that even citizens with average income are in fact left out of certain services, more specifically personal services, and excluded from joining the decision process affecting them.

Where does this analysis lead to? Traditional conceptualization of the principle of the consumer's sovereignty – the very foundation of liberal thinking – no longer makes sense today: it has lost its grip on reality. What we need is to build bridges spanning from a labour in quest of genuine significance to a consumption that cannot be an end in itself. That is where civil economy can offer a remarkable, perhaps unique, contribution by turning the consumer into a social actor well aware of the influential power he or she holds over what is produced and how it is produced. The Fordist consumer delegates the firm to represent his or her own interest, with the state intervening to ensure protection. The post-Fordist consumer is a 'global' entity who finds in civil society not only a place of protection, but, in particular, of *empowerment*, even in a formal sense. From this angle the consumer is 'post-Hegelian' by definition. If one thinks of the expanding practice of various forms of critical consumption, ethical finance, *TransFair*, LETS (Local Exchange Trade System), time banks and so on,[22] one realizes the practical extent of this argument.

A CONCLUDING REMARK

In the previous pages I always used the expression civil economy, less frequently non-profit organizations, never 'third sector', the reason being that 'third sector' is a theoretically feeble (state and market, supposedly the two others, are not sectors) and culturally ambiguous concept because it endorses the notions of marginality: where the state cannot enter and where the private firm has no interest to operate, there the non-profit organization carves itself a niche. As if to say that third sector's origin and *raison d'être* lie in a twofold failure: of the state and of the contract, as indeed Anglo-Saxon economic literature has been theorizing for some time.[23]

However, one should resist this conceptualization in the light of two basic considerations. First, the argument leads to contradicting in practice the subsidiarity principle that everybody claims to accept and subscribe to. The present antinomy situation of subsidiarity will not pass unnoticed, the universal acknowledgement of its value and significance collides with substantial difficulties in implementing it. The other consideration relates to the civilization challenge we cannot ignore: to improve the civil quality of our societies. This is why we need to broaden the general notion we have of market economy that a certain *vulgate* of the liberal thought tradition handed down to us, a vulgate according to which the market is coextensible *only* to the sphere of private enterprises, that is, those operating for profit.

What is disturbing is that, today, neoliberal market ideology is claiming that the market performs not only an economic function but also basic social and political functions, such as creating freedom and democracy and redistributing income – if only we wait long enough! So the role of government can be diminished as an obstacle to the new society to be created by the private market.

Worse, because we are concentrating on remedial work, we tend to see our central remedial problems as ones of ethics, implying that if only individuals, businesses and government were less greedy, we could have a human world. Certainly, if greed lessened, it would be a better world, but marginally so, unless the less greed also freed up people's social imagination into rethinking the basic economic model itself and not just its concrete ramifications.

As we have seen, the proposal here advanced is to consider the individual-in-society, not the relationless individual the basic player in society. Market economies capable of meeting a post-Fordist society's well-being expectations needs to breathe with two lungs: private economy and civil economy whose governing principles were expressed above. We need both principles and their 'contamination' into practical life if we are to look for the means to make competition civilized, to overcome the polemological version of market that, faced with unacceptable social and human costs, can no longer satisfy the canons of economic rationality. Today it is more far-sighted and less expensive to be cooperatively competitive than conflictually competitive. In the long-run perspective it is not only more 'benevolent' but also more rational to organize the economic process inviting civil society to collaborate rather than to entrust it with mere interstitial functions, resting on incentive schemes alone. I believe this should be the horizon from which a vigorous action could start for a revival of civil society in the post-Fordist epoch.

NOTES

I would like to express my gratitude to Ferruccio Marzano for the opportunity to participate in a most stimulating conference in memory of Fausto Vicarelli, a gifted economist and a sincere friend whose life testified to the best in altruistic behaviour and reciprocity. I am also grateful to my discussants, N. Acocella and A. Roncaglia, and to the other participants in the debate for their observations and suggestions. The usual disclaimer applies. An extended and partly different version of the present essay is being published in Italian as Zamagni (1997).

1. Wolfe (1989), p. 102.
2. Scazzieri (1996a, b); Porta and Scazzieri (1996, 1997); Poni (1995); Poni and Scazzieri (eds) (1994); Nuccio (1995). See also Roncaglia (1989).

3. Bernardino da Siena (1989). On L. Bruni's thought, see Baron (1968). For a general outline of civil humanists see also Baron (1970).
4. Romagnosi (1834), pp. 9–11.
5. Smith (1976), (orig. ed. 1759), p. 86.
6. For an essential presentation see Screpanti and Zamagni (1994). A central element in the re-definition of the economic question is the hegemonic acceptance of the general equilibrium theory developed by Leon Walras (1874), a theory that allows no room for the concept of civil society or for moral rules of behaviour.
7. It may be worthwhile to add that in the Keynesian conceptualization State is not the equivalent of 'government'. According to Keynes the State's peculiar feature is represented neither by the mechanism nor by the function, but by the motivations that underlie behaviours. The State is therefore a nexus of institutions – which can be privately owned – operating for the common good. What Keynes has in mind when he speaks of socialization of the economy, is not the public sector's expansion as we understand it today, but the growth at the level of civil society of the motive of public service. For an interesting discussion of Keynes's concept of State and its economic role see Skidelsky (1989).
8. Arrow (1972), p. 343. On this subject see also how Coleman formalizes the concept of trust, highlighting its economically significant peculiarities, Coleman (1990).
9. Roniger (1992).
10. Kolm (1994), pp. 67–95. See also Kolm (1984).
11. As we know, according to the 'rational choice' theory, the agent does not select the rationality criterion: this is, by hypothesis, the maximization of self-interest. By this freedom of choice becomes a 'constrained freedom'. One historical case exemplifying this point is reviewed by McIntyre (1995), pp. 537–57.
12. Manghi (1995), pp. 433–59. On this subject and how to approach it in the economic discourse, see Zamagni (1995), with essays giving an account of a great many attempts made to recognize behaviours that egoism cannot possibly explain.
13. We owe to Sen one of the first attempts to advance a relational approach to reciprocity. See Sen (1967), pp. 112–24. See also Tirole's stimulating study representing the first attempt to define a model for the concept of group reputation as an aggregate of individual reputations, Tirole (1996), pp. 1–22.
14. It may be interesting to report J.S. Mill's thinking, so far ahead of his time. In his celebrated 1859 essay *On Liberty*, Mill clarifies that majority's tyranny is a sign not so much of the way democracy operates, but of the hegemony of the 'trader's spirit', namely of that special kind of human nature I defined above as 'culture of contract'. Mill writes 'whenever any variety of human nature comes to prevailing in a given community, it becomes overbearing and practically compels everyone to submit to or imitate it', quoted in Jellamo (1995), p. 30.
15. For an interesting discussion about alternative *governance* structures in a post-Fordist society, see Streek and Schmitter (1991).
16. Cf. Pagano (1990). Positional goods peculiarities account for what Frank

calls 'vice-chairman post inflation', namely the proliferation of political parties and groups within them as attempts to increase the supply of that positional good that is power or social status: the Italian case is most illuminating. Frank (1985).

17. Gershuny (1983).
18. Cf. Uhlaner (1989), pp. 253–85, for an interesting application of the theory of relational goods to voting participation.
19. Recent OECD papers, (1994a, b), point out that the significance of service compensation *vis-à-vis* job loss in industry has shrunk in all advanced countries in the course of the 1980s. One might remark that the US experience allows the abatement of long-term unemployment by sustained job-destruction and -creation dynamics – (*temporary lay-offs* and *downsizing* practices) – but at the same time it is responsible for widespread insecurity in labour relations, for unacceptable loan differentials, for growing exclusion of large population segments (the so-called *working poors*). Freeman's provocative assertion is stimulating: with regard to alarming figures of adults jailed or on bail in the US (4.6 million in 1993) as compared to unemployment figures (4.2 million), he argues that 'The equivalent of European long-term subsidized unemployment is, in the US, the jail population. Europeans provide the jobless with welfare state services; we jail them and give them free board, lodging and TV. The problem is unresolved'. (Freeman (1994).
20. Gershuny (1982, 1987). We owe this author the credit for the first systematic study of present trends concerning time utilization in advanced economies.
21. On this see Pagano (1985) and (1993), pp. 38–48.
22. A *Lets* is an association organizing barter of goods and services based upon the reciprocity principle. First created in Canada where they have 10 such associations, *Lets* rapidly spread all over: in England there are about 300, 100 in the US, 200 in Australia and so on. One of the reasons of their success is that they permit the exchange of services or professional performaces that have no price in the private market – human resources that otherwise would be unused, not to say wasted. The Time Bank experience belongs to this context.
23. On this see Keynes's opposing stance as expressed in his famous 1926 essay *The End of Laissez Faire*: 'I believe in many cases the ideal dimension for organization and control units lies at an intermediate point between the individual and modern State. I think progress is the growth and recognition of entities whose acting is inspired solely by public well-being *as they see it*' (added italics). See also Lord Beveridge's interesting position, that would much rather have '*social service state*' than *welfare state* to signify that the state cannot assure welfare, but civil society can.

REFERENCES

Arrow, K. (1972) Gifts and Exchanges, *Philosophy and Public Affairs* **1**, 343–62.

Baron, H. (1968) *From Petrarch to Leonardo Bruni*, Chicago-London, Chicago University Press.

Baron, H. (1970) *La crisi del primo rinascimento italiano. Umanesimo civile e libertà repubblicana in un'età di classicismo e tirannide* (The Crisis of the First Italian Renaissance. Civil Humanism and Republican Liberty in an Age of Classicism and Tyranny), It. tr., Florence, La Nuova Italia.

Bernardino da Siena (1989) *Prediche volgari sul campo di Siena* (Vernacular Sermons in the Siena Campo), in C. Delcorno (ed.), Milano, Rusconi.

Coleman, J. (1990) *Foundations of Social Theory*, Cambridge, MA, Harvard University Press.

Frank, R. (1985) *Choosing the Right Pond: Human Behaviour and the Quest for Status*, New York, Oxford University Press.

Freeman, R.B. (1994) Blue Collars Become Scarce, *International Herald Tribune*, 4 December.

Gershuny, J. (1982) Social Innovation, *Futures* **9**, 178–89.

Gershuny, J. (1983) Technical Change and Social Limits, in A. Ellis and K. Kumar (eds), *Dilemmas of Liberal Democracies*, London, Tavistock.

Gershuny, J. (1987) Technical Change and the Work-leisure Balance, in A. Silberston (ed.), *Technology and Economic Progress*, London, Macmillan.

Hirsch, F. (1976) The Social Limits to Growth, Cambridge Mass., Harvard University Press.

Jellamo, A. (1995) Mill e il dispotismo delle masse (Mill and Mass Despotism), *Critica Liberale*, February.

Keynes, J.M. (1926) *The End of Laissez-faire*, London, Macmillan.

Kolm, S. (1984) *La bonne économie. La réciprocité générale*, Paris, PUF.

Kolm, S. (1994) The Theory of Reciprocity and the Choice of Economic Systems: An Introduction, *Investigaciones economicas* **18**, 67–95.

Manghi, B. (1995) Altruismo (Altruism), *Rassegna Italiana di Sociologia* **36**, 433–59.

McIntyre, M. (1995) Altruism, Collective Action, and Rationality, *Polity* **27**, 537–57.

Mill, J.S. (1859) *On Liberty*, It. tr. Milan, Il Saggiatore [1981].

Nagel, T. (1970) *The Possibility of Altruism*, Princeton N.J. Princeton University Press.

Nuccio, O. (1995) *La civiltà italiana nella formazione della scienza economica* (Italian Civilization in the Formation of Economic Science), Milan, Etas Libri.

OECD (1994a) *Job Study*, Paris, OECD.

OECD (1994b) *Employment Outlook*, Paris, OECD.

Pagano, U. (1985) *Work and Welfare in Economic Theory*, Oxford, Blackwell.

Pagano, U. (1990) The Economics of Positional Goods, *Mimeo*, Cambridge.

Pagano, U. (1993) E' la razionalità economica ragionevole? (Is Economic Rationality Reasonable?), *Ragion pratica* **1**, 38–48.

Poni, C. (1995) Standards, Trust and Civil Society: Measuring the Thickness and Quality of Silk Thread, *Mimeo*, Bologna.

Poni, C. and Scazzieri, R. (eds) (1994) Production Networks: Market Rules and Social Norms, *Mimeo*, Bologna.

Porta, P. and Scazzieri, R. (1996) Concorrenza e società civile (Competition and Civil Society), in A. Quadrio Curzio (ed.), *Alle origini del pensiero economico in Italia* (At the Origins of Economic Thought in Italy), Bologna, Il Mulino.

Porta, P. and Scazzieri, R. (1997) Towards an Economic Theory of International Civil Society, *WP3*, University of Milan.

Romagnosi, G.D. (1834) *Collezione degli articoli di economia politica e statistica civile* (Collected Articles on Political Economy and Civil Statistics), Florence, Stamperia Pitti.

Roncaglia, A. (1989) Italian Economic Growth: a Smithian View, *Quaderni di Storia dell'Economia Politica* **VII**, 225–34.

Roniger, L. (1992) *La fiducia nelle società moderne* (Trust in Modern Societies), Messina, Rubbettino.

Scazzieri, R. (1996a) *Sulla teoria economica della società civile* (On the Economic Theory of Civil Society), Accad. delle Scienze dell'Istituto di Bologna (Ac. of Sciences, Bologna Institute).

Scazzieri, R. (1996b) Tecnologia, conoscenza e società civile: uno schema analitico (Technology, Knowledge and Civil Society: An Analytical Framework), *Nuova Civiltà delle Macchine*.

Screpanti, E. and Zamagni, S. (1994) *An Outline of the History of Economic Thought*, Oxford, Oxford University Press.

Sen, A. (1967) Isolation, Assurance and the Social Rate of Discount, *Quarterly Journal of Economics* **80**, 112–24.

Skidelsky, R. (1989) Keynes and the State, in D. Helm (ed.), *The Economic Borders of the State*, Oxford, Oxford University Press.

Smith, A. (1976) *The Theory of Moral Sentiments*, in D. Raphael and A. Macfie (eds), Oxford, Oxford University Press, (orig. ed. 1759).

Streek, W. and Schmitter, P. (1991) Community, Market, State – and Associations? The Prospective Contribution of Interest Governance to Social Order, in G. Thompson *et al.* (eds), *Markets, Hierarchies and Networks*, London, Sage.

Tirole, J. (1996) A Theory of Collective Reputations (with Applications to the Persistence of Corruption and to Firm Quality), *Review of Economic Studies* **63**, 1–22.

Uhlaner, C.J. (1989) Relational Goods and Participation: Incorporating Sociability Into a Theory of Rational Action, *Public Choice* **62**, 253–85.

Walras, L. (1874) *Eléments d'Economie Politique Pure*, 3rd ed., Paris, R. Pichon-R. Durand, 1896.

Wolfe, A. (1989) *Whose Keeper? Social Science and Moral Obligation*, Berkeley, University of California Press.

Zamagni, S. (ed.) (1995) *The Economics of Altruism*, Aldershot, E. Elgar.

Zamagni, S. (1997) Economia civile come forza di civilizzazione della società italiana (Civil Economy as Civilization Thrust in Italian Society), in P. Donati (ed.), *Rapporto sulla società civile in Italia (Report on Civil Society in Italy)*, Milan, Mondadori.

Comment

Nicola Acocella

To better understand Zamagni's contribution an explicit definition of some concepts is in order. The civil economy is a set of interpersonal relationships (in particular, of material flows) based on the principle of reciprocity. This principle requires the existence of material interpersonal flows (transfers) based on *solidarity*: each member of a social organization feels obliged to share her wealth and labour power with the other components and expects to share their wealth and labour power in similar circumstances (Grossi, 1984; Polanyi, 1944). However, no one takes account of past flows or asks for any compensation other than a generic readiness of other members to do the same in similar conditions. Voluntariness, the undetermined and unessential (in strict and immediate terms) nature of the equivalent and some degree of unselfishness are, therefore, the characteristic features of civil society.

Zamagni's main thesis is that these relationships play an important role for the very existence and development of an economic and social system. In many circumstances an 'irrational' (from the standpoint of conventional wisdom) attitude of the kind underlying the reciprocity principle not only does not lead to economic disaster, but produces better results than those deriving from the exchange of equivalents (the familiar market exchange), by avoiding situations of 'social deficiencies', increasing positive liberty, boosting employment and satisfying human needs.

A corollary of this thesis is that the civil economy should be subsidized in order to compete with the private economy. An implicit assumption for this conclusion is that the positive results of the civil economy only accrue in the long run, whereas there are set up costs in the short run which are absent for the private economy that is already in operation. Moreover, the running costs of the civil economy are not sufficiently lower.

Zamagni's main thesis is largely based on propositions that should be tested but sound likely at least to some extent. As for the subjective aspects of that thesis – in particular, the quality of life in a solidaristic system is better than in a competitive or coercive system

– I largely share the underlying values. Therefore, I have no profound reason to dissent from Zamagni's main thesis.

Some statements that Zamagni has superimposed on, or associated to, this thesis can however be questioned. In fact Zamagni uses them to derive the corollary I have mentioned and many statements having important practical consequences. I will consider only some of the problems raised by Zamagni's analysis. First, he says that the civil economy, together with the private economy, is part of the market economy, in contrast with the government.

This can be so, obviously, only if the similarities between the civil and the private economy are greater than those between the civil economy and the government. The civil economy shares reciprocity with the private economy while diverging from it:

a) for the essential and predetermined (synallagmatic) nature of the equivalent in market exchange, which is the standard, although not unique, relationship of the private economy;
b) for the intentions and the motivations of the persons involved, which, in the case of the private economy, are selfish and altruistic or at least solidaristic in the case of the civil economy.

As for this second reason of divergence, it is true that solidarity takes an intermediate position between selfishness and pure altruism; because of this intermediate position, it is a difficult category to set. One possible solution would be that each one decides according to her preferences – as far as value judgements are concerned – and convictions. At this level of analysis it seems to me that the motivations of persons operating in the civil economy are closer to those of individuals when they decide to establish a public body. The drive for solidarism (concern for other people) is closer to the collective aim of public bodies than to the selfish motivation of private ones.

The question cannot, however, be settled only, or mainly, on the basis of ethical or psychological attitudes. As political economists we are not asked to say if a solidaristic person is a masked egoist or a quasi-altruist or if she should be one or the other. We are dealing with institutions and we must ask what role the civil economy can play with respect to the real conduct and performance of the private economy and the state. From this point of view there are both market and government failures. The civil economy, as Zamagni says, can temper market failures. One can add that it can also temper government failures. In both cases, however, it serves collective aims.

Zamagni might support his assimilation of the civil economy and the private economy with the argument that both are based on elements of voluntary cooperation, whereas the state is characterized by its power to impose. Such an argument would however ignore: i) that market exchange can hardly be conceived as a cooperative act; ii) that there are coercive elements in real private economies, linked to the existence of corporate hierarchies, market power, the pressure put by some agents on others because of unemployment and other situations of need. In particular, the difference between taxes and monopoly prices is much slighter than that, say, between the objectives and the conduct of a voluntary organization and a public organization for the relief of migrants. On the other hand, one can hardly accept the argument that the prevailing feature of the state is its power to impose. Zamagni too easily dismisses the contractualistic and democratic perspectives.

Finally on this question, one can ask why we want to aggregate the civil economy to the private economy or to the government. It can serve the analytical purpose of giving a more correct representation of how individuals behave, overcoming the deformations of the *homo economicus*. Alternatively, it can serve a policy purpose, by specifying some characteristics that should be satisfied by the civil economy in devising policy schemes: for example, the government must decide whether certain organizations that appear to be largely private in the operations they perform should none the less be considered as part of the civil economy. Zamagni seems to have both of them in mind: he refers first to the former (at the end of his second section) and then to the latter. His likely line of reasoning is the following: on the one hand, the civil economy complements the private economy in determining market performance; the consideration of the civil economy alongside the private economy can give a better representation of the non-state sector, avoiding the misrepresentation of this sector that can derive from an exaggeration of the selfish motivations of individuals; on the other hand, since the civil economy has a better performance than the state in pursuing altruistic ends and since there are set-up costs in establishing the civil economy, the state should help it to take off.

For both analytical and policy purposes a specification of the actual configurations of the civil economy is in order. According to Zamagni these range from the cooperative firms to 'voluntary organizations' and the family. This specification raises some problems. In particular, it seems too extreme to think of *some* of the forms that mutuality takes on in reality (also as an effect of the conditioning exerted by the private economy) as embodying the principle of solidarity, in a way and to such an extent to avoid market failures. Let us take cooperatives as an example. They – like many other agents (too easily qualified as non-profit organizations) – do indeed tend to earn profits, even 'monopoly' profits. From this point of view the element of solidarity they embody is very limited; in the end some individuals are involved in economic exchanges in their own interest, possibly to the detriment of others. To this end they can add a high mark up to their costs or even have a 'speculative' conduct that can do harm to other agents. If Zamagni thought of the strong private interests that often characterize some forms of the 'non-profit' sector, when assimilating this sector (and the economy of which it is considered to be an expression) to the private economy, he is perfectly right. But in this case the emphasis on the solidaristic nature of this sector should have been tempered.

In addition, one could question the implicit assumption made by Zamagni in prescribing a subsidization of the civil economy. The whole subject of the setting up and running costs of the civil economy deserves indeed further analysis.

To conclude, assimilating the civil economy to the private economy and differentiating it from the state has at least two negative consequences:

a) It unduly accentuates the authoritative character of the state, attenuating its very role of a 'nexus of institutions working for the public good' that Zamagni seems to prefer; this characteristic is always present in reality to some extent and would be enhanced by a convergent action of the civil economy performed by suitable non profit organizations.
b) It can generate dangerous mixtures of the civil and the private economy, by inducing the most unscrupulous private agents to assume improper features, to simply capture public favour or the public funds available for the development of the civil economy.

These critical remarks do not intend to question the relevance of the civil economy and of the opportunities it can further, in a world where 'the trampling, crushing, elbowing and treading-on each other's heels . . . are . . . anything but the disagreeable symptoms of one of the phases of industrial progress', certainly not 'the most desirable lot of human kind' (Mill, 1970, Book 4, Chapter VI, Section 2).

REFERENCES

Grossi, F. (1984) *Sistemi produttivi e organizzazioni sociali*, Milano, Angeli.

Mill, J.S. (1970) *Principles of Political Economy*, Harmondsworth, Penguin Books [Reprint].

Polanyi, K. (1944) *The Great Transformation*, New York, Rinehart.

Comment

Alessandro Roncaglia

Zamagni's main thesis is that the civil economy, characterized by reciprocity, is a third way between the market, where self-interest dominates, and the State, that is the area of command. And in order 'to build a civil economy' Zamagni reproposes Roniger's 'focussing process', namely to concentrate as a first step on short-range, interpersonal, trust-producing activities such as those typical of cooperatives or non-profit organizations.

I disagree both with Zamagni's peculiar notion of 'civil economy' and with the 'focussing strategy' he proposes. The reader must be warned, though, that Zamagni's paper is a multifaceted one, with a number of different and sometimes contrasting lines of reasoning eclectically recalled in its three sections; yet, it is natural for a commentator to concentrate on points of disagreement.

In illustrating my doubts, I will follow Zamagni in referring to the history of economic thought, and specifically to Adam Smith's notions of self-interest and benevolence. These lead to a lay notion of 'civicness' as a necessary component of a market economy. A distinction thus emerges between 'civicness' and reciprocity, as shown by instances of 'non-civic reciprocity'. The conclusion is a relationship between the market, the state and non-profit activities which differs from the one Zamagni suggests with the 'focusing strategy'.

For those accepting the monodimensional notion of the 'economic man' as a utility-maximizing machine, it may appear natural to counterpose self-interest and benevolence as separate, contradictory motivations of human behaviour. Yet, this view is untenable both in itself and as an interpretation of Adam Smith.

True, benevolence (or 'sympathy', meaning – from its Greek etymology – 'to share feelings') is at the centre of the *Theory of Moral Sentiments* (1759), while self-interest is the crucial force in the *Wealth of Nations* (1776). Yet, the two viewpoints were not considered contradictory by Smith himself, who kept revising the two works for successive editions during his lifetime, or by his contemporaries, or by the scholarly editors of the Glasgow edition of his writings (1976–83).

The point is that Smith's analysis is part of a centuries-long debate on 'passions and interests'. Participants in this debate commonly admitted multiple motivations of human behaviour, recognizing the complexity of human beings. Thus the relationship between self-interest and benevolence is established by Smith with his 'ethics of sympathy', recognizing the intrinsic social nature of humans and the relevance of their shared feelings. Self-interested behaviour analysed in the *Wealth of Nations* is thus to be distinguished from selfishness, since the former is checked and kept within boundaries of laws and customs, supported by widespread acceptance of moral commandments and civic feelings. The very survival of a market economy depends on the good functioning of the checks and balances on self-interested behaviour, both internal and external to each agent, namely on a sufficient degree of 'civicness'.

In other words, selfishness designates an overruling passion driving human behaviour; self-interest is instead the result of social institutions and customs developed under the stimulus of, and supported by, a complex set of motivations among which there is room for respect for other humans and for shared feelings of common belonging. It is the recognition of these boundaries to action and of this commonality of interests which characterizes civic behaviour.

There are a few hints in the direction of this interpretation of Smith's thought and of this notion of civil society in the second (historical) section of Zamagni's paper.[1] However, in subsequent sections and in developing his main argument he goes on to consider separately the various motivations behind human behaviour, contrasting the market economy based on self-interest and the public economy based on command to the 'civic economy' based on reciprocity.

As in the ritual exchange of gifts in primitive communities, relations based on reciprocity are not simultaneous and thus necessarily require mutual trust. According to Zamagni, while the market is 'trust-consuming', non-profit activities are 'trust-generating'. Small-group relations create 'trust networks'. This is why non-profit institutions are more appropriately called 'civic economy'.

Two aspects of this theory will be isolated for criticism: first, the idea that market relations are 'trust-consuming'; second, the idea that reciprocity relations by their very nature favour 'civicness'.

As for the first point, we may recall that Zamagni's thesis, according to which market relations are 'trust-consuming', runs counter to a well-established idea, that of the *doux commerce*.[2] According to this idea, with the spreading of market relations agents become used to pursuing their own interests by entering into exchange agreements with others, in the absence of links stemming from family, friendship or clan, while respecting rules established both by the law and by the customs and habits of their community. This behaviour is considered conducive to the development of a 'civil' society, namely a society where violence is banished and each person respects the rights of others.

While this idea is largely accepted, it must of course be noted that the opposite idea has also been defended, mainly within the Marxist and the Roman Catholic traditions of opposition to the market economy.[3] We may thus call a lay idea of the civic society the one defended, among others, by Adam Smith and illustrated above. According to this tradition, civicness is a prerequisite, as well as a result, of economic development in a market economy.[4]

Once this is understood, the criticism to Zamagni's second thesis is immediate. Reciprocity relations do not, by themselves, favour social well-being. All depends on whether they are part of a civic society (in our meaning of the word), or of a system of clan egotism. Examples of 'civically-perverse' reciprocity unfortunately abound in our societies. For instance, reciprocity and trust relations are basic in academic power groups, in masonic lodges or in the mafia.[5] Here reciprocity becomes necessary precisely because of the illegal (or at best illicit) nature of the activities of these groups, which makes it quite difficult to enter into exchange relations protected by law.

This is why the 'focusing strategy' may be dangerous. Once reciprocity relations are counterposed to market ones, clan fidelity takes precedence over meritocracy. Where competition does not act as a constraint to egotistic clan behaviour, the results can be quite disrupting. Even more than for market relations, where competition may act as a constraint, in the case of reciprocity relations a 'laic civicness' must be a prerequisite, and not a hoped-for result.

All this points to the dangers of isolating non-profit activities as a third way opposed to the market and the state. In a civic society, where self-interest is accompanied and driven by higher moral feelings, the role of the state in ensuring not only obedience to the law but also a widespread feeling of social cohesion and commonality of interests (though in the presence of conflicts arising from participation in a competitive market arena) is decisive for the development of a sound system of market relations. Since participation in the market arena unavoidably involves conflicts, this implies for instance a competitive policy ensuring as far as possible equal opportunities for all participants, a social security policy providing for the disadvantaged and a policy aimed at preventing both the conversion of economic power into political power and the derivation of unfair economic advantages from political power.[6]

At the same time, the development of the market economy provides the necessary material foundations for the welfare institutions of a civic society. When mere survival is not a pressing problem for most citizens, the development of non-profit making, social welfare enhancing, activities is easier. Such activities then rely on both the market and state intervention. They should thus hopefully not be based on 'networks of local trust' opposed to both market and state, thereby creating a dangerous feeling of extraneity towards both of them. Non-profit activities should rather stem from the same lay spirit of commonality and civicness which is a requisite for the good functioning of the market economy.[7]

'Civicness' is a set of virtues, and cannot be reduced to reciprocity – exactly as 'self-interest' is a complex motivation for human behaviour, and cannot be reduced to egotism. It is the assumption of a 'monodimensional man', typical of marginalist economics, that leads us astray. The risks stemming from this mistake, as shown above, are quite considerable.

NOTES

1. We may recall, however, that Screpanti and Zamagni (1989, p. 70) adopt the opposite interpretation based on the counterposition of self-interest and benevolence, thus remaining within the mainstream marginalist view of a monodimensional 'economic man'.
2. The strong historical roots of this idea, as well as the opposite lines of reasoning, are illustrated in Hirschman (1982).
3. As Hirschman (1982) recalls, criticism of the commercial society may be accompanied by praise of ancient virtues (in Hirschman's terminology, 'feudal blessings' correspond to the persistence in modern economies of pre-capitalistic influences): thus reciprocity could be ennobled by reference to feudal chivalry.
4. This tradition is not new in Italy. Cf. for instance Sylos Labini (1989), Roncaglia (1989). In this context, 'competition' means the absence of barriers favouring privileges of entrenched groups against equality of opportunity. Competition thus constitutes the objective of a reformist policy rather than a natural characteristic of market economies.

5. In fact, when Zamagni speaks of 'exchange of favours', if we isolate the quotation from the context we are reminded of the uncivic Italian habit of recommendations ('raccomandazioni') rather than of Tuscan industrial districts. 'Negative reciprocity' takes place whenever group well-being is pursued at the expense of other groups; commonly social costs are then higher than group benefits.
6. Connected to these aspects is the vital link between political and economic liberties: a link clearly present in Smith, but quickly forgotten after the French revolution rendered it 'dangerous'. Cf. Rothschild (1992).
7. It must also be recognized that 'local networks' may breed distortions in the use of resources, even more than market and state activities. Consider for instance the actual role of 'bank foundations': too often local luxury consumption takes precedence over the financing of capital accumulation and the development of the local community; in any case it does not contribute to territorial re-equilibrium with transfers in favour of backward areas of the country. The common answer to this – namely, that such issues are the realm of state intervention, while local institutions are better apt to take care of local, often relatively unimportant, matters – strikingly contradicts Zamagni's confidence in the role of the non-profit sector.

REFERENCES

Hirschman, A.O. (1982) Rival Interpretations of Market Society: Civilizing, Destructive, or Feeble?, *Journal of Economic Literature* **20**, 1463–84.

Roncaglia, A. (1989) Italian Economic Growth: a Smithian View, *Quaderni di storia dell'economia politica* **VII**, 225–34.

Rothschild, E. (1992) Adam Smith and Conservative Economics, *Economic History Review* **45**, 74–96

Screpanti, E. and Zamagni, S. (1989) *Profilo di storia del pensiero economico*, Rome, La Nuova Italia Scientifica.

Sylos Labini, P. (1989) Sviluppo economico e sviluppo civile, *Moneta e credito* **XLII**, 291–304.

Comment

Felice R. Pizzuti

Zamagni's construction rests upon a broader conception of the market and activities carried out in the economic sphere, compared to that traditionally considered by economic theories. In some respects, it is an impressive conception but one in which we lose the centrality and generality of the two basic features of the market: a) the exchange of equivalents and b) the attitude of the parties to reach an equilibrium whereby their own specific self-interest is maximized.

According to Zamagni, there is much more to the market and the economy; human actions are not guided only by self interest (the prime mover of the private component of the market and the economy) but also by altruistic moral sentiments – such as love, friendship and solidarity – that animate civil society and enable it to grow. Donations, volunteer work and transfers based on solidarity would be part of the related area within the civil economy. However, Zamagni includes those kinds of behaviour among economic and market activities, which stimulate movements of labour, capital, goods and services, but are devoid of the features that characterize the market – namely they do not involve the typical and necessary equivalence of exchanges, nor do they imply any antagonism between the parties.

Zamagni maintains that the civil component, defined as the free expression of moral sentiments such as altruism, has traditionally been present in the market. It is only since the middle of the last century, with the development of the capitalist market, that this narrow conception of the market, identified with its private component based only on self interest, has gained prominence. The same view of the economy polarized between the private market and the state would be a consequence of that narrow view of the market and of the 'myth' of the state as the only agent of the common interest.

Actually, capitalist development has caused neither the disappearance of the social dimension of the market (which, if understood correctly, has increased hand in hand with the huge development of the market as a place for the meeting and exchange of the products of individual activities) nor the furtherance in itself of individualistic motives (as the primary engine for exchange in the market). The elements of market sociality represent an outcome of the interaction of selfish behaviour; that outcome is not related to the presence of behaviour subjectively altruistic that, as such, lie outside the market, namely, among the non-economic dimensions of human behaviour.

The peculiarity of the capitalist market is that, within its framework, labour is an exchangeable commodity; indeed, the importance of the labour market becomes critical within the capitalist economy and the society that is founded on it.

In short, while the development of some relationships existing within civil society is highly desirable (albeit not all: suffice it to mention those caused by hatred, envy, revenge and so on), they cannot be mixed either with the relationships arising from market exchanges or with the role of public authorities whose purpose is to regulate the market and act as a substitute for it when the individual approach is ineffective and/or inefficient in promoting the welfare of the community.

Finally, it might be appropriate to specify that, even if all human behaviour was inspired solely by altruistic criteria, there would still be the need for a general coordination of individual choices. A greater willingness of individuals to cooperate could facilitate this task, but could not replace it.

To include behaviour whose objective is not the exchange and the definition of 'civil economy' among market activities would require a related economic theory. To this end, Zamagni submits the reciprocity principle as an explanatory category. However, if it is acknowledged that in the civil economy a reciprocity rationale is nevertheless at work and that there exist bi-directional transfers governed by some compensation criteria, while denying that those flows and their offsets can be analysed on the basis of the rationality principle, the reciprocity principle is left undefined analytically as are the laws of the civil economy which would be based on that principle.

Zamagni seems to deal with this problem by adopting a negative approach; he stresses two basic differences existing between the reciprocities of the civil economy and the exchange of equivalents in the private economy. First, while in an exchange of equivalents the price is set prior to the transfer of the commodity, 'in the reciprocity relation the transfer precedes, both logically and temporally, the exchanged object'. Within the civil economy, those who initiate a relation do so on the basis of an expectation of reciprocity that, obviously, is based on a high level of trust in the other operators.

The second but fundamental element of diversity as well as of economic superiority that would characterize reciprocity relations is provided by the very role of trust. This, in fact, would foster cooperative behaviours and, by changing the economic game, would lead it toward more efficient outcomes.

Not only does the presence of operators who are not self-interested facilitate cooperation, but it also makes it rational; it would be more rational for a prisoner to chose to cooperate, in facing the well-known dilemma, if he were sure that the other prisoner was guided by a spirit of cooperation.

The question that remains unanswered in Zamagni's construction is how to account for the basic role that this trusting attitude plays in relations that one way or another develop in a market and economic setting, since this attitude is more typical in relations such as friendship and solidarity.

Clearly, it is not enough to say that these are relational goods pertaining to the civil economy, not to the private economy guided by self-interest; some theoretical explanations are necessary as to why market operators behave as if they were all members of the same family.

The basic misunderstanding seems to lie in the above-mentioned confusion between the causes for voluntary actions – such as those prompted by love, friendship, solidarity, altruism and trust – and the economic rationale of the exchange which, by definition, rests upon the pursuit of an individual gain by self-seeking parties entering into it.

What is being delineated here is an actual contradiction in market relations that Zamagni seems to want to reject when he states: 'Today it is more far-sighted and less expensive to be cooperatively competitive than frictionally competitive'. Instead, it is the lack of compatibility between the terms cooperation and competition that springs up in these very words, as opposed to the consistency, typical of the market, between friction and competitiveness.

It is quite possible that the members of an association with strongly appealing ideal and social objectives – to the point where those who share those objectives give donations and time for volunteer work – establish a higher form of cooperation than is normally found among economic operators. This case, however, lies beyond the realm of the economic rationale of the exchange; we are actually in the area of volunteer work and associative activities where individual choices are not guided by personal interest but by the interest shared by all the members of the association. Besides, these group interests are not necessarily appreciated by the community in which this association operates. Members of organized crime syndicates can also establish close ties based on trust among themselves, which certainly increases their efficiency. The task of defining what is socially useful or desirable rests upon the community's representative bodies, not on single groups of people joined in an association. Benevolent groups can enter into economic relations among themselves and with other operators through the market, and there is no reason to think that their objectives might be pursued by following different rules from those that govern the market. Why, for instance, should a consumer have more 'trust' in a supermarket run by a cooperative as opposed to one run by a corporation? Should there be situations of inefficient friction also in these cases, then only an entity that operates to maximize the welfare of the community as a whole could call on the single groups to behave cooperatively.

Zamagni seems to tend to underestimate this role of the public operator and advocates the development of the civil economy alongside with the private one; free competition between the two market sectors would determine their relative development. Calling for free competition would imply tax neutrality between the two sectors, and no special support for either which, if present, would give rise to clear problems of unfair competition and, consequently, to allocation inefficiency. However, a common demand that the multifaceted world of *non-profit* organizations is putting forward with increasing vigour, and with the support of some ideas of the 'civil economy', deals exactly with a general favourable tax treatment in comparison with other enterprises. Should those moral sentiments present within civil society, rightly appreciated for the very reason that they are inspired by altruism and not selfishness, become an effective cover to promote self-seeking economic interests at variance with the welfare of the community, there would be two serious consequences: not only would the productive efficiency of the economic system be reduced, but the disappointment originated by the manipulation of good sentiments would accelerate civil society's decadence, not its growth.

Part V

Testimonials

9 A Letter to the Conference

Hyman P. Minsky

16 October 1996

Dear Professor Marzano,

As you know, my health precludes my participation in the conference in honour of professor Fausto Vicarelli on November 21–23 to be held in Rome.

Quite soon after your invitation, I learned of my illness and I made the news available to all concerned. There was a slight chance that the cancer would be under control but unfortunately it is not.

You asked if I could make a statement that could be read at the conference. The following is such a statement:

Fausto Vicarelli was a deep and important thinker who was engaged in integrating ethics and economics. Without ethical considerations, doing economics is a vacuous occupation; and in no place are ethics more important than in issues of social commitment. Ethical considerations enter into every phase of economics, in particular how we handle financial relations which often obscure the relationships between the contributions that are made to the economy and the take-outs that the people are entitled to from the economy. The right to take-outs from economic outputs are obscured by a fog of financial and proprietal engagements. One's ability to take out, to receive from the joint products of society are obfuscated by financing relations. This Vicarelli knew; this we should all remember.

In particular, social commitments obscure rights and privileges, and nowhere is this clearer than in the world with uncertainty, which is the essential aspect of economies that abandon simple financing patterns. This is becoming clearer everyday as capitalism becomes more complex and as capitalism becomes the well-nigh universal form of organization of the world economy. As we can see from Vicarelli's last project, he had much to contribute to the discussion of rational expectations, which occupied economists over much of the decade since Fausto's death. I feel certain that had he lived, Vicarelli, like Sargent, would have continued to cut through the fog of the extreme rationality of rational expectations. The idea that rational expectations are perfect knowledge would certainly have been too much for Vicarelli.

Fausto was a dear person, beloved by all who knew him. I consider it a great privilege to have been a friend of Fausto's during his lifetime.

Sincerely,

Hyman P. Minsky

10 Miscellanea

Antonino Tripoli

None of the founder members of the 'Fausto Vicarelli Association' had suspected during his lifetime how important an economist Fausto Vicarelli was; it was only after his death that we realized this. For us he had simply been a friend, in the very best and truest meaning of the word, a friend who was always ready to listen with sincere interest to your problems, just as he was with everybody else.

Fausto was an example to us all. He taught us what social commitment means, how to defend human rights and how to live a coherent life. He showed us how to deal with problems directly, how to avoid compromises and how to overcome our egotism and seek justice for all, instead of privileges for the few. Most important of all, he never taught these things explicitly, but by the example of his actions.

When he died we felt somehow as if we had lost our guide, our mentor. Then after a while we realized that the best way to remember and honour him would be to follow his example and put into practice his teachings. Hence the Fausto Vicarelli Association was founded. Its aims are basically twofold: firstly to encourage and support research by young economists through a yearly prize to be awarded to the best degree dissertation in economics and second, to further social activities, such as those we are involved in with Albanian schools at the present time. In addition, four years ago the Association organized an academic conference on 'Economics and the fulfilment of human beings' to commemorate Fausto's very personal approach to economic problems. Our participation in the 1996 International conference is the second important meeting of this type and we believe that there will be other similar occasions when we may meet and once again discuss Fausto's legacy to economics and social commitment.

On a more personal level I would like to add that my involvement in the Association has given me a full understanding of economics as well as a greater awareness of the richness of Fausto's personality. I must admit to being rather illiterate in economics. My field is high tech and I had always been convinced that the improvement of human conditions depended on progress in medicine, technology, judicial and social sciences and in the evolution of more advanced forms of government.

For me economics was an arid subject, linked to accounting and mostly concerned with producing budgets, balances and more or less reliable forecasts, but with very little social significance. Through my contact with Fausto Vicarelli when he was alive and even more through considerations made after his death, I started realizing what kind of an impact solutions of economic problems and particularly decisions of economic policy can have on the fate of the community. I came to understand why the factors of social progress I mentioned above can remain ineffective without a 'correct' allocation of resources behind them and how important a moral approach to economics is.

Finally I came to realize how important it was to bring together the two aspects of Fausto's person which I had failed to connect before: on the one hand, his very warm interest and deep concern for all, and, on the other, his profession as an economist inspired by his commitment. In other words for Fausto the study of economics was a social service of paramount relevence. His writings, behind the highest scientific rigour, reveal the pursuit for a solution to people's problems through the establishment and application of correct economic laws.

I would now like to send an important message to the young people of the present generation. Whatever your profession may be, you must always remember that a lot can and must be done to improve human conditions both for yourselves and especially for your fellow human beings. As the conference has demonstrated clearly, there are numerous problems waiting to be solved and people are looking for some indications as to their remedies. The fulfillment of this task could be your objective and it would be the best way to honour the intellectual and moral heritage of Fausto Vicarelli.

FRANCO BENTIVOGLI

Ten years have passed since the premature death of Fausto Vicarelli, whose extraordinary human qualities, social conscience and high standing as an economist are inseparable in the memories of those fortunate enough to have known him or especially to have been his friends.

Perhaps it is not true that the death of a friend leaves a great void, though it certainly leaves a long train of sadness and sorrow. Fausto's death, however, has not left us empty-handed. The gift of his friendship remains, and his example still summons us to be active and involved, not to give in to weariness, nor to tread water in the lee of great ideas.

Those who knew Fausto never remember him simply for his accomplishments as an economist, though he certainly was a brilliant one, but above all for his humanity, his sense of friendship, his disinterestedness. Fausto was a true and close friend to people of all kinds. 'He was,' in the words of one of his friends, 'the most ordinary and common man I ever met, and yet the most extraordinary and uncommon one'.

Reporting his death, an economic newpaper wrote, 'He did not belong to the ivory tower. He was one of those rare economists who have their roots in the civil society'. Indeed his work was not limited to the University or the Research Department of the Bank of Italy; it carried over to the arena where economic policy is made in the real world, with the labour movement – the CISL trade union confederation and its metalworkers affiliate, the FIM-CISL – to which, with characteristic commitment, rigour and generosity, he donated his expertise and analytical powers.

Fausto Vicarelli never considered any aspect of his involvement in society as last on the list, whether it was his professorship at the University, his research at the Bank of Italy, an economics lecture to young trade unionists, speaking about solidarity and economic policy to a gathering of young people at the Cittadella in Assisi, or about the problems of underdevelopment in Brazil to a radio network.

His commitment to those at the bottom was full and unreserved, whether the subject was the economic problems of the nation, those of his neighbourhood or those of the Third World. He had not a whiff of the opportunistic calculation that is found so often among successful people and that makes them so out of touch with ordinary ones. I remember a letter Fausto fired off to *Mondo Economico*, published in the issue of 20 December 1984, in which he stoutly defended Father Leonardo Boff, the Brazilian theologian, whose book *Church, Charisma and Power* had received a harsh review. Fausto accused the reviewer of being 'a classic example of how intellectuals often use their dialectics to save their soul by walling out the disturbing truths of reality'.

Fausto Vicarelli was much more than just one of the many economists who have worked with the FIM and CISL. His role was never limited to economic advisor. He worked on strategic planning and leadership training, and he was an active, critical participant in our research work to recast union policies in order to meet the national and international challenges of the 1980s.

I remember his contributions to important moments of our movement, from the FIM's organizational meetings in Rimini and Vico Equense to its seminars on the role and problems of the trade unions in the accumulation process, to his lectures on industrial economics and policy at the Florence Study Centre, the national school of the CISL, to his contributions to research on the trade unions' economic policy.

I particularly remember the lectures he gave with such generous enthusiasm at the Umbrian Romitorio, the FIM's training school in Amelia. Those who attended his classes appreciated his depth of thought, his simplicity of language, his talent for communicating with one and all. His skills as an economist and teacher were complemented by his warmth and concern. It is the custom at the Romitorio for participants to evaluate the teacher at the end of a course: they always gave Fausto top marks. I may add that Fausto Vicarelli and Federico Caffè were surely the best-loved and most highly appreciated teachers ever to give courses for young metalworker activities.

Fausto willingly placed his knowledge at the service of the trade unions, but never with a desire to win favour. In other words he was not a 'court economist' but a scholar with very clear ideas about the aims and rules of economics – a clarity that demanded harmony and practice.

Fausto's relationship with our movement also illustrates the CISL's distinctive trait: its readiness to confront the problems of the economy with an open mind, rejecting a retreat into a fundamentally defensive stance but at the same time refusing to bow to the views of the great economic interests or to those who sing the praise of the invisible hand, able, so to say, to balance all things on its own.

Fausto was well aware of the difficulties faced by a trade union when it addresses the problems of income distribution, capital formation and unemployment, that is to say the difficulty of distinguishing between the protection of short-term and long-term interests, though both are equally important for workers.

Coming to grips with these problems is very hard for a union. It requires close involvement of the workers and 'implies the spread of a new approach to industrial crisis and new culture of participation in the production process. What is more, the labour movement must involve the political parties in this march'. Fausto Vicarelli considered this *the challenge*: 'to propose a new strategy aimed against nostalgic Manchesterian revivals but also against unconditional welfarism as a system'.

For Fausto, unemployment was the paramount problem. But, he added, it is senseless to consider unemployment only with an eye to the next six months or to call for stop-gap measures. Appropriate policies backed by consistent behaviour are needed. It is clear, Fausto continued, that unemployment has structural features and that policies and behaviour to combat it cannot be based on short-run tactical instrument, but have to be much broader in scope.

'The task at hand,' Fausto observed, 'is to manage the *fourth* industrial revolution and to avoid being overwhelmed by it, as happened in the mid-1800s and the 1930s. To do this, it is necessary to avoid making two errors in particular: to believe that a single move or economic policy instrument can by itself resolve the employment problem, when a synergy of conduct and forces is required; to mark time in disputes over principles or in a show of pride, when, on the contrary, it is indispensable to look ahead and harness human invention and industry for the benefit of mankind'. He perceived the challenges of the future and was convinced that great resources of research, innovation and courage had to be mobilized. He was fond of quoting Keynes: 'We have to invent a new wisdom for a new age. And in the meantime we must, if we are to do any good, appear unorthodox, troublesome, dangerous, disobedient to them that begot us'.

In the academic world Fausto Vicarelli is well known in Italy and abroad as a great authority on Keynes. He often emphasized the decisive role assigned by Keynesian theory to economic policy as an effective instrument of intervention in the economy. He did not believe in ineluctable 'laws of nature', which many theories insist are inherent in the workings of the economy. Nor did he accept their determinism, which leaves no room for man's will and effort to affect the course of economic developments.

Fausto contented that economics in not a neutral science and should always explicitly state the values on which it is premised. In one of his articles he quoted Myrdal: 'There is no way of studying social reality other than from the viewpoint of human ideals. A "disinterested social science" has never existed and, for logical reasons, cannot exist'.

If I have concentrated on Fausto Vicarelli's extraordinary personal qualities, it is not by chance. We live in times when the so-called civil society is all too often dominated by people willing to sell or sacrifice everything – human relationships, friendship, values – in order to gain power and success. Against the background of this sordid marketplace, this daily trade in cynicism, Fausto's life stands out all the more clearly as an example of disinterestedness and transparency.

Fausto was a man of deep religious faith, worn lightly, without ostentation, and recognizable in the discreet yet intense practice of brotherly love. This was, as I said, his style; but it was also the best way of being a man of faith. This, I think, is the best legacy he has left us.

NICOLA GENOVESE

My memories of Fausto Vicarelli are linked to the unforgettable experience of his visits to the University of Messina when he gave two lectures on Keynesian theory. The first took place in 1978 shortly after the publication of the first edition of his book *Keynes. The instability of capitalism*, when the lively debate over *La controversia keynesiana*, edited by Vicarelli in 1974, was still raging. The second of these lectures was held in 1981 when the monetarist critique of Keynesian theory, spearheaded by Friedman and, in a more intransigent form, by Lucas, was rampant and Vicarelli was preparing a reply to it with editing a new book *The Relevance of Keynes Today* which was published in 1983 for the centenary of J.M. Keynes's birth.

I used the word 'experience' with reference to Vicarelli's lectures because they coincided with two critical moments in the evolution of macroeconomic studies and of his own scientific works. The first of these critical moments was marked by the phenomenon of 'stagflation' which had perplexed Keynesian economists when faced with an increase in unemployment at the same time as an increase in the rate of inflation. The second moment was marked by an almost complete U-turn in economic theory, which found acceptance in the political world with the arrival of the Reagan administration in the USA and the Thatcher government in the United Kingdom. The prevailing style of expression was reminiscent of the English Treasury in the 1930s with the capitalist system once again viewed as stable and economic policy ineffective, even harmful.

In the midst of these fundamental turning points Fausto Vicarelli adopted a truly coherent attitude and it is difficult to give an account of his visits and convey the emotion experienced while listening to an economist expounding with such calm eloquence his theses clearly inspired by his ideals and determined to seek the 'true Keynes'.

In fact from the very first meeting he expressed his conviction that what had been disturbed by events was in fact the 'traditional Keynesianism' of the so-called 'neoclassical synthesis' which had carefully conserved features of the 'conventional wisdom' prior to the *General Theory* and against which Keynes himself had fought so assiduously.

The first lecture in 1978 focused on the central theme of the book mentioned above, *The Keynesian Controversy*, which had been edited by Vicarelli. The title had been deliberately chosen in order to relaunch the debate which had developed after the publication of the *General Theory* between Keynes and representatives of the neoclassical world (or the classics as he called them). Vicarelli and the other authors of the book wanted to re-open this debate with the authors who had interpreted Keynes with Walrasian models along the lines of Hicks-Modigliani-Klein.

As is well known, at that time other authors (Leijonhufvud, Clower) had tried to project a different kind of view of Keynes from the one shared by Keynesians up to then or to create a Keynesian counterrevolution. However these authors gave an interpretation which considered unemployment as a phenomenon of disequilibrium and suggested causes for it which only partially differed from those used to justify unemployment by exponents of orthodox economics, such as Marshall-Edgeworth-Pigou, who had been criticized so harshly by Keynes in the *General Theory*.

Vicarelli explained that, while it was right to criticize the traditional Keynesian model which gave too much importance to price and wage rigidity as well as to the liquidity trap in explaining unemployment, the path followed by Clower and Leijonhufvud to analyse the thought of Keynes through a model of general economic equilibrium was not acceptable. In fact in this way unemployment came to be seen as a state of transition towards a situation in which markets acquire the necessary information in order to elaborate and transmit an equilibrium price vector which guarantees full employment. He also commented on the proposal put forward by these authors that economic processes should be studied in conditions of uncertainty and he predicted future developments which were to lead to the so-called 'microfoundation' of macroeconomics and to the 'New Keynesian macroeconomics', though he judged them to be incapable of catching the true meaning of Keynes's thought.

I was particularly struck by the fact that Vicarelli's research on the true teaching of Keynes was never abstract nor simply theoretical for purely exegetic purposes. On the contrary, as he himself confirmed on this occasion, he was looking for a solution to contemporary problems, even if they did seem far from those analysed in the Keynesian model. He approached the question of inflation from a completely different angle to either Hicks, who looked for its cause in the labour market, or to Joan Robinson, who suggested studying the level as well as the composition of effective demand.

He believed that a correct interpretation of Keynes would give a better understanding of the connection between growth and price increases through an analysis of the relationship between the interest rate, the profit rate and the price level.

In fact his lecture ended with an analysis of this relationship by means of an original model which included all the main features of Keynesian thought (effective demand, short-run and long-run expectations) and a mechanism for the determination of relative prices similar to that proposed by Sraffa in *Production of Commodities by Means of Commodities*. In this way he also managed to show to what extent the picture of reality given by the *General Theory* constitutes a real alternative to the one suggested by the neoclassical school and not simply a particular case of it.

There is no need to re-examine this model since it has entered into the annals of the analysis of Keynesian thought, but I do remember that in the first lecture Vicarelli was not completely satisfied with it. In fact he was worried about its deterministic implications and the influence that Garegnani's thought had exerted on it, especially as Garegnani had blamed Keynes for the neoclassical synthesis of unemployment theory, an opinion which Vicarelli did not share. He was also worried about the way in which long-term expectations had been modelled as well as the constraint imposed on the model by the presence of the long-term tendency towards a levelling of profits. The reason for his discontent was to be revealed in the second lecture.

In view of the economic situation in the early 1980s, we looked forward with great interest and curiosity to hearing Fausto Vicarelli talk once again about Keynesian theory at a time when very few, either at home or abroad, still professed to be a follower of Keynes.

To our surprise he was not at all interested in the numerous controversies surrounding macroeconomic theory with its different schools and the new problem of microeconomic foundations. Instead he talked about his book *Keynes. The Instability of Capitalism* which he was revising for a new English edition. He talked at length of Keynes's works prior to the *General Theory* and of this great economist's experiences both in the academic world and in the various positions he held as a Civil Servant of the British government and as consultant in important international organizations, of which he had learnt through the publication of the *Collected Writings of J.M. Keynes*.

At the end of his lecture Vicarelli said that this study of Keynes and of all his works, which he considered to be linked by a common line of thought to the *General Theory*, had convinced him of the necessity to get rid of the constraints imposed by the 'equilibrium principle' in order to interpret, or at least begin to appreciate, Keynes's ideas. Instead it was essential to understand that Keynes had shown how to determine the conditions of a capitalist economy in any particular period on the basis of the short-term expectations, which are usually realized, and the long-term expectations, considered as exogenous, on which the liquidity preference and the marginal efficiency of capital, respectively, are based.

Vicarelli had actually first sketched out this concept in the last chapter of his book on Keynes and refined it in his paper published in the collection of essays edited in 1983, but it still seemed highly problematical, especially with regard to the long term.

I would like to conclude with some comments about the importance today of Vicarelli's dedicated search for the 'true Keynes'. First of all, we can see it all around us, with the growing number of conferences on Keynesian economics which are being organized both in Italy and abroad sixty years on from the publication of the *General Theory*.

Furthermore, in a world which desperately pursues monetary stability, where competition has become global, where state intervention tends to be limited to a bare minimum and interest rates have reached high real levels, it seems quite reasonable to suppose that conditions could develop to cause a substantial fall in effective demand with disastrous consequences. We must, therefore, work to re-establish Keynesian ideas and to make use of them in order to have policies which correct the contradictions inherent in capitalism.

It seems appropriate to close with the words of Keynes which Vicarelli quoted at the end of his 1974 book and which easily lend themselves to the present day situation as we live through great transformations.

> *We have changed by insensible degrees our philosophy of economic life, our notions of what is reasonable and what is tolerable; and we have done this without changing our technique or our copybook maxims. Hence our tears and troubles.*

11 Closing Remarks

Ferruccio Marzano

The present conference represents one among several initiatives which have been taken in memory of Fausto Vicarelli on the tenth anniversary of his untimely death. Each conference has been intended to stress specific aspects of Fausto's scientific and human personality, as well as to focus on certain periods of his multiform activities. Besides what has already been recalled by various contributors in the preceeding pages, in my concluding remarks I shall dwell very briefly on three points.

First, I wish to say that I met Fausto at Harvard in November 1961, when we were both visiting that prestigious American University as 'foreign students'. Although we came from very different backgrounds, there we shared not only the same research programme – both had been sent to work with Professor Gottfried Haberler on problems of international economics, Fausto by Professor Volrico Travaglini, and myself by Professor Giuseppe Ugo Papi – but most importantly a common interest in proceeding along a multiplicity of research lines and experiences, without being 'constrained' by any specific, pre-determined approach.

Such a perspective led to both of us following a number of most diverse post-graduate courses and seminars not only at Harvard, but also at the not far away MIT, where we met two other Italian economists who were visiting scholars there in the same academic year: Pierangelo Garegnani and Duccio Cavalieri. Besides our periodic meetings with Professor Haberler, I particularly remember our attending lectures by Professors Gerschenkron, Kuznets, Leontief, Dorfman, Duesenberry, Houthakker, at Harvard, as well as the 'famous' seminars on capital theory run by Professor Samuelson at MIT. I may add that, during *that* year 1961–62 spent at Boston, Garegnani's outlook on capital theory was to have a noticeable influence on my scientific formation; I presume the same was true for Fausto.

Actually, in that period, the well-known 'capital theory controversy' between the two Cambridges was very topical. The years of the 'Keynesian controversy' were to come later, in the mid 1970s.

Anyhow, my recollection is that, in both controversies, Fausto's deeply believed in the role of confrontation and dialogue, in the continuous search for new ways of understanding reality, and in particular capitalist economies. Whatever his specific field of interest was, he was always guided by this conviction and the methodology which would naturally follow from it.

More generally, in my view and as papers and debate at the conference have shown, Vicarelli's scientific outlook may be described as a triangle with reality, theory and moral values located in its three vertexes. In such an outlook, economic theory should consistently aim to explain reality; but this should be done on the basis of value premises which should always direct the economist's research in certain directions instead of others. In Vicarelli's opinion – and I entirely agree with him – such a 'research programme' has to be found above all in Keynes's economics, provided it is correctly understood on the basis of a *literary* interpretation of Keynes's works and in particular of his *General Theory* and provided it is also seen within each interpreter's own value judgements.

Within this framework, the conference proceedings can be seen to fall into two groups. In the first group, which would include Dr Fazio's 'opening address' and the papers by Tobin, Musu, Davidson, Kregel, Nardozzi, the central idea has always been concerned with an attempt to compare Keynes's, Vicarelli's and other similar economists' thought with that of the 'opposite stance' just on the basis of their particular way of providing an account and an explanation of the 'real world' and in particular of the capitalist world. In each paper, although in different ways, this confrontation seems to have seen the 'success' of Keynes's, Vicarelli's and similar authors' thought *vis-à-vis* the opposite side.

In a second group of papers, such as those by Lunghini, Zamagni, Atkinson, as well as in the 'testimonial contributions' by Minsky, Tripoli and Bentivogli, the aim has been to deal with what should, according to Fausto Vicarelli, be the second 'horn' of an economist's outlook, that is to say the relationship between theory and moral values. In this respect, the 'winning idea' had to be the conviction that an economist should be mostly concerned with the moral implications of his thought and, therefore, with the social involvement of his activities as much as with the real significance of his work.

Finally, let me call attention to the fact that there is a single, more specific sense in which Vicarelli's thought is to be understood as a 'proper' development of Keynes's thought, that is to say, his adherence to Keynes's representation of a capitalist economy as a 'monetary production economy' and more particularly as a 'monetary entrepreneurial economy'. One of the main points of such an outlook is that a capitalist economy is characterized by certain specific *institutions* which structure it into specific ways and interactions. Hence the key role of such *institutions* as entrepreneurial decisions and particularly investment decisions, financial and especially liquid fund allocations, and more generally agents' different behaviour patterns under conditions of uncertainty and short-run *as well as* long-run expectations. From this point of view, we know that, in the last years of his life, Fausto was engaged in an attempt to go more deeply into such problems, and in particular into the role that Keynes's ideas on probability (Keynes, 1921) would have played in shaping the methodology of the *General Theory* (Vicarelli, 1983).

Let me conclude by expressing my hope that the next conference in memory of Fausto's ideas and teachings may be properly dedicated to this latter group of problems.

REFERENCES

Keynes, J.M. (1921) *A Treatise on Probability*, London, Macmillan; also in *The Collected Writings of John Maynard Keynes Vol. VIII,* London, Macmillan [1973].

Vicarelli, F. (1983) Dall'equilibrio alla probabilità: una rilettura del metodo della Teoria Generale, in F. Vicarelli (ed.), *Attualità di Keynes,* Rome-Bari, Laterza; Engl. tr. *Keynes's Relevance Today,* London, Macmillan [1985].

Author Index